M Meldrum   M Lejk   P G

SSADM Techniques

an introduction to Version 4

Chartwell Bratt

Studentlitteratur

Chartwell-Bratt (Publishing and Training) Ltd
ISBN 0-86238-224-6

Printed in Sweden
Studentlitteratur, Lund
ISBN 91-44-38061-5

Printing 2 3 4 5 6 7 8 9 10 | 1998 97 96 95 94

To our families

Preface

This book aims to provide an understanding of the techniques used in SSADM Version 4 and to place the techniques within the framework of SSADM. It is intended to provide an introduction to the techniques and their place in SSADM. The text is primarily aimed at undergraduate students but material from the book has been successfully used on a postgraduate IT conversion course and in the training of practitioners. The text does not aim to comment on the usefulness or otherwise of SSADM. Many courses use SSADM standards to teach techniques but do not teach SSADM as such. This text should provide material for any course teaching system analysis and design techniques.

Although this text provides a useful starting point for learning the techniques used in SSADM, we do not claim to comprehensively cover each technique. The serious student of SSADM must have access to the SSADM manuals published by NCC/Blackwell.

The first chapter provides an introduction to SSADM and sets the context in which the techniques are used. Chapters 2 to 15 cover the techniques in the order in which they would appear in a project using SSADM. One technique, The Data Flow Model, has been split into two chapters. The first chapter concentrates on the conventions for drawing the diagram, the second on the full use of the technique in SSADM. We have found it useful to teach this technique in this way, using the material in Chapter 3 in the first Systems Analysis and Design unit of a course and Chapter 4 in the second year course. We have tried in all the other technique chapters to describe the basic principles of the techniques first and then to introduce some of the complexities.

The text makes extensive use of practical examples and sets regular exercises for students. Answer pointers for selected exercises and overhead masters of many of the figures are available for lecturers adopting the text. Case studies are used throughout and these have been simplified since our aim is to provide an understanding of the techniques, not to provide a realistic fully documented system.

We have used several case studies since this allows the text to be used by students who are not covering all of the techniques in one course unit. The case studies are used to provide exercises for many of the techniques but we have tried to avoid too much cross-referencing to descriptions in other chapters.

In a text which provides so many examples it is difficult to avoid ambiguities in descriptions. The exercises have been successfully used on a number of courses at all levels. Variations in interpretation of the case studies have provided good discussion points for classes in areas such as the weakness of narrative for system description and the benefits of the techniques in exposing such problems. The case studies are based on systems which should exist in institutions using the text. Your own institution's system requirements can be used to vary, or add to, the case studies.

Where possible these techniques should be taught using automated tools since this removes much of the drudgery of the documentation. Students should at least be given a demonstration of the facilities provided by such tools.

Acknowledgements

Colleagues and students at the University of Sunderland. Thanks are especially due to Roger Foster for technical help.

Colleagues and Students at Manchester Metropolitan University. Thanks are due to all staff in the Department of Business Information Technology for their support and encouragement. The User Support Officers in Aytoun are thanked for their technical assistance with the production of the manuscript.

Philip Yorke of Chartwell-Bratt.

Our families for their support during the preparation of this book. Stuart Meldrum for proof reading the final-draft.

Louise Graham for her help and support.

Mike Hill of the CCTA for his advice on the early stages of the book.

NCC/Blackwell for the SSADM Version 4 manuals.

Exerts from the SSADM Version 4 Structural Model are reproduced with the permission of the Controller of HMSO.

Contents

CHAPTER ONE

Introduction to SSADM

1.1 Introduction

SSADM stands for Structured Systems Analysis and Design Method. It is a method used for the analysis and design of computer-based systems. SSADM is not the only method available but it is very sound and is being increasingly adopted in the public and private sectors.

Systems analysis and design is a wide-ranging and complex field. Practitioners need a variety of skills in order to effectively carry out their work. Analysts must have social skills such as diplomacy, the ability to put people at their ease, confidence to hold their own at Board level. SSADM does not attempt to help the analyst acquire such social skills. However, analysts must be technically competent in order to translate user requirements into a successful computer-based system. They also need to be able to effectively control their work and, at project leader level, the work of others. It is these areas of technical competence and control that SSADM addresses.

It is necessary for the analyst to have a framework in which to work since systems analysis and design is a complex operation and systems projects can last for long periods of time. Analysts need to know where to start, what to do next, how to document what they find and how to cross-reference the various documents produced. Although this may seem obvious, many organisations (particularly smaller ones) have no, or very scant, guidance or standards in this area. The emphasis is often placed on producing working systems as quickly as possible. It is when these "working" systems do not meet user requirements and prove to be unsatisfactory that the lack of proper analysis and documentation is highlighted. The amount of effort involved in correcting these omissions can often be more than that required to produce the initial system. It is for reasons such as this that attention should be paid to properly planned, documented and structured systems analysis and design.

SSADM provides a very effective framework in which an analyst can work. It is a structured set of

- structural standards : to guide the analyst through a project by detailing the Steps which may need to be undertaken, the techniques to employ at each Step and the documentation to produce.

- procedural standards : to provide the analyst with a range of techniques which can be used to model, describe and develop existing and required systems.

- documentation standards : to provide a complete set of documents to be used in a project, this is the SSADM Dictionary.

SSADM is not intended to cover the complete Information Systems Life Cycle. There are areas such as project management which SSADM does not cover. SSADM will provide raw data which can be used as inputs to complementary methods and techniques in areas such as project management, testing, quality assurance, capacity planning, training and standard setting.

1.2 Background to SSADM

SSADM is owned by the Government, in particular the Central Computer and Telecommunications Agency (CCTA) which is part of HM Treasury. It was developed for the CCTA in 1980 and the CCTA remain the design authority for the Method. The current version of SSADM (1991) is Version 4 which is documented in the SSADM Manual published by NCC/Blackwell.

Although the CCTA owns SSADM, it has adopted an "open" strategy in which SSADM is publicly available and can be used without a licence or payment to CCTA. Anyone can develop SSADM interface guides to link to other methods and techniques. Guides can also be produced for 3GL environments, Database Management Systems (DBMS) and for application generators. The SSADM Design Authority Board will recommend the guides which most actively reinforce the Method.

Development of SSADM is an ongoing process in which comments and proposals from users are considered. It is a user-oriented method and all new proposals for developing SSADM are assessed with reference to:

- ease of use
- compliance with standards
- software support
- flexibility
- quality

This continuous development ensures that the Method is not left behind in the ever-changing world of computer systems. In addition, work is in progress to produce common standards with equivalent French methods in preparation for the European Single Market.

1.3 Structural standards

SSADM consists of 5 CORE MODULES. Each Module is divided into STAGES, each Stage is divided into STEPS and each Step is further divided into TASKS. The 5 Core Modules and the Stages are shown in Figure 5.1.

Appendix 1 gives the Activity Descriptions from the Structural Model of SSADM. For each Module the Structural Model gives the objectives, summary description of activities, participants, preconditions, products and activities. Note that the tasks within each are not listed. Readers are referred to the SSADM Manual for a complete list of Steps and tasks.

Module		Stage	
FS:	**Feasibility Study**	**0**	**Feasibility**
RA:	**Requirements Analysis**	**1**	**Investigation of Current Environment**
		2	**Business System Options**
RS:	**Requirements Specification**	**3**	**Specification of Requirements**
LS:	**Logical System Specification**	**4**	**Technical System Options**
		5	**Logical Design**
PD:	**Physical Design**	**6**	**Physical Design**

Figure 1.1 Core modules and stages of SSADM

Each Module, Stage, or Step can be considered as a 'black box'. Each has defined inputs and products and a set of tasks to be performed. Modules, Stages and Steps can be selected as being appropriate to a particular project. For instance Stage 1, Investigation of the Current Environment, can be omitted when there is no current system to be investigated. Within a Stage the Steps and Tasks can be selected as appropriate and carried out as rigorously as necessary. Experience in using the Method provides the best basis for selecting the necessary activities, the selection being based on the products provided by the activity. However the given inputs for each selected Module, Stage and Step must be available. Below is a brief summary of each Module.

1.3.1 Module FS - Feasibility Study

The Feasibility Study examines a proposed information system to determine whether the system will meet the specified business requirements of the organisation and whether a case exists for the development of such a system. A Feasibility Study is recommended to precede a Full Study for all projects except those with a low risk. The current system and the required system are explored and documented only in sufficient detail to enable the problem to be defined. Different solutions to the problem are identified.

1.3.2 Module RA - Requirements Analysis

Requirements Analysis involves setting up the analysis phase of the project by creating the necessary plans and agreeing the initial scope of the study. A detailed investigation of the existing system is undertaken in terms of system processes and data structure and this is documented together with any problems and requirements which have come to light. The Stage is terminated with a formal review.

A physical description of the existing system is converted into a logical description. The conversion from physical to logical removes the physical trappings and constraints to reflect the underlying policy of the existing system. The security, control and audit requirements of the system are considered and these, together with any other problems/requirements are incorporated into the documentation. A number of business system options are produced which reflect alternative ways of solving the problems and implementing the requirements. The user selects an option.

1.3.3 Module RS - Requirements Specification

The selected business system option is documented in full detail. The input and outputs can be examined with the users using techniques such as prototyping to indicate the format of screen displays and reports. The data model is developed and all access paths are defined. Any process which might change the data is identified and documented. The Requirements Specification must be completely accepted by the users before any further progress is made.

1.3.4 Module LS - Logical System Specification

Logical System Specification addresses the possible approaches to the physical implementation of the required system. A number of technical options are created specifying languages, packages, development environments and implementation platforms. An option is selected on grounds of cost and performance. In parallel with this the Requirements Specification is further detailed into implementable components. These components define the operation of the system within enquiry and update specifications.

1.3.5 Module PD - Physical Design

Physical Design converts the logical design into physical data, processes, inputs and outputs using the language and features of the chosen technical option. The data and process designs are developed incrementally and constantly tested and reviewed. The designs are then tuned in order to meet the design objectives. The file/database definitions and program specifications can then be completed. The system test plans, operating instructions, implementation plans and manual procedures are then defined.

1.4 Procedural standards

The Modules, Stages and Steps described in the last section refer to a number of techniques and documents which are used in the Method. As this book concentrates on the techniques of SSADM, they will be explained in detail in later chapters. However, the main techniques and a brief description of each now follows.

(a) business system option — This shows a proposed solution to the problem under investigation in terms of groups of processing requirements (functions)

(b) data flow modelling — Data Flow Diagrams (DFDs) represent flows of information through a system and between the system and the outside world. These are supplemented by documentation, such as Entity Descriptions, to give the Data Flow Model.

(c) dialogue design — Dialogue Structures are built up from definitions of the input/output structure for enquiries and updates. This is closely related to function definition which identifies processing requirements at a high level. Logical dialogue designs are used as the basis for physical dialogue design

(d)	entity-event modelling	Describe the effect of events which change the data in the system. These events identify processes in the system. Techniques used are Entity Life Histories and the Effect Correspondence Diagram
(e)	function definition	Documents information about user interactions with the system which is collected from Data Flow Models and grouped into sets of system processes which are seen as a unit by the users.
(f)	logical data modelling	The information stored and used in the system is modelled looking at the data groups and their relationships. A Logical Data Structure is produced as well as supporting documentation describing entities and relationships.
(g)	logical database process design	Takes the Requirements Specification and uses it to create a logical design of the required processing for data, input to and output from, the database. This design is implementation independent and is used as the basis for physical design.
(h)	process specification	The access paths to data required for enquiries and updates are identified to provide Enquiry Structures and Update Structures. The processes required in the system are thus identified and described.
(i)	relational data analysis	Relational Data Analysis (RDA) (normalisation) rationalises data and creates unambiguous logical data sets.
(j)	requirements definition	Identify requirements which meet the needs of users and the business as a whole. The requirements are quantified and provide a basis for decision-making for the new system. The Requirements Catalogue is updated and modified as the systems life cycle progresses.

(k)	technical system option	This defines the hardware and software environment in which the system will be physically realised.
(l)	physical data design	Takes the Logical Data Model (described in (f)) of the required system and turns it into a product specific database design within the selected technical environment.
(m)	physical process specification	Takes the Logical Design of the required system (described in (h)) and turns it into product specific process specification.

1.5 Documentation Standards

SSADM has 5 main products:

- Feasibility Report
- Analysis of Requirements
- Requirements Specification
- Logical Systems Specification
- Physical Design

These are the Module products. Each of these can be broken down into a number of documents which are produced by a Stage. The Stage products consist of documents produced by a task. The documents may vary depending on the needs of a project and the activities undertaken, but each activity has a defined product. The SSADM Dictionary in the SSADM Manual contains a Product Breakdown Structure which shows the relationship between Products in a hierarchic way. It also contains Product Descriptions which define the purpose of the contents, the standards for presentation and the quality criteria to be applied. Sample forms are also included in the Dictionary.

1.6 The philosophy of SSADM

SSADM is based on a number of fundamental principles which place it apart from traditional methods of systems analysis and design.

(a) SSADM is requirements driven and focuses on the requirements of the future system.

(b) SSADM distinguishes between the logical and physical aspects of a system. It places a great deal of importance on this distinction and this is one of its great strengths. An existing system is first described physically (i.e. as it is) and from this a logical description is derived. This mirrors the underlying policy rather than the implementation of that policy and gives a clear picture of the essence of existing procedures. The required system is developed as a logical model and it is this that is used as the basis for the final physical design. SSADM does not rule out situations where there is no existing system.

(c) SSADM provides 3 views of a system. Many structured methods rely on one technique such as Data Flow Diagramming or entity modelling as the basis for development. SSADM uses 3 different views of a system based on:

- functions
- events
- data

These 3 views are developed in parallel and checked one against the other for consistency as they are naturally inter-related. This cross-checking ensures the completeness and accuracy of the system model. This is another of SSADM's strengths.

Functions are the users' views of the system processing. For instance a user of a sales order processing system might see the function 'Record Customer Order'. This in fact could be a set of processes with one set of processes for existing customers and another when a new customer places an order. The new customer might have to have a customer record created before the sales order is recorded and a different credit checking process might be used to that for existing customers.

The analyst must explore the processes which lie behind each of these user functions. The users' main contact with the system is through system inputs and outputs so dialogue and report definition and design are important factors here.

Events are triggers which generate a change in the data in a system. These can be real business events such as 'Receipt of Customer Order' or system generated events such as the end of year trigger for a management accounting system. SSADM uses techniques such as Entity Life Histories to help check that all possible events have been considered. For instance if a customer record exists on the system, how and when is it created?; how and when is it removed from the system?; can details about the customer be changed, such as credit status?.

Data is manipulated and maintained by the system to carry out the system objectives. It is important to understand the data in a system and examine how the data is grouped together and the relationships between the data groups. SSADM builds a Logical Data Model of the data structures in a system. The data can then be examined to see how it needs to be processed. A well designed data structure leads to a more flexible system design and more efficient processing.

(d) The Method ensures regular reviews where work done is critically appraised in terms of quality and completeness. The definition of products for each Module, Stage and Step makes project planning and control easier since progress can be measured in terms of units completed. SSADM can be interfaced with an appropriate project management method.

(e) The approach taken is top-down starting at a high-level and then gradually decomposing down to increasing levels of detail.

(f) User participation is actively required at all points in the Method. Other methods may pay lip-service to user involvement, but in SSADM it is built into the Method. One of the three views of the system, functions, looks at the system processes from the users points of view. Input and outputs are defined from an early Stage and the use of prototyping is favoured. Users are also actively involved in the decision making process. The diagrammatic techniques such as Data Flow Diagramming can be easily understood by users.

(g) Because of the variety of implementation environments which exist, conversion of logical to physical design will depend upon the target environment. The SSADM Interface Guides provide rules and guidelines for defining various databases and files, programs and runflows.

(h) SSADM is designed to be used with IT support. This can range from use of word processing for documentation, diagramming tools, data dictionary software or CASE tools. Using SSADM as a purely paper-based methodology is not recommended since the volume of paperwork generated would swamp any analyst.

(i) The Structural Model of SSADM provides a rigorous description of the Method and is intended to assist with the setting of standards. It assists in interfacing with complementary methods and techniques.

1.7 Example

To illustrate principle (c) above, the three views of a system, consider the case of a student records system.

1.7.1 Data

Investigation of the system identifies a number of things about which data is kept including the following:

students
lecturers
courses
assignments
examinations

These things, called ENTITIES, will form the basis of the system data structure and this is unlikely to change much with time. The major techniques for examining data structures are Logical Data Modelling and Relational Data Analysis.

1.7.2 Functions

Is this all we need to describe and understand the system? Obviously not. We need to know what data enters and leaves the system. We also require to know what happens to this data inside the system i.e. what processes act upon it. Some typical processes may well be:

> maintain student personal details
> record coursework marks
> calculate students' final marks
> record examination results

These processes are grouped from the user viewpoint and are the FUNCTIONS required in the system. This aspect will be examined using Data Flow Models, Dialogue Design and Function Definition.

1.7.3 Events

Would this be sufficient to describe the system? There is one vital factor missing - a sense of time. The Data Flow Model and the Logical Data Model pay no attention to time. There is nothing in the Data Flow Model to stop the processes just described occurring in the sequence:

> calculate students' final marks
> record examination results
> record coursework marks
> maintain student personal details

The students' final marks can only be calculated after the coursework marks and examination results have been recorded. This third view of the system is addressed by the Entity Event Model which examines the EVENTS which affect each entity and trigger the processes on the Data Flow Diagrams.

These three views of the system interact with one another and SSADM uses the cross-referencing between them to check the validity and completeness of the system under investigation.

1.8 Benefits of SSADM

Some of the benefits of SSADM are listed below:

(a) It makes planning easier by providing a structured framework.

(b) It provides management with an opportunity for reviewing project progress. At each Stage it is possible to assess what tasks should be completed and what deliverables are due.

(c) It improves the quality of systems by accurately identifying user needs and producing a flexible result.

(d) It provides a means of communication between all parties concerned with systems development.

(e) Using a proven method means that the most effective way of doing things is defined in advance thus reducing the risk of wasting resources.

(f) Once established, it increases the productivity of development staff. The techniques used are widely known and there is an available pool of labour with the appropriate skills.

(g) By providing a standard framework, it is useful for trainees and experienced analysts.

(h) SSADM is an open method and is continuing to develop.

1.9 Use of SSADM in practice

The Steps and even Stages of SSADM are not all applicable to every project. Such questions as:

- "What if there is no existing system?"
- "What if the final hardware/software environment is laid down in advance?"
- "What if the system is going to be implemented using package software?"
- "What if the statement of requirements is going to be issued to outside suppliers?"
- "What if the system is a very small system?"

all imply some modification or truncation of the Modules, Steps and/or Stages. If it is decided to miss out various Steps, Stages or even Modules in SSADM, at least the question would have been asked:

> "Is this Step/Stage/Module necessary or relevant to my particular project?"

By asking the question, an essential element of project management has been addressed. The decision can be made on the basis of the products which are necessary.

Often some parts of a system will require IT support such as word processing or electronic mail. The use of such software needs to be less formally specified than defining a sales order entry section of a system. In such cases it can be useful to use SSADM linked to other techniques such as soft systems analysis. SSADM can be used on any size of project by careful selection of the appropriate activities.

SSADM is still developing and weaknesses identified by users in Version 3, such as Logical Dialogue Design and the links with program design methodologies eg Jackson Structured Programming, have been addressed in Version 4. The Method will continue to develop.

Although many organisations are now using SSADM they are often not using the Method in full. Techniques such as Data Flow Diagrams, Relational Data Analysis and Entity Modelling are well established and generally do not cause problems. Other techniques such as Entity Life Histories and Effect Correspondence Diagrams are less well known and cause more problems to new users of SSADM. Several books on SSADM are now available and a system for registering SSADM trainers and setting examinations in SSADM has been established.

The use of SSADM may be a requirement in contracts to software houses, particularly for government projects. An increasing number of job advertisements now request a knowledge of SSADM.

1.10 Summary

SSADM is a formal systems analysis and design method which provides a set of techniques within a framework of control and review points. The Method is an open method but development is controlled by the CCTA.

SSADM consists of up to 5 Modules which are subdivided into Stages and then Steps. Each Step consists of a number of tasks. The Method provides 3 views of a system - data flows, data structures and time cycles using a variety of interlinking techniques. This is provided within a framework which consists of structural, procedural and documentation standards.

1.11 Keywords

Structural Standards
Procedural Standards
Documentation standards
Physical Design
Logical Data Model
Data Flow Model
Entity Event Model
Open method
Stage
Step
Requirements Analysis
Requirements Specification
Feasibility Study
Logical Design
3 Views of a System
Products
SSADM
Module
Task

1.12 Exercises

1. Who owns SSADM and how does an organisation obtain permission to use it?
2. Outline the set of three standards provided by SSADM.
3. Name the Core Modules of SSADM.
4. Describe the modular structure of SSADM.
5. Name the main techniques provided by SSADM.
6. Outline the philosophy of SSADM.
7. Describe the three views of a system provided by SSADM.
8. Outline the benefits of using SSADM.
9. Are all the activities in SSADM compulsory?
10. What type of IT support complements SSADM?
11. Does SSADM produce a physical system?
12. What is the difference between a logical and a physical design?
13. Name the five main products of SSADM.
14. What is meant by saying that SSADM is a 'product driven method'?
15. How are users involved in SSADM?

CHAPTER TWO

Requirements Definition

2.1 Introduction

The Requirements Definition Technique is used to establish requirements for the proposed system. The requirements should meet the users' needs within the overall business objectives. Requirements are expressed in quantifiable terms. Use of this technique ensures that analysis is centred on requirements for the future system. The information gathered using this technique becomes the basis for decision-making throughout the project.

The technique is used throughout SSADM but the bulk of the work is carried out during the Requirements Analysis module. It is an iterative technique, increasing detail is added as requirements analysis progresses. The requirements are recorded in the Requirements Catalogue.

Throughout this Chapter reference is made to the Car Allowance Case Study. This Case Study describes the system for authorising employees in a large organisation to claim for business journeys made using their own vehicles. The details are described in more detail in Chapter 4, section 6.

2.2 Car Allowance System Case Study

Utility Corporation has decided to investigate the computerisation of the Company Car Allowance System. This system allows employees to claim an allowance from the company for using their cars on company business. The current system is manual except for the payment of cheques which is carried out on a mainframe based system used to produce all of the company's cheques.

The system requires employees to apply to become an authorized user before they can claim the allowance. The Administration and Transport Departments deal with the authorization of users. Transport gives all users new to the scheme a driving test and checks all cars over 3 years old. Administration receives the application forms and arranges the authorization procedure with Transport. Once all the Transport checks have been completed, the user is awarded a user allowance grade. The allowance is then authorized by the Administration Manager. Copies of the authorization document are held in the Transport, Finance and Administration Departments. The details held in each department conflict. The new system should aim to reduce duplication of information between the departments.

The allowance is meant to be attached to a particular job, but, currently, once a user has been authorized the authorization information is not updated. The user can still claim car allowance as long as the appropriate department manager signs the form. The new system will require all authorized users who change jobs to apply for a car allowance in their new job. Previously authorized users will not require to sit another driving test.

Another problem with the current system occurs when an authorized user changes a car. All changes of car should be notified to Administration and a test arranged when the car is over 3 years old. In practice, authorized users only notify administration when the change of car means they are entitled to a different band of allowance. The new system should ensure that claims are only paid on authorized vehicles.

Claims are currently handled in Finance Department as they come in, applicants can claim no more than once per month. Claims are batched and dealt with once or twice a week as the Finance Clerk's other work permits. The new system should allow the Finance Clerk to spread the processing of claims in this way. Currently a cheque requisition form has to be prepared for each claim and authorized by a Senior Accountant, the cheques are produced by a mainframe based system. Part of the brief for the new system is to investigate the printing of cheques directly from the new Car Allowance System. The security and audit requirements need to be carefully considered here. Eventually the system may allow claims to be paid with monthly salaries but this is not feasible with the current payroll system.

The new system requires some additional reports. Each employee should receive a monthly statement with their cheque. In addition employees should receive an annual statement at the financial year end. Departmental Managers should receive monthly and annual printouts detailing claim totals and miles covered by each employee.

Finance currently receive several enquiries each week about the progress of claims through the system. It would be helpful if the Finance Clerk had on-line enquiry facilities to check the status of a claim.

The current procedures involving authorization by management of applications and claims must be retained in the new system, as should the split in responsibility for processing applications and claims. These procedures are essential to prevent fraudulent claims.

The new system should run on a personal computer on an existing Local Area Network. The files will be held on a file server. The system should be running by the start of the next financial year (10 months time). The existing application forms and claim forms should be used in the new system.

2.3 The Requirements Catalogue

Requirements must be expressed in terms which:

- are quantifiable
- minimise duplication in the specification
- are sufficiently detailed on which to base decisions

The Requirements Catalogue is used to record the information gathered about requirements. The information in the Requirements Catalogue can be reviewed or updated at any time. A sample of the information shown on a Requirements

Catalogue Form illustrating a requirement which has been satisfied is shown in Figure 2.1. The Priority is defined by the user for each requirement using terms such as high/low or compulsory/desirable/optional.

In addition the Source and Owner of a requirement should be recorded. The Source is the person, document etc who/which identifies the requirement. The Owner of a requirement is the individual or a group, such as a committee, responsible for making decisions about the requirement. Each requirement should be given a unique reference number.

2.4 Fact Finding

The requirements are established using fact finding techniques. As the system investigation continues more details can be included on each Requirements Catalogue entry or existing details can be amended. The fact finding techniques chosen are at the discretion of the analyst and could include any of the following:

- interviewing
- analyzing documents from the current system
- questionnaires
- work logs specially designed for this system investigation
- shadowing a user or carrying out a user task
- observation
- prototyping
- ideas sessions where participants brainstorm possible requirements
- the analyst's personal knowledge of facilities available in similar systems elsewhere. Knowledge gained from journals, conferences, previous work experience etc

Note that it is important to quantify requirements and rigorously analyze the need to meet this requirement. The question "why" is probably the most important an analyst can ask. A potential user manager might ask that he/she be able to query the proposed employee car allowance system to find out who drives blue Vauxhall Cavaliers. This requirement would involve storing extra information about the car, ie the colour, which no other requirement specifies. On further questioning the manager it may be established that he does not really require this information. The analyst should always remember that ownership of requirements must always rest with the users of the proposed system.

Functional requirement
Provide Admin. Clerk with on-line facility to create new car allowance users.

Non-functional requirements

Description	**Target**	**Acceptable Range**	**Comments**
Service level	0700-1900 Mon-Fri		Occasional weekend
Availability	60%	50-60%	
Security	control access		
Audit	log new car users log creator's ID		

Benefits

Provide better service to claimants
Reduce time spent checking hardcopy records.

Comments/suggested solutions

Provide enquiries function for both Admin and Finance

Related documents

Related requirement references
17

Resolution
Enquiries function provided, options for claim or authorization details.

Figure 2.1 Extract from Requirements Catalogue

2.5 Functional Requirements

The functional requirements are those which dictate what the system should do. They might be for any of the following:

Functional Requirement	Comment
hardcopy output	**ad hoc and regular reports; forms such as invoices and payslips**
enquiries	**on-line interrogation of system data**
updates	**changes to the system data**
data	**data to be stored, data structures,**
data transfer	**communications with other systems**

Functional requirements for the Car Allowance System might include the following:

hardcopy output	**monthly statement for each employee** **annual statement for each employee** **monthly analysis for each manager** **annual analysis for each manager**
enquiries	**on-line access for Finance to check claim progress details**
updates	**Administration to enter new or amended authorization details** **Transport to enter transport authorization** **Finance to enter claim details**
data	**Hold details about employee, car details, claim details, department details.** **Employee's authorization history details to be held.**
data transfer	**Possible direct link to pay system, claims paid with monthly salary.**

2.6 Non-Functional Requirements

Non-functional requirements address other facilities which the system should have such as security, response time etc. Some non-functional requirements are system-wide and should be recorded as such in the Requirements Catalogue. Other non-functional requirements will be directly related to one or more functional requirements. An example might be response times, the needs may vary from one part of the proposed system to another. The Analyst should carefully consider the non-functional requirements and ask questions such as "Is 95% availability required for the whole system, or just for part of it?"

The following sections discuss some possible non-functional requirements which should be considered.

2.6.1 Constraints

2.6.1.1 Interfaces with other systems/external entities

Requirements here may be :

- that data is presented in a particular way to another system or external entity, eg for an Inland Revenue return.
- that data be transferred using communications facilities, tape etc, eg a payroll system may require sending monthly salary details to the bank on tape so that employees can be paid directly into their bank accounts.
- that data is received in a particular format eg. a customer using electronic data interchange (EDI) may present orders in a format which needs to be converted before being processed in the system.

The Car Allowance system will require to produce cheques using the existing pre-printed cheque stationery. The existing application and claim forms should be used.

2.6.1.2 Conversion from current system.

Special requirements for conversion must be recorded. It is important that users obtain an acceptable level of service while conversion is taking place.

The method of conversion should be carefully considered and requirements documented.

In the Car Allowance System employees will still expect to be paid claims promptly during the conversion process. A retrospective parallel run is recommended since this provides extended system testing, training on the new system and allows the work on maintaining the new system files to be scheduled round the existing workload. The current files must be maintained until the end of the current financial year, this will mean that both the new and old files must be updated during the conversion period. The new system will takeover at the start of the next financial year. Creation of the computer based files for the system will involve contacting some employees to confirm current car details since the present duplicate sets of records have missing and conflicting information.

2.6.1.3 Archiving

Data retention requirements must be recorded and decisions made as to what data must be kept eg for legal or operational reasons.

The Car Allowance System is recording financial data. The claim details can be archived at the end of each financial year , but data must be retained for the period required by law. Authorization history details should not be archived annually since they will be checked when an application is received.

2.6.2 Service Level

Service level incorporates requirements such as response time, system availability, reliability etc which will affect the quality of the service provided to users. This information is essential to capacity planning and physical design.

In the Car Allowance System the Administration, Transport and Finance Departments will require on-line access during normal working hours, Monday to Friday. Claims could be entered as soon as they are received by the Finance Department. Payments will be made on a weekly basis so cheques will be produced in a weekly batch run from the previously-entered claim details.

2.6.3 Security

Security requirements include access restrictions; data back-up; recovery; contingency planning; audit and control requirements. For example the system may require a series of passwords which are regularly changed. It may also require an audit trail of any record creations, amendments or deletions. A cheque requisition system may require dual authorization before payment is released.

The Car Allowance System must retain the split responsibility for authorising allowances. Administration will deal with the process for creating an authorized user on the system. Finance will deal with the payment of claims. Listings will be required for new users, amendments to user details, claims paid etc. A system of passwords which are changed regularly must be set up. Current procedures with authorization signatures for allowance applications, amendments and cheque requisitions must be retained in the system.

2.6.4 Legal Requirements

Legal requirements may affect data retention, processing requirements, data validation procedures etc. Careful consideration must be given to relevant legislation and its effect on the system. Legislation considered might include The Data Protection Act 1984, health and safety legislation, employment legislation, consumer protection legislation, etc.

The Car Allowance System is recording details about identifiable individuals so the Data Protection Act must be carefully considered. The system should be registered under the Act if necessary.

2.7 Quantifying Requirements

Wherever possible requirements should be quantified. This helps to reduce ambiguity and provides a basis for deciding whether an implemented system meets requirements. The new system's performance should be regularly monitored to see if the requirements are still being met. The quantities recorded in the Requirements Catalogue provide the basis for comparison.

Requirements can be readily measurable in factors such as target response times. In some cases the measurement may not be so obvious, for instance a target of increased customer satisfaction could be measured by recording the number of customer complaints before the new system is implemented and using this as a benchmark to assess whether the new system really does increase customer satisfaction.

The current Car Allowance system will provide statistics for the number of authorized users, claims per week etc. These should remain approximately the same in the new system.

2.8 Resolution of Requirements

As the project progresses various requirements will be resolved and this should be recorded. For instance once the documents, such as the Employees' Monthly Statement, have been designed, the Requirements Catalogue should be annotated to indicate this and the design document reference number entered in the Related Documents Field.

In the Car Allowance System the low priority requirement to pay employees' claims with their monthly salary may be considered not to be feasible at present for technical reasons, eg the introduction of a new payroll system in two years time. The justification for not meeting the requirement, at present, should be recorded in the Requirements Catalogue.

2.9 Use of Requirements Definition during SSADM steps.

2.9.1 Feasibility Module

Requirements definition is used during the Feasibility Study Module for the following:

- reviewing Terms of Reference
- establishing business objectives
- identification of users of the proposed system
- survey of current system (if any) to identify problems
- identification of functional and non-functional requirements

The information gathered is recorded in the Requirements Catalogue. The Feasibility Report should include requirements, problems and constraints.

2.9.2 Requirements Analysis Module

2.9.2.1 Step 110 Establish Analysis Framework

Creation of Requirements Catalogue, if one has not been carried forward from the Feasibility Report. The starting point is the Project Initiation Document (and related documents) which is reviewed for requirements. Clarification should be sought on any requirements which are unclear.

2.9.2.2 Step 120 Investigate and Define Requirements

Detailed investigations will throw up new requirements and /or problems and will allow completion of Requirements Catalogue entries. Requirements may be modified as fact finding progresses. Where there is no current system this step forms the basis for the investigation of requirements. The functional requirements must be expressed in sufficient detail to enable the definition of Business Systems Options in Step 210. Non-functional requirements must be recorded in sufficient detail to allow the Definition of Business Systems Options and to provide a reasonable basis for cost estimation.

The User Catalogue is created on the basis of users identified during this requirements definition process. The User Catalogue is discussed in more detail in Chapter 3.

2.9.2.3 Step 150 Derive Logical View Of Current Services

Logicalisation may result in the identification of physical constraints which should be recorded in the Requirements Catalogue.

2.9.2.4 Step 210 Define Business System Options

The requirements Catalogue provides a basis for the definition of the Business System Options.

2.9.3 Requirements Specification Module

2.9.3.1 Step 310 Define Required System Processing
Step 320 Develop Required Data Model

The Requirements Catalogue is updated to reflect the selected Business System Option. Any requirements which have been modified or not met must be annotated with the reason. The Requirements Catalogue should be cross referenced to Data Flow Diagrams and the parts of the Logical Data Model which support a requirement. More details should be established for non-functional requirements for inclusion in the Required System Logical Data Model.

2.9.3.2 Step 330 Derive System Functions

The Function Definition technique uses the Requirements Catalogue to identify enquiries and updates, along with related non-functional requirements. Function Definitions which resolve requirements are then cross referenced in the Requirements Catalogue.

2.9.3.3 Step 350 Develop Specification Prototypes

Prototyping may identify some additional requirements and these should be recorded in the Requirements Catalogue.

2.9.3.4 Step 370 Confirm System Objectives

The Requirements Catalogue is checked to ensure that all requirements, functional and non-functional have been recorded and described in full detail.

2.9.4 Logical Systems Specification Module

2.9.4.1 Step 410 Define Technical System Options

Some requirements can only be resolved by aspects of the technical environment. These are addressed during the definition of Technical System Options. An example might be a requirement to restrict access to terminals which can only be resolved by using measures such as magnetically encoded keys or cards to restrict terminal access.

2.9.4.2 Step 510 Define User Dialogues

Any requirements which can be resolved in user dialogues are considered during this step.

2.9.5 Physical Design Module

The Requirements Catalogue is reviewed during the Physical Design Module to ensure that any outstanding requirements are resolved. Users may require to make decisions which optimise the solution for one requirement which can not be met in full if another requirement is met. Desired service level may be a problem area to be resolved.

2.10 Summary

Requirements Definition aims to identify and specify a set of requirements for the proposed system which meet the needs of users and the business objectives as a whole. It results in the creation of the Requirements Catalogue which defines functional and non-functional requirements.

Requirements Definition is an iterative technique. Requirements are added, deleted, amended and updated as systems investigation progresses. The resolution of requirements in the proposed system is recorded in the Requirements Catalogue and related documentation is cross referenced.

The completed Requirements Catalogue provides a basis for measuring new system performance.

2.11 Keywords

Requirements Catalogue	Requirements Analysis
Functional requirements	Fact finding
Non-functional requirements	Business System Options
User Catalogue	Function Definition
Prototyping	Technical System Options
Current Environment	Required System
Project Initiation Document	Resolution of requirements
Service level	Legal requirements
Security requirements	Constraints

2.12 Exercises

1. What data should be recorded in the Requirements Catalogue?

2. What are the functional requirements of a system?

3. What are the non-functional requirements of a system?

4. What fact finding techniques could an analyst use to establish requirements?

5. Who owns a requirement?

6. Prepare a Requirements Catalogue for a system to be implemented on your home computer to keep track of the family's record/tape/compact disk collection.

7. Prepare a Requirements Catalogue for the Car Allowance System using the information contained in this chapter.

8. Use the information in the Case Study in Appendix 2 to complete as much of the Requirements Catalogue as possible. Identify the information which is missing and suggest appropriate fact finding methods to obtain it. Consider the non-functional requirements carefully.

9. Use a database package on a personal computer and set up a system which will allow you to record and maintain a Requirements Catalogue.

CHAPTER THREE

Dialogue Design

3.1 Introduction

Dialogue Design in SSADM starts as early as Stage 1, Investigation of the Current Environment. It has two phases, Dialogue Identification and Dialogue Design. Dialogue Identification is completed by the end of Stage 3, Specification of Requirements. The Dialogue Design is carried out during Stage 5, Logical System Specification, and is used as an input to Stage 6, Physical Design.

SSADM assumes that the analyst has access to such computer aids as screen painters and dialogue simulators. In this environment it is easy to change screen designs and exchanges of data between user and computer. Therefore the accent in dialogue design is no longer on documenting the form of the human-computer exchanges; but rather on making sure that the data required really does exist in a suitable form.

The other thrust of dialogue design within SSADM is to follow good practice in human computer interaction. This second aim is achieved by the use of a Style Guide. This lays down the rules which should be followed in screen design. Ideally, it should cover the entire installation; but it may be for one application or user department only.

This Chapter is placed early in the book since Dialogue Design starts with the establishment of the User Catalogue which is carried out early in Stage 1. Sections 3.1 to 3.3 can be read before any of the remaining chapters in the book. Section 3.4, Dialogue Identification, is best read in parallel with

Chapters 4 to 11, Chapters 4 to 8 are particularly relevant. Section 3.5, Dialogue Design, should be read in conjunction with Chapters 12 to 15. The Car Allowance System Case Study described in Chapter 2, section 2 and Chapter 4, section 6 is used to provide examples throughout this chapter.

3.2 Prototyping

Use of computer aids is meant to make it easier to demonstrate and test the dialogue without attendant programming costs. The term "prototyping" is used to describe this process. SSADM does not specify precisely what is meant by prototyping. The term has been used widely and loosely in the data processing industry. It can mean anything from a complete application produced by an application generator, or a sub-system, or merely a demonstration with a greater or lesser degree of function.

The use of prototyping means that dialogue design becomes an iterative process. Every input to the process is capable of being changed by the demonstration of the current prototype, and will feed back into the next generation of the prototype. Prototyping is discussed in more detail in Chapter 10.

3.3 Style Guide

SSADM strongly recommends the use of an Application Style Guide. This is a set of standards for dialogue design based on the Installation Style Guide but tailored to the specific application. Many installations already have a set of standards for dialogue design to ensure some standardisation of appearance and use across systems.

The concept of a Style Guide comes from the publishing industry. It is a design aid which tries to ensure a high standard of product presented to the public. In the case of newspaper publishing it also ensures that the product is consistent. The public does not expect a newspaper to contain too many surprises. A publishing Style Guide might include such items as type faces to be used, hyphenation rules, paragraph sizes, justification (eg straight right edge or ragged ends to lines), punctuation conventions, use of foreign words, rounding of numbers, use of jargon, use of abbreviations, and the method of introducing abbreviations.

3.3.1 Printed Output

Many installations have established standards of good practice for the layout of computer printed reports. These will include the setting of maximum line lengths, and page depths. This simplifies filing requirements and the purchasing of stationery.

When reports are printed centrally, another useful aid is the use of standard report header and trailer pages. These ensure that circulated reports are in fact complete, and are addressed to the correct destination. The pages carry data such as the name of the report, dates of production and printing, and the titles of the recipients of the various copies.

Within an application it is useful to standardize report headings and field layouts. This involves some agreement on nomenclature, ie, what each field actually means and what it should be called. Similarly there should be some agreement on the identification of reports within an application and the report names.

3.3.2 Screen Layout

A Style Guide is also important for the layout of data on a screen. There are some simple rules for interactive screen layout which have been around since the early seventies, but are continually breached. For instance it is unwise to carry more than one main idea on a single screen. Allowing more than about six data items to be input at one time is a recipe for disuse or disaster. Bells, whistles, high intensity, reverse image, flashing screens and fields should be used sparingly. All of these features may be tremendous selling aids, but they can be an enormous affliction to those who have to put up with them as part of their daily work. Similarly colour can be of great assistance to those who are not colour blind, but even then, not if overdone. There should be only a limited number of different colours per screen (maybe three or four) and the fields to be emphasized should be in the brighter colours.

When in doubt, remember the old adage "to emphasize everything is to emphasize nothing". In a well run organisation the Style Guide should spell out how all of these features are to be used.

3.3.3 User Interface

The Style Guide should define what type of user interface is to be used for each application. By user interface is meant the choice of whether to use menus, icons, natural language, coded language, form filling type screens or a mixture of two or three of these. Each of them might be useful in a particular context, but it is necessary to define the place of each.

Many software systems now allow the user to define icons. While this can be a very powerful tool, it can also become a major hazard to communication. If each analyst defines a unique set of icons, every system has to be learned from scratch. Icon definition must be controlled, and subject to the Style Guide.

As in printed reports, there could be standards laid down for screen layouts for an application: where frequently used fields are positioned, where error messages are displayed, the level of detail in error messages, a standard "Help" facility, a standard way of quitting the system, and maybe a standard way of undoing an action. Often a user realizes that an action was wrong, just after committing a data entry.

It might be that an "undo" function will be difficult to implement, but in any case, it is wise to define a standard method of recovering from particular error situations. For example, if it was thought necessary that some error was of sufficient importance that it merited a sound alarm, perhaps it deserves some deliberate action to acknowledge the error and then clear it.

3.3.4 Technical Aspects

Access control is an important part of security planning, which takes place early in the SSADM development phase. The results of this consideration should be included in the Style Guide, in order to make sure that important decisions, which have already been taken, are conveyed to those responsible for implementing them.

Response time is also a candidate for inclusion in the Style Guide. Like security, it forms part of the System Specification and ought to be passed on to the people who are going to produce the system. If response time is not planned and tested, it will be a problem to rectify the matter when the shortcomings are finally recognized.

Certainly the designers should know if delay loops are going to be needed to prevent inordinately rapid response. (When the system is lightly loaded, delay loops can be used in order to make the response time as uniform as possible).

Standard "wait" messages should be written to reassure the user during temporary system overloads. Otherwise the user will think the system has not received the message and will start tapping the enter key with unpredictable results.

3.4 Dialogue Identification

Dialogue Identification must be completed by the end of Stage 3, Specification of Requirements. It is an iterative process and is carried out alongside the other techniques used during Stages 1 to 3. Dialogue Identification consists of four tasks:

- Produce User Catalogue
- Identify User Roles
- Identify Dialogues Required
- Identify Critical Dialogues.

3.4.1 Produce User Catalogue

The User Catalogue is established as early as Step 120, Investigate and Define Requirements. It lists the job titles of those who will use the system, and the activities that each user performs with respect to the system. In Stage 1, Investigation of Current Environment, the users of the current system are identified. As systems investigation progresses the User Catalogue is updated and amended until it reflects the users of the Required System. Where there is no existing system the User Catalogue is drawn up from the job descriptions for the new system.

In a large complex system, it may be useful to group users in some way. Supporting documentation, such as organisation charts, may be used to clarify complex relationships. The creation and amendment of the User Catalogue may identify organisational problems which have to be referred to user management for solution.

A User Catalogue showing some of the activities for the Current Environment Car Allowance System is shown in Figure 3.1. This chart highlights one of the main problems in the current system, the duplication of activities in the Administration, Finance and Transport Departments.

Job Title	Job Activities Description
Administration Clerk	**Action applications** **Action change of car details** **Action withdrawals of authorization**
Transport Clerk	**Action car check** **Action driver check** **Action change of car details** **Action withdrawals of authorization**
Finance Clerk	**Action change of car details** **Action withdrawals of authorization** **Action claim**
Administration Manager	**Authorize application**

Figure 3.1 Section of User Catalogue for Current Environment Car Allowance System.

A User Catalogue for the Required Car Allowance System is shown in Figure 3.2. The job activities are similar to those in the current system but duplication of activities has been removed by having one central computer-based set of files. Some additional activities have been identified during Requirements Definition and they have been included in the User Catalogue.

3.4.2 Identify User Roles

Once the User Catalogue has been established, it can be used to identify User Roles. A User Role is a group of job holders who share a large proportion of common tasks. This process groups together job-holders who need to access the same functions. The identification of User Roles helps to prevent duplicating the specification of dialogues because they are required by two different sets of users. This activity is carried out during Stage 3, Step 310, Define Required System Processing. By this time the Logical View of the Required System has been agreed.

Job Title	Job Activities Description
Administration Clerk	**Action applications** **Action change of car details** **Action withdrawals of application** **Action change of authorization details**
Transport Clerk	**Action driver check** **Action car check**
Finance Clerk	**Action claim** **Issue monthly employee statements** **Issue monthly departmental reports** **Issue annual departmental report** **Issue annual employee report**
Administration Manager	**Change authorization bands**
Accounts Manager	**Change pay rates**

Figure 3.2 Section of User Catalogue for Required Car Allowance System.

Where two job titles both carry out broadly similar tasks, they belong to the same User Role. All the users carrying out a similar task may not belong to the same User Role. For instance a senior manager may be able to carry out the tasks of a subordinate during peak work loads or absence, but this does not mean they have the same User Role, the levels of security clearance may be different. Figure 3.3 shows part of the User Roles Documentation for the Required Car Allowance System.

User Role	Job Title	Activities
Application authorization	**Admin. Clerk**	**Action applications**
		Action change of car details
		Action withdrawals of application
		Action change of authoriz. details
	Transport Clerk	**Action driver check**
		Action car check
	Admin. Manager	**Authorize application**
Accounts Officers	**Finance Clerk**	**Action claim**
		Issue monthly emp. statements
		Issue monthly dept. reports
		Issue annual dept. report
		Issue annual emp. reports
Accounts Manager	**Accounts Manager**	**Change pay rates**
Administration Manager	**Admin. Manager**	**Change authorization bands**

Figure 3.3 User Roles for the Required Car Allowance System.

3.4.3 Identify Dialogues Required

Dialogues are identified by creating a User Role/Function Matrix. The User Roles are identified from the User Roles Documentation and the functions are identified from the Function Definitions. The X symbol shows which User Roles can initiate a function. This cross-reference between a user and a function indicates the need for a dialogue.

Picking out each X in a row will identify all the dialogues required for a particular User Role. Where two User Roles can initiate a function, one dialogue may be able to serve both User Roles. The User Role/Function Matrix should be checked carefully with the users to check that the functions and dialogues identified are correct. Part of the User Role/Function Matrix for the Car Allowance System is shown in Figure 3.4.

User Role \ Function	Register authorised user	Register car allowance claim	Produce departmental monthly report	Produce employee monthly statement	Produce departmental annual report	Produce employee annual statement
Application authorisation	X					
Accounts Officers		X	X	X	X	X
Accounts Manager						
Administration Manager						

Figure 3.4 Part of the User Role/Function Matrix for the Car Allowance System

3.4.4 Identify Critical Dialogues

The dialogues which are regarded as critical to the required system should be identified on the User Role/Function Matrix. This can be done by circling the X on the matrix, or by changing the X to a C. Critical dialogues can be identified using factors such as frequency of use, involvement of a large number of data items, User Roles sharing a dialogue, complexity, importance to the business and a change in the way users perform tasks. Critical dialogues can be input to Technical System Options to help identify the effect of various options. Some critical dialogues may also be used in Prototyping. Critical dialogues for the Car Allowance System are highlighted in Figure 3.5.

3.5 Inputs to Dialogue Design

The products of Dialogue Identification are input to Dialogue Design along with some other SSADM products. It is perhaps misleading to talk of inputs to or outputs from the design process. By using a prototyping approach the design process is iterative. All the output feeds back into the next iteration as input and can be changed by design.

User Role \ Function	Register authorised user	Register car allowance claim	Produce departmental monthly report	Produce employee monthly statement	Produce departmental annual report	Produce employee annual statement
Application authorisation	(X)					
Accounts Officers		(X)	X	X	X	X
Accounts Manager						
Administration Manager						

Figure 3.5 Critical dialogues for the Car Allowance System.

For example, the designers may have decided upon some error signalling protocol, which specifies audible alarms for some situations, and flashing coloured screens for others. It might have seemed a good idea when tried in the design office on one terminal. When the prototype is tested with real operators and real data, the ensuing noise and lighting effects may be more typical of the amusement arcade than the workplace. As a result both prototype and Style Guide need rewriting. Prototyping can also feed information about Menu and Command Structures back into the Dialogue Design.

Another input to the Dialogue Design technique is the Function Descriptions, which tell the designer what the dialogue is attempting to achieve. They are supported by Input/Output Structures which relate directly to the structure of the dialogues. Input/Output Structures are a representation of the function designer's view of the data which the function needs or provides. As part of SSADM's checking facilities, the dialogue and function designers should come to the same required view of the data, otherwise further investigation is required.

The Requirements Catalogue will have been developed earlier in the system life cycle and it should be a prominent input to the dialogue design. The Requirements Catalogue states what the users want out of the system, and as such it is the foundation of the system. Every idea that the designer generates should be checked to make sure that it meets what the users really want.

It is far too easy to get carried away with the technicalities of the new system. Every so often the designer should step back and compare what he has produced with the expectations of the system's sponsors. It is possible that those expectations will be changed in the light of what is feasible, or of new insights into the system aims, but any changes need to be agreed formally.

3.6 Activities of Dialogue Design

The foundation of Dialogue Design is the set of Input/Output Structures created during Function Definition (see Chapter 8). These Input/Output Structures are amended by the activities of dialogue design and become Dialogue Structures.

Dialogue Structures are a reworked version of the Input/Output Structures, where the data items being transferred are grouped into logical components. These can then be thought of as major elements of the underlying dialogue. Any inconsistency found in the Function Definition can be reconciled at this point.

There are six activities in dialogue design:

- i) List dialogue elements
- ii) Identify Logical Groupings of Dialogue Elements
- iii) Prepare Dialogue Control Table
- iv) Design Menu Structures
- v) Design Command Structures
- vi) Define dialogue level 'Help'.

3.6.1 List dialogue elements

The Input/Output Structure Descriptions output from Function Definition will provide a list of the dialogue elements and associated data items. This information should be recorded on a Dialogue Element Description, see Figure 3.6 for a sample description. Each bottom level box on the Input/Output Structure corresponds to a dialogue element.

Dialogue element	Data item
Payroll no.	**payroll no.**
Employee details	**employee name** **job title** **job location** **allowance grade**
Car details	**car make** **car model** **engine cc.** **registration no.**
Total claim detail	**total mileage** **total claim value**
Journey detail	**start odometer reading** **finish odometer reading**

Figure 3.6 Dialogue elements for "Registration of claims" dialogue.

3.6.2 Identify Logical Groupings of Dialogue Elements

The next step is to take the Input/Output Structure and identify the Logical Grouping of Dialogue Elements. The following rules should be observed when grouping dialogue elements(examples are taken from Figure 3.7):

- dialogue elements in sequence may be grouped together (see Car-claim-1)
- a dialogue element may not be in two logical groups eg "Total claim details"(input) may not be in both Car-claim-2 and Car-claim-3.
- dialogue elements may not be omitted from a sequence when forming a logical group
- a logical group may be formed from dialogue elements which are close together eg Car-claim-1.

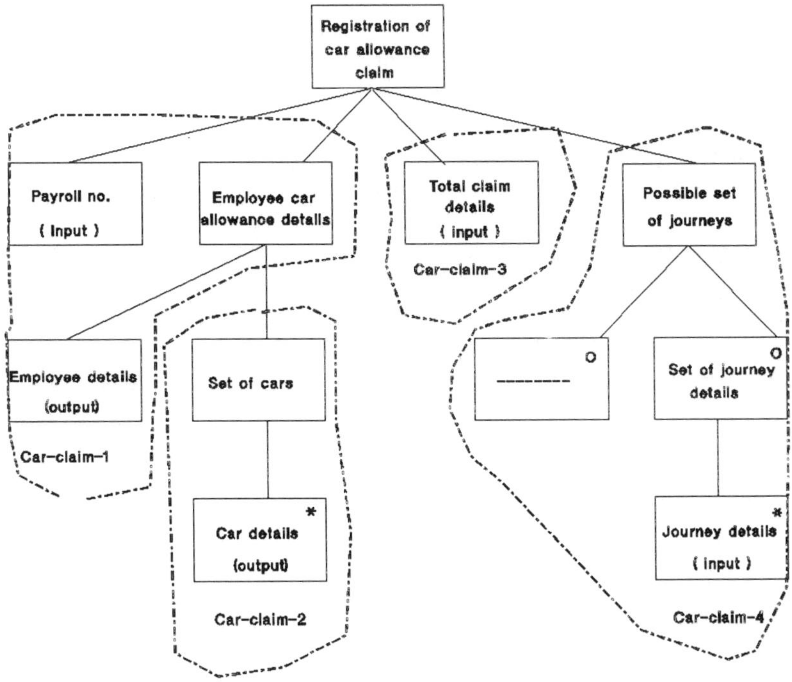

Figure 3.7 Logical Grouping of Dialogue Elements for "Registration of claims"

The primary objective of producing the Logical Grouping of Dialogue Elements is to define the navigation within the dialogue. If one user activity follows another then they should be grouped together, eg in Car-claim-1 the input of the "payroll number" will be followed immediately by the output of the "employee details". Car-claim 2 consists of up to two sets of car details, it makes sense to put this in a separate group since the iteration provides useful information on the Dialogue Control Table for later use in Physical Design. Many of the groupings will involve pairs of input and output. Where an input involves a lot of data items it may be better in a group on its own.

Having been grouped, the Dialogue Element Description is updated with the Logical Grouping of Dialogue Elements ID, see Figure 3.9. A dialogue will then consist of a number of Dialogue Elements.

3.6.3 Prepare Dialogue Control Table

The summary of the Logical Grouping of Dialogue Elements is called the Dialogue Control Table. This shows the normal path through the Dialogue Elements, and a number of optional paths (if they exist). There is also provision for including the likelihood of using the optional paths, and the frequency of use of the various elements.

The Dialogue Control Table in Figure 3.8 shows that 85% of claims take the default pathway using Car-claim-1, 2 and 3. The remaining 15% of claims also use Car-claim-4 and take alternative pathway 1. The minimum, maximum and average occurrences of each Logical Group of Dialogue Elements is also shown. For instance Car-claim-2 shows that the details of at least one car and a maximum of two cars should be displayed.

LGDE ID	Occurrences			Default pathway	Alternative pathways		
	Min	Max	Ave		Alt 1	Alt 2	Alt 3
Car-claim-1	1	1	1	X	X		
Car-claim-2	1	2	1	X	X		
Car-claim-3	1	1	1	X	X		
Car-claim-4	0	50	15		X		
Percentage path usage				85	15		

Figure 3.8 Dialogue Control Table

The Dialogue Element Description should now be annotated to show if a Logical Grouping of Dialogue Elements is mandatory (M) or optional (O). This can be derived from the Dialogue Control Table. Any Logical Grouping of Dialogue Elements which has an X against it on every pathway is mandatory. If there is no X on some pathways then that Logical Grouping of Dialogue Elements is optional. Figure 3.9 shows the completed Dialogue Element Descriptions. An iteration in the Dialogue Structure shows that a dialogue element can occur zero, one or many times so any grouping which includes an iteration may need to be annotated M/O.

Dialogue element	Data item	LGDE	Mandatory/ optional LGDE
Payroll no.	**payroll no.**		
Employee details	**employee name** **job title** **job location** **allowance grade**	**Car-claim-1**	**M**
Car details	**car make** **car model** **engine cc.** **registration no.**	**Car-claim-2**	**M**
Total claim detail	**total mileage** **total claim value**	**Car-claim-3**	**M**
Journey detail	**start odometer reading** **finish odometer reading**	**Car-claim-4**	**O**

Figure 3.9 Dialogue Element Description for "Registration of claim".

3.6.4 Design Menu Structures

Menus are defined to be a hierarchical structure used to access dialogues and some off-line functions. The starting point for the construction of menus is the User Role/Function Matrix. The first-cut grouping of functions is taken by recording all the functions initiated by a particular User Role. This is easily identified since each row on the matrix represents a User Role and an X represents a function initiated by that User Role. There should be one Menu Structure for each User Role in the system.

For example, from the matrix in Figure 3.4 the following dialogues in the Car Allowance System are initiated by the Accounts Officers:

- Registration of car allowance claim
- Department monthly reports
- Department annual reports
- Employee monthly statement
- Employee annual statement

Having identified the dialogues, they must be grouped in a hierarchical structure for each User Role. The following guidelines are useful when defining the menu structures:

- consult with the user. Groups should support the way the user works

- examine the Required System Dataflow Diagrams to identify groups of dialogues which logically belong together

- groups can contain different numbers of elements

- groups can contain submenus

- consider the results from any prototyping of menus

- incorporate relevant information from the Style Guide on menu construction

The results should be documented as a Menu Structure. Menus are identified by a box with square corners and a reference such as MEN1. Dialogues are identified by a box with rounded corners and a reference such as DIAL01. Figure 3.10 shows the Menu Structure for the Accounts Officer User Role in the Car Allowance System.

Check the Menu Structure against the appropriate row on the User Role/Function Matrix. There should be one dialogue box for each X on the matrix.

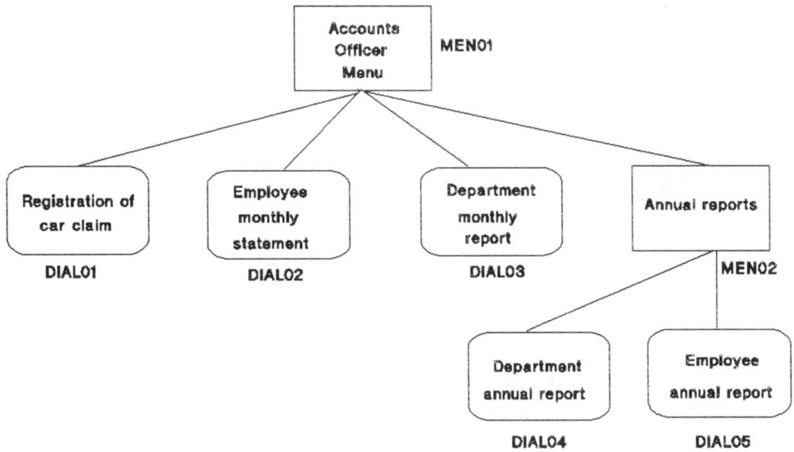

Figure 3.10 Menu Structure for Accounts Officer User Role

3.6.5 Define Command Structures

Command Structures indicate the path that control can take when a dialogue terminates. This could support giving control to another menu or jumping sideways to another dialogue. The Command Structures and Menu Structures together provide a full picture of all the possible paths through the system.

Every dialogue can have a Command Structure. It shows any subsequent dialogues and menus. The information is gathered from Function Descriptions and users. The structure is documented on a Command Structure Form.

In the Car Allowance System, after the completion of the "Registration of car allowance claim" dialogue, the options open to the user are:

- to record another claim, ie. return to the beginning of the dialogue
- to quit and return to the main menu

This is shown in the Command Structure for the dialogue in Figure 3.11.

Option	Dialogue or Menu	Dialogue/Menu name
Record another claim	**Dialogue**	**Registration of claim**
Quit to Accounts Officer Menu	**Menu**	**Accounts Officer Main Menu**

Figure 3.11 Command Structure for "Registration of claim" dialogue.

All dialogues listed must appear on the User Role/Function Matrix for that User Role. All the menus listed must be valid for the User Role.

Each Menu Structure identified should end up with a number of Command Structures appended.

3.6.6 Define dialogue level 'Help'

Document any requirement for help relating to matters such as the location of a dialogue in the Menu Structure, how to move through the Menu Structure or guidance on which task to move to next.

3.7 The place of Dialogue Design in SSADM

3.7.1 Feasibility Study

The intended users of the required system are identified in the User Catalogue. This is used to help with defining the scope of the problem, selecting Feasibility Options and is part of the final Feasibility Report.

3.7.2 Requirements Analysis

3.7.2.1 Step 120 Investigate and Define Requirements

The intended users of the new system are defined in the User Catalogue.

3.7.2.2 Step 160 Assemble Investigation Results

The User Catalogue is one of the SSADM products reviewed for completeness and consistency.

3.7.2.3 Step 210 Define Business System Options

The User Catalogue, as one of the outputs of Requirements Analysis, is input to the definition of Business System Options.

3.7.3 Requirements Specification

3.7.3.1 Step 310 Define Required System Processing

This step requires the User Catalogue as one of its inputs. The Dialogue Design technique is used to define the User Roles.

3.7.3.2 Step 330 Derive System Functions

Using the results of Function Definition, produced during this step, the required system Dialogues can be identified. This is done by cross referencing the User Roles and the functions on a User Role/Function Matrix. Critical dialogues are highlighted on the matrix.

3.7.3.3 Step 350 Develop Specification Prototypes

Selected dialogue menus and command structures are prototyped. The results of prototyping are used to modify the logical dialogue design as necessary.

3.7.3.4 Step 360 Assemble Requirements Specification

The User Role/Function Matrix becomes part of the Requirements Specification Document.

3.7.4 Logical System Specification

3.7.4.1 Step 410 Define Technical System Options

The critical dialogues highlighted on the User Role/Function Matrix are a useful input to the definition of Technical System Options.

3.7.4.2 Step 420 Select Technical System Options

Once a Technical System Option has been selected, the Application Style Guide is developed based on the Installation Style Guide.

3.7.4.3 Step 510 Define User Dialogues

All the Dialogue Design tasks discussed in section 3.6 are carried out during this Step.

3.7.4.4 Step 540 Assemble Logical Design

The products of the Dialogue Design technique become part of the Logical System Specification Document.

3.7.5 Physical Design

3.7.5.1 Step 630 Create Function Component Implementation Map

Physical dialogue design and error handling are specified during this Step.

3.8 Summary

Dialogue Design is the technique that specifies the user interaction with the system. It involves two phases, Dialogue Identification and Dialogue Design. Dialogue Identification is completed by the end of Stage 3, Specification of Requirements. Dialogue Design is carried out during Stage 5, Logical System Specification, and is used as an input to the Physical Design.

3.9 Keywords

Dialogue identification	Requirements Catalogue
Dialogue design	User Catalogue
Application Style Guide	User Role/Function Matrix
Installation Style Guide	Input/Output Structures
User Role/Function Matrix	User Role
Function Definition	Menu Structures
Dialogue level 'Help'	Command Structures
Dialogue Element Description	Dialogue Control Table
Logical Grouping of Data Elements	Dialogue Structure
Critical Dialogues	

3.10 Exercises

1. Identify the activities involved in Dialogue Identification.

2. Describe the activities involved in Dialogue Design.

3. Prepare a User Catalogue for the Current Environment Telephone Allowance System described in Chapter 5, section 2.

4. Prepare a User Catalogue for the Required Telephone Allowance System described in Chapter 5.

5. Identify the User Roles for the Required Telephone Directory System and create a User Role/Function Matrix showing the critical dialogues.

6. Prepare a User Catalogue for the Required Student Administration System described in Appendix 2. Identify the User Roles and create a User Role/Function Matrix showing the critical dialogues.

7. For the Car Allowance System, carry out the Dialogue Design techniques, discussed in section 3.6, on the dialogue which creates a new authorised car user.

8. For the Car Allowance System, carry out the Dialogue Design techniques on the dialogue which can change the car details of an authorised user.

9. Complete the Dialogue Design for the Required Telephone Allowance System (see questions 4 and 5)

10. Complete the Dialogue Design for the Required Student Administration System (see questions 6).

CHAPTER FOUR
Creating a Data Flow Model.

4.1 Introduction

Chapter 1 discussed the three views of a system taken by SSADM. Data Flow Diagramming is the technique used to describe one of these views, that of the information flow through the system. Data Flow Diagrams have often been used as the central technique for structured methods, however they give only a partial description of the system and SSADM provides strong links with other techniques which complete the system description.

There are two chapters on the Data Flow Model in this book. This chapter will describe the need for Data Flow Diagrams and how to draw them for a current physical system. Chapter 5 will describe how Data Flow Diagrams are used in the different stages of SSADM.

4.2 Need for Data Flow Diagrams

Narrative descriptions of a system are a poor way of conveying to a user what an existing system does, or a new system will do. Using English to describe a system provides the reader with a large volume of reading material and it is difficult for the reader to see how all the parts of the system fit together. It is also extremely difficult to describe something precisely in English, ambiguities can arise no matter how carefully a document is written.

A technique is required which allows the reader to see a structured model of the system that provides an overview of all the component parts, but also allows the reader to see a detailed model of a particular component part. Such a model would be even more useful if it could be understood by everyone involved in the systems development process, from the systems analyst to the user. Since English is a poor method of describing a system, a pictorial model might provide a clearer and less ambiguous view of the system.

Data Flow Diagrams provide a clear pictorial model of the Data Flows in a system. The diagrams are structured in a hierarchical way so that the user can see an overview of the whole system and its relationship with the system environment by looking at the Context Diagram and level one Data Flow Diagram. Detailed models of component parts of the system can be seen in lower level Data Flow Diagrams.

Data Flow Diagrams do not give any indication of sequence or frequency of processing. SSADM uses other techniques alongside Data Flow Diagrams to provide a complete view of the system.

4.3 Data Flow Diagram Symbols and Conventions.

There are six symbols used to draw Data Flow Diagrams.

4.3.1 External Entity

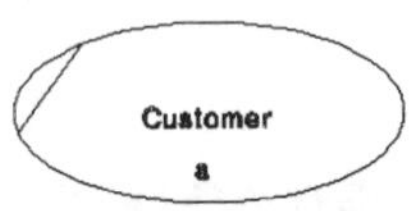

An external entity is represented by an oval. An external entity is a source or recipient of data outside the system currently being described.

An external entity could a person or organisation such as a customer, a supplier or a manager. An external entity can also be another system, manual or computerised, with which the current system exchanges data. The name of the external entity is in the centre of the box. A lower case alpha character may be used to uniquely identify an external entity. A particular external entity may appear several times on a Data Flow Diagram so that crossed flow lines can be avoided, this is indicated by a line across the top, left of the oval.

4.3.2 Process

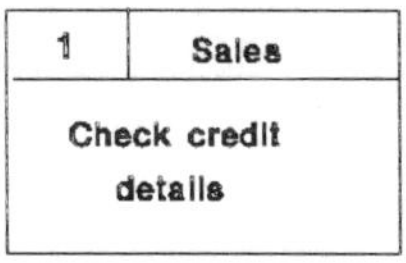

A process is represented by a rectangle. A process is an operation which transforms a data flow into one or more different data flows.

Each box is uniquely identified with a number in the top left. The location of the process is described in the top, right of the box. The label in the lower portion of the box identifies the process. The name of a process should be kept as short as possible and consist of an active verb such as "check", "complete" etc followed by a noun or short phrase, eg "Check Quantity-in-Stock", "Complete Order-Details".

Take care to avoid vague descriptions such as "process invoices", this could mean a number of different processes at different parts of the system. The description should be precise eg "Produce Customer Invoices". Each process has a unique number and the location of the process is also identified. A location can be either a user department or an existing computer program.

4.3.3 Data Store

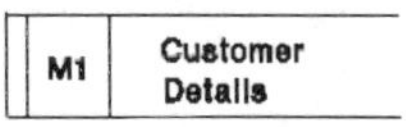

A store of data is represented by an open ended rectangle. A store is any temporary or permanent collection of data which occurs in the flow of data through the system, that is anywhere data is at rest in the system. A data store can be a manually maintained collection of data such as a card index mailing list or a ring binder containing price lists or even an in-tray on someone's desk. A data store can also be a computer based file of data. There are two types of data stores:

- main data stores
- transient data stores

A main data store contains data held centrally which is used by a number of different processes. Each main data store is uniquely numbered starting with 'M' for manual files and 'D' for computer based files. Data stores can be duplicated on a Data Flow Diagram to avoid crossed flow lines. A duplicated data store is indicated by a double vertical bar at the left hand side of the symbol.

A transient data store holds data temporarily before using it in a process and deleting it. An example might be an in-tray which holds customer orders from the day's mail until the clerk has time to process the order. The processed order is not put back in the in-tray. A transient data store is identified by putting a 'T' before the number. If the data store T1 is also a manual file, such as the in-tray, it would be numbered T1(M).

4.3.4 Data Flow

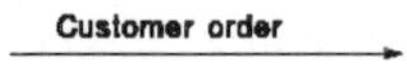

A named arrow represents a data flow. A data flow is a group of data items moving from one part of the system to another. The arrow does not indicate an action and should be named with a noun and adjectives, no verbs permitted. Where even one data item on a data flow differs from another data flow the names should be unique to avoid confusion. Data flows do not require to be named if their content is obvious from the diagram, but it is good practice to name each data flow. If you are using a diagramming tool to prepare your diagrams you may be forced to name each data flow.

A double headed arrow may be used on a high level Data Flow Diagram to indicate that there are both input and output flows in a lower level diagram. However, if a process reads a data store and then updates it, only the data flow with the update is shown. A double headed arrow should not be used on a bottom level Data Flow Diagram.

4.3.5 Physical Resource Flow

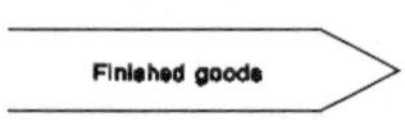

The broad arrow represents a physical resource flow such as the movement of components between the stockroom and the production line. This symbol is rarely used since physical materials are usually accompanied by a data flow such as a stock requisition note and it is the flow of information which is our main concern. The physical resource flow may be useful when developing an initial Level One Data Flow Diagram, particularly in systems which are concerned with the flow of materials. The physical resource flow can be used in preliminary discussions with users to help establish the existence of the data flows with which they are associated. Physical resource flows may come to or from an external entity or a physical resource flow but a process must always be at one end of the arrow.

4.3.6 Physical Resource Store

The closed rectangle represents a store of physical resources. This might be a warehouse or a loading bay or some other area where goods are kept in the system. The only possible input to or output from a physical resource store is a physical resource flow.

4.3.7 Links Between Symbols

Data flows and physical resource flows can be used to provide the links between symbols in SSADM as shown in Figure 4.1.

	Process	Data Store	External Entity
Process	YES	YES	YES
Data Store	YES	NO	NO
External Entity	YES	NO	YES

Figure 4.1 Permissible links between DFD symbols

An external entity can never be linked to a data store since a process within a system must always be present to access a data store. For the same reason two data stores cannot be directly linked, a process is required to move data from one to the other. Two processes can be directly linked but this can indicate two processes which are closely coupled and can be merged (see Chapter 5). It is often useful to show links between two external entities. An example is a sales order processing system where the system under investigation does not include warehouse procedures. Instead of only showing delivery instructions going from sales to the external entity Warehouse, it may be useful to show that the Warehouse sends the goods with a delivery note to the external entity Customer as shown in Figure 4.2.

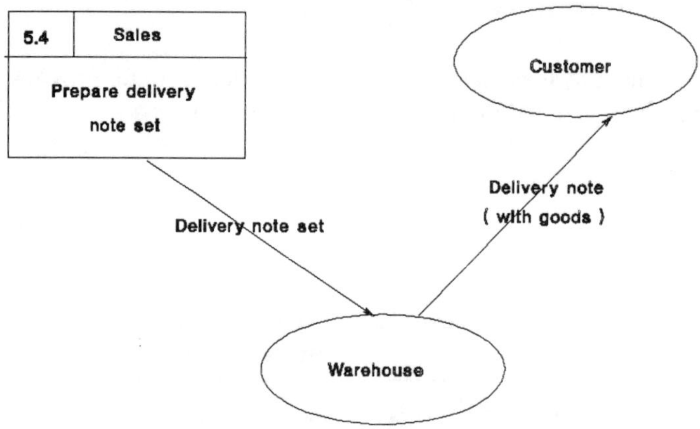

Figure 4.2 Linking two external entities

Figure 4.3 shows some possible links between processes and data stores. When a data store is amended or added to, the arrow head on the data flow should point towards the data store. When a data store is referred to by a process then the arrow head should point away from the data store. Only the net result of processing against a data store requires to be shown on the Data Flow Diagram. If a process reads a data store and then immediately updates it then only the update data flow requires to be shown on the Data Flow Diagram.

In Figure 4.3(a) the data flow direct from one process to another indicates that process 2 deals with the output from process 1 as soon as it is received. In

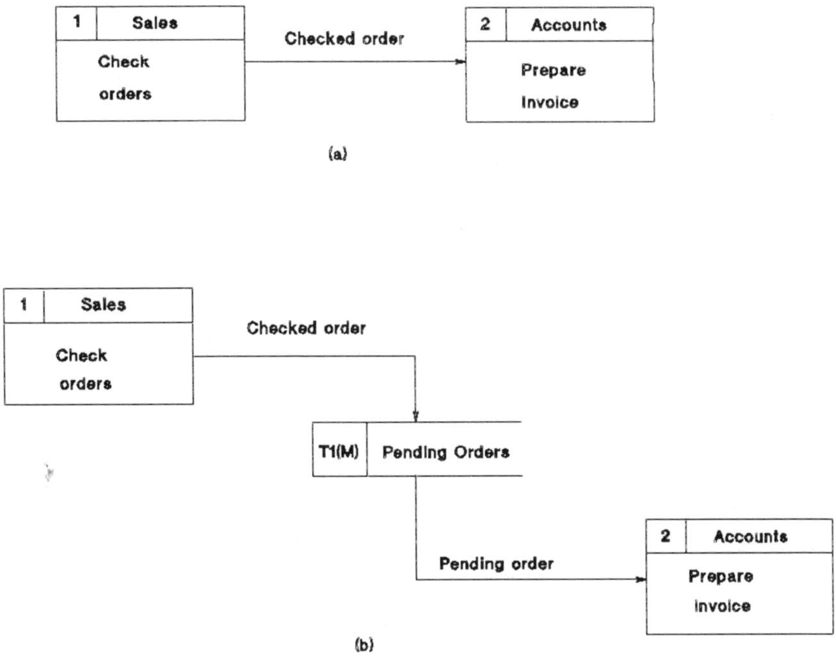

Figure 4.3 Data store to process links

Figure 4.3(b) process 1 adds to a data store and process 2 refers to or retrieves data from the same data store. This can be used to indicate batching where process 1 creates a temporary data store and from time to time process 2 picks up data from this data store.

The temporary nature of the data store is indicated by numbering it T1(M). It can also be used to show that process 1 adds to or amends data in the data store and process 2 refers to this data store without changing it, for example process 2 could use the data in a calculation but not change the data, in this case the data store is not temporary and would be numbered M1.

4.4 Exercises

1. Identify the errors in the following symbols.

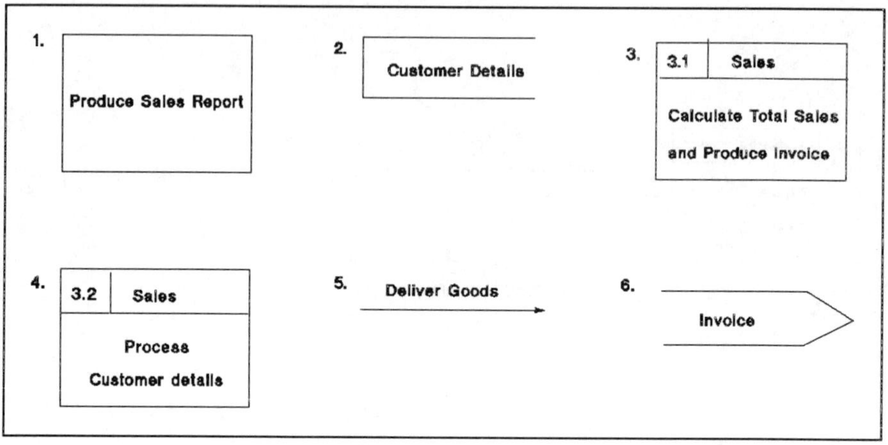

2. Are the following combinations of symbols permitted?

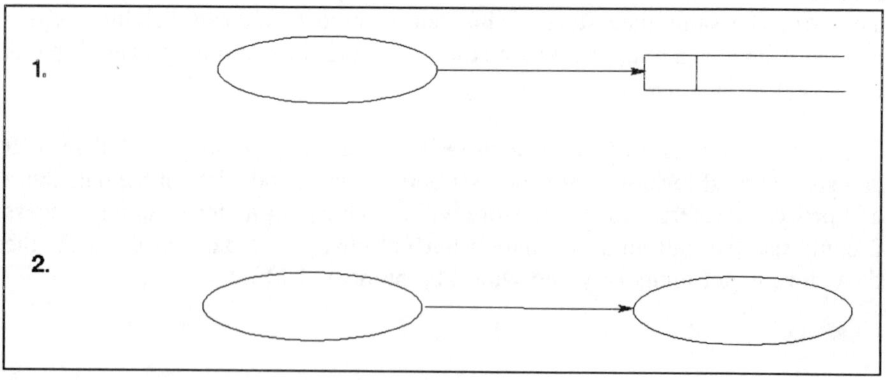

3.

4.

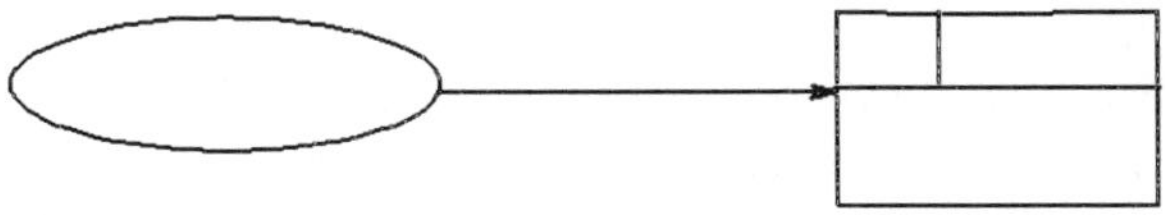

5.

6.

7.

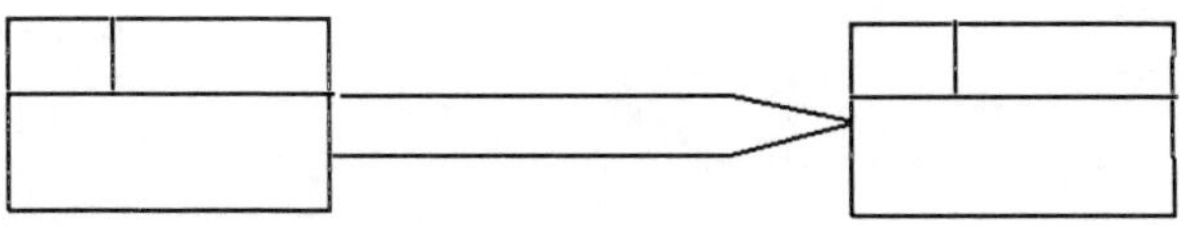

4.5 Hierarchy concept.

Data Flow Diagrams represent a model of the information flow in a system. It is important that the model is not cluttered with too much detail since it would then become difficult to understand. However, detailed information about the information flow is still required. To solve this problem Data Flow Diagrams are built in a structured manner with a top level diagram (Level 1 Data Flow Diagram) giving an overview of the major component parts of the system. The information flows between these component parts are clearly identified, as are the information flows to and from the External Entities. Lower level diagrams (Level 2 Data Flow Diagrams) are then constructed to show the detail of the information flows in each component part. This process of decomposition can be extended to even lower levels of detail if required. The numbering system for the processes on each level reflects the hierarchical structure shown in Figure 4.4.

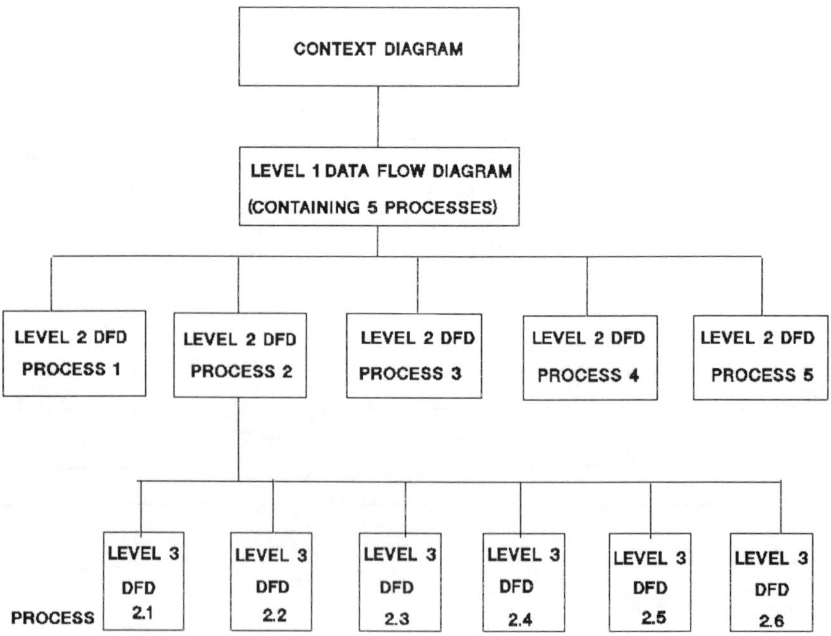

Figure 4.4 Hierarchical structure of a set of DFD's.

The process number indicates the process box on the higher level diagram which is being expanded. The level two diagrams for processes 1, 3, 4 and 5 will generally also be expanded to level 3. A well balanced set of Data Flow Diagrams would decompose all level one processes to the same extent. It should not normally be necessary to go beyond level 2 or 3. Elementary Process Descriptions are used to further expand each of the lowest level processes on a set of Data Flow Diagrams (see section 4.21.2). The lowest level processes are indicated with an asterisk in the bottom right hand corner of the process box.

It is possible to extend the hierarchy concept further to make the level one diagram easier to read. A single data flow can represent two or more data flows on a lower level diagram. It may be possible to group entities together on a level one diagram. For instance the level one diagram may have entity (a) Customer, while on the lower level diagrams this is shown as (a1) Industrial Customer, (a2) Commercial Customer, (a3) Domestic Customer. It is also possible to group data stores, data store 1 Customer Accounts may decompose to data stores 1a Industrial Customer Accounts, 1b Commercial Customer Accounts and 1c Domestic Customer Accounts. The numbering system for data stores is similar to that used for processes.

4.6 Case Study - Car Allowances System

The following description of the current environment of a Car Allowances System will be used and developed throughout this chapter. Documents are underlined. The description has been drawn up as a result of interviews with staff in the Administration and Finance Departments.

Utility Corporation is a large company providing a service to the public. Employees of the company may be required to use their own car for business purposes, in which case they are entitled to claim a car allowance.

Employees appointed to a new post must apply for a car allowance using the Car Allowance Application Form which is a four part set printed on NCR paper. This form is signed by the employee's manager who then sends the Manager Signed Four Part Application Form to the Senior Administration Officer, Central Administration Department. The Senior Administration Officer carries out a number of checks and then sends the Checked Application Form to the Transport Department for authorization of the driver and the car. The Senior Administration Officer keeps a log of all Car Allowance Applications received and records the progress of the application in this log. The Transport Signed Application Form is returned to the Senior Administration Officer. The Senior Administration Officer then calculates the allowance grade due to the employee by referring to the current Car Allowance Regulations, and arranges for the final authorization signature from the Administration Manager. Once the fully authorized set is ready the Senior Administration Officer retains Copy 1 in the Admin. Car Users File, sends Copy 2 to the Transport Manager, Copy 3 to the Finance Department and Copy 4 to the applicant's manager. Administration, Finance and Transport Departments each file their copy of the allowance authorization.

An employee's Car Allowance Claim Form is signed by the employee's manager who then sends in the Manager Signed Claim Form to the Claims Clerk in the Finance Department. Claims are processed on the day they arrive. The claim forms undergo a variety of checks against the Finance Car Users File which contains the original authorization copy 3. The checks made on each claim are to ensure that the driver is authorized on the grade claimed and that the form has been signed by an appropriate manager. Checked Claim Forms are then given to the comptometer (adding machine) operators in the Finance department. They check that the mileage for individual journeys given on the form adds up to the total miles claimed. Mileage Checked Claim Forms are then returned to the Claims Clerk who prepares a Cheque Requisition Form which is passed to the clerk who deals with the computerised cheque requisition system. The claim forms are held temporarily until the cheques are returned. The computer printed Cheque is delivered to the Claims Clerk. The clerk checks the claim form against the cheque and then attaches a pre-printed Compliments Slip to the Cheque and sends it directly to the employee. The Paid Claims Form can then be filed in alphabetical order with all the other claim forms for that month in the Car Allowances Paid File.

Employees changing their car should send in a New Car Details Letter to the Central Administration Department, in practice this only happens when the change of car will result in a change of the mileage rate payable to the employee. The Senior Administration Officer takes a photocopy of the new car details and sends the copy to Transport and keeps the original in a pending file. When Transport sends back the New Car Authorization, the Senior Administration Officer calculates the new allowance grade and prepares a 4 part Regrade Letter. Copy 1 of the Regrade Letter is filed in the Admin. Car Users

File with the Employee's original New Car Details Letter, Copy 2 is sent to Transport, Copy 3 is sent to Finance and Copy 4 is sent to the Employee.

The area of the system being examined with a view to computerisation is all the car allowance processing tasks which are carried out in Administration, Finance and Transport.

4.7 Document Flow Diagram

There are several approaches to drawing Data Flow Diagrams. The method suggested in this book starts with examining the flow of documents in a system. This approach is very useful since, where there is an existing system, documents are often the starting point for discussion with users during systems investigation. The first step is to identify the documents then find out where they originate and their destination. The names of the documents have been changed slightly if the document has been amended in any way, for example by the addition of a signature. Figure 4.5 shows the documents identified.

SOURCE	DOCUMENT	DESTINATION
Employee	Car allowance application form	Manager
Manager	Man-signed application form	Admin.
Admin.	Checked application form	Transport
Transport	Trans-signed application form	Admin.
Admin.	Authorized application copy 1	Admin.
	" " copy 2	Transport
	" " copy 3	Finance
	" " copy 4	Manager
Employee	Car allowance claim form	Manager
Manager	Man-signed claim form	Finance
Finance	Checked claim form	Compt. Ops
Compt Ops	Miles checked claim form	Finance
Finance	Cheque requisition form	Cheque System
Cheque System	Cheque	Finance
Finance	Cheque with compl. slip	Employee
Employee	New car details	Admin.
Admin	New car details original	Admin.
Admin	" " " copy 1	Transport
Admin	" " " copy 2	Finance

Fig. 4.5 Document Flow for Car Allowance System

The next step is to put this information in the form of a diagram. The Document Flow Diagram is not an end product of SSADM ie it will not appear in the final system documentation. It is a useful diagram to discuss with users when an analyst is trying to understand an existing system and it provides a good basis for drawing a draft level 1 Data Flow Diagram. All the sources and destinations are identified by an oval and the documents are on named arrows between the ovals. Any documents which have the same source and destination are not shown on this diagram, they are retained within that location and identify potential data stores when the Data Flow Diagrams are drawn. The Document Flow Diagram for the Car Allowance System Case Study is shown in Figure 4.6.

It may be useful to draw separate Document Flow Diagrams for different parts of a complex clerical system. The boundary of the system under examination can now be discussed with users and drawn with a dotted line on the Document Flow Diagram as shown in Figure 4.6.

4.8 Context Diagram

The Context Diagram is a top level view of a system which shows the data flows to and from External Entities. These can be considered to be the system's major inputs and outputs. It is not essential to draw a Context Diagram but many analysts find it useful since it highlights the data being passed between the system and the system environment and clearly identifies the boundaries of the system. External Entities outside the organisation and other systems with which the system interacts are clearly identified. Context Diagrams are also known as Level 0 Data Flow Diagrams. A Context Diagram is often drawn after some of the lower level Data Flow Diagrams have been completed and a fuller understanding of the systems data flows has been achieved. The Car Allowance system has been simplified and it is useful to draw a Context Diagram before drawing the levelled set of Data Flow Diagrams. A Context Diagram for the Car Allowance System can easily be drawn up from the Document Flow Diagram in Figure 4.6. Everything within the boundary line is included within a single process box. All data flows which cross the system boundary are shown. Input sources and output destinations are identified as External Entities. The Context Diagram is shown in Figure 4.7.

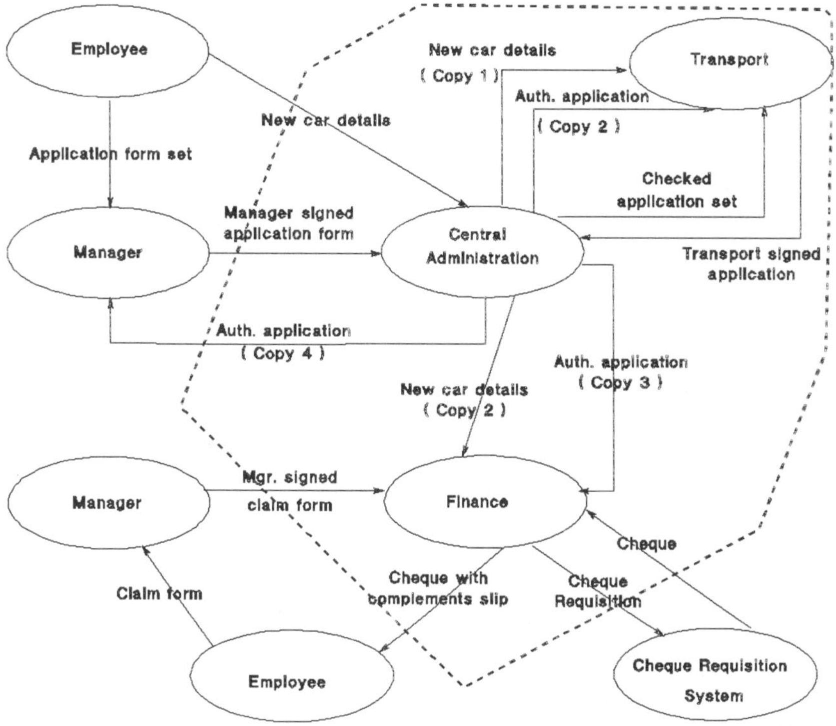

Figure 4.6 Document Flow Diagram

4.8.1 Explanation of Context Diagram

The External Entities identified are Employee, Cheque Requisition System and Manager. We are not concerned with the processes these External Entities use to produce inputs to, or receive outputs from, the Employee Allowances System. Manager is shown twice on the diagram to avoid having too many data flows to and from the one symbol. Note that duplication of an external entity is indicated by a slanted line across the top left corner of the oval. The Cheque Requisition System is an entirely separate system from the Employee

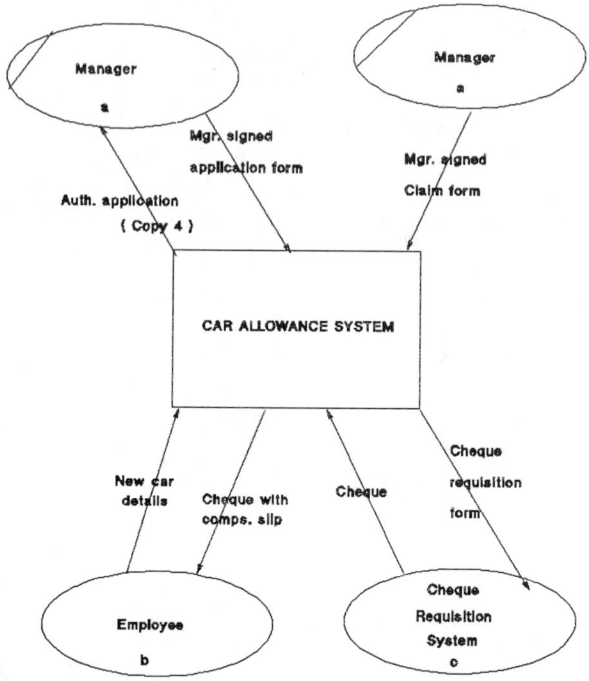

Figure 4.7 Context Diagram

Allowances System. The Cheque Requisition system produces the Cheque as an output. The model of the information flows in the Employee Allowances System is not concerned with how this output is produced only with identifying the source of the output and identifying any input which it needs to provide to the Cheque Requisition System.

Anything inside the boundary of a system is not an external entity. The Central Administration Department, the Transport Department and the Finance Department are all concerned with processing for the Car Allowances System and so are within the system boundary. The processing carried out in these departments will be described in more detail in the Level 1 and Level 2 Data

Flow Diagrams. The departments will be shown as the location in the appropriate process boxes. Manager is an external entity for this system as an employee's manager sends the application and claim forms in to the Administration Department. The Manager is the source of the forms as far as the Administration Department is concerned. We are not investigating the procedures each manager carries out when deciding to put an employee forward for a car allowance. However we have lost the information that employees send forms through their manager, the level 1 Data Flow Diagram can be used to give this information so that our picture of the system is complete.

4.9 Exercises

1. Draw a document Flow Diagram for the current environment of the Telephone Directory System described in Chapter 5, section 2.

2. Draw a Context Diagram based on your answer to exercise 4.9.1.

3. Identify the External Entities, inputs and outputs for the Student Administration System described in Appendix 2.

4. Draw a Document Flow Diagram based on your answer to exercise 4.9.3.

5. Draw a Context Diagram based on your answer to exercise 4.9.4.

4.10 Level 1 Data Flow Diagram, Identifying the Parts

A Level 1 Data Flow Diagram is the top level Data Flow Diagram. It gives an overview of the whole system which is being modelled, showing its major processes and data stores. The system's relationship with its environment is indicated by the data flows to and from External Entities. All the data flows on the Context Diagram should appear on the Level One Data Flow Diagram. If any extra data flows across the system boundary are identified then the

Context Diagram should be redrawn. The first step in drawing the Level 1 Data Flow Diagram is to identify a receiving process for each input to the system and a generating process for each output. This is shown in Figure 4.8.

INPUT	**RECEIVING PROCESS**
Man-signed appl. form	**Check application form**
New car details	**Record change of car**
Man-signed claim form	**Check claim details**
Cheque	**Despatch payment**

OUTPUT	**GENERATING PROCESS**
Auth. appl. copy 4	**Authorize car allowance**
Cheque/compl. slip	**Despatch payment**
Cheque req. form	**Prepare cheque requisition**

Figure 4.8 Car Allowance System receiving and generating processes

As few processes as possible have been identified. "Despatch payment" has been recorded as a receiving and generating process since the receipt of the cheque from the Cheque Requisition System triggers the process to despatch cheques with complements slips to employees. The outline of the Level 1 Data Flow Diagram can now be drawn as shown in Figure 4.9. Note that there are no links between the processes. The next stage is to use our Document Flow Diagram to find any missing internal data flows. Any data stores should also be identified.

4.11 Exercises

1. Use the Telephone Directory System discussed in Chapter 5, section 2 and prepare an outline Level 1 Data Flow Diagram.

2. Using the Student Administration System described in Appendix 2, and your answers to the exercises in section 4.9 draw up a list of receiving and generating processes for the system inputs and outputs.

3. Draw an outline Level 1 Data Flow Diagram using your answer to exercise 4.11.2

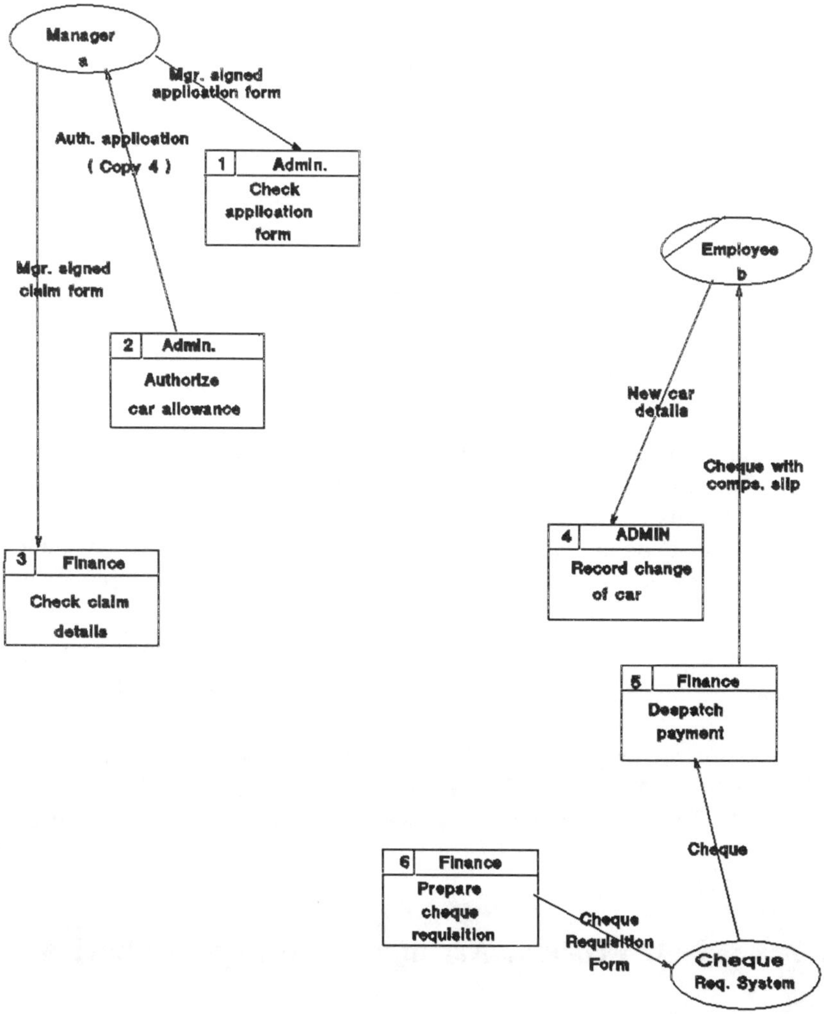

Figure 4.9 Outline Level 1 Data Flow Diagram

4.12 Completing the Level One Data Flow Diagram

4.12.1 The Missing Components

Only three stages remain to complete the diagram

- the identification of any data flows between processes
- the identification of any data stores required by more than one process
- the identification of any processes which only deal with internal inputs and outputs.

We need to take each process in turn and consider its relationships with all other processes, its requirement to store data and its requirement to access stored data. The Document Flow Diagram can be used to help identify internal data flows. If one process is created for each source or destination inside the system boundary then we have a good basis for the Level 1 Data Flow Diagram. The table in Figure 4.5 identifies the possible existence of some data stores where the source and destination of a document are the same location.

4.12.2 Process 1, Check Application Form

The input to this process is the Manager-signed Application Form. On the Document Flow Diagram in Figure 4.6 we find that the Checked Application Set goes to Transport. Figure 4.9 has no process for Transport so a new process is required which can be called Arrange Transport Authorization.

4.12.3 New Process, Arrange Transport Authorization

From the Document Flow Diagram the output from this process is the Transport Signed Application Form. This output goes to the Administration Department so that the allowance can be authorized. There is no suitably named process to deal with this so another new process can be created named Authorize Allowance.

4.12.4 Process 2, Authorize Allowance

From the Document Flow outputs from this process can be seen to be the separated Authorized Application Copies 1 to 4. Copy 4's destination, Manager, is included in Figure 4.9, but the destinations of the other three copies are not included since they are internal data flows. Copy 1 is filed in the Administration Department so a data store Admin Car Users is required. Copy 2 is sent to Transport Department where it is filed so a new process Record Allowance Details (location Transport)is required and a data store Transport Car Users. Copy 3 is sent to Finance Department and again a new process Record Allowance Details (location Finance) is required and a data store Finance Car Users.

4.12.5 Process 4, Record Change Of Car

This process has the input New Car Details. The output related to this on the Document Flow Diagram is the New Car Details Copies 1 and 2. Copy 1 is sent to Finance and could be dealt with by the process identified in 4.12.4 , Record Allowance Details (location Finance) since the activity involves adding more information to the Finance Car Users data store. Copy 2 is sent to Transport and can be dealt with by the process identified in 4.12.4 Record Allowance Details (location Transport). The original copy of the New Car Details is filed in the Admin Car Users data store.

4.12.6 Process 3, Check Claim Details

The input to this process is the Manager-signed Claim Form, as shown in Figure 4.9. The output from the checking process stays within the Finance Department but is sent to a different section, the Comptometer Operators. For clarity in the first draft Data Flow Diagram this will be shown as a separate process Check Mileage Total.

4.12.7 New Process, Check Mileage Total

The output from this process is Mileage Checked Claim which is sent back to the Finance process Prepare Cheque Requisition.

4.12.8 Process 6, Prepare Cheque Requisition

This process has the output Cheque Requisition identified on Figure 4.9. The Mileage Checked Claim Form must be held in a temporary data store at this point so a new data store Unpaid Claim Forms is required.

4.12.9 Process 5, Despatch Payment

The only data flows not identified in Figure 4.9 concerning this process must involve data stores. When the Cheque is received the Unpaid Claim Form must be extracted from the temporary data store and transferred to a long term data store Paid Claims.

The resulting draft Level 1 Data Flow Diagram is shown in Figure 4.10.

4.13 Comments on the Draft 1 Level 1 Data Flow Diagram

The Document Flow Diagram should be checked to ensure that all documents have been included in the Level 1 Data Flow Diagram. The Admin Car Users data store has been shown twice to avoid having long or crossed flow lines. The symbols both have the same reference number and the duplication is indicated by an extra bar on the left of the symbol.

All the data flows on the diagram have been named. Note that data store 2, Transport Car Users is only used by one process. On a level one Data Flow Diagram it is only necessary to show data stores which are shared between processes. The Transport Car Users data store is considered to be internal to the Record Allowance Details process and is only shown on the level 2 Data Flow Diagram which shows the detail of this process.

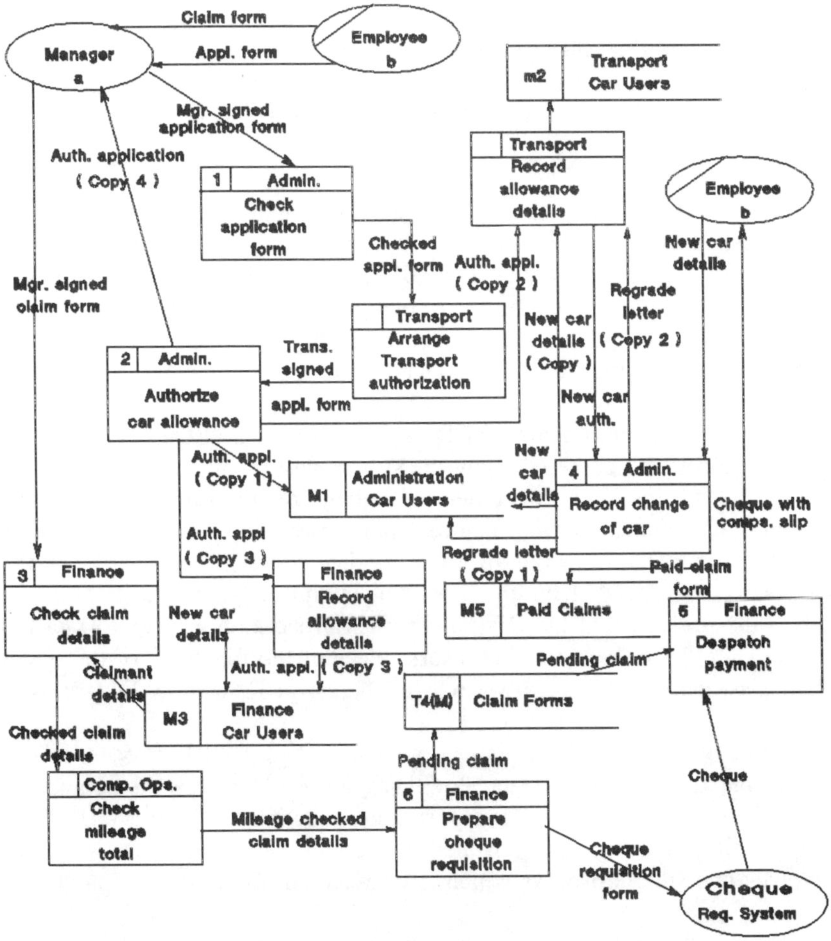

Figure 4.10 Draft Level 1 Data Flow Diagram

4.14 Levelling A Data Flow Diagram

A Level 1 Data Flow Diagram should have a maximum of 15 processes. If possible it should fit onto one A4 page or it will loose its readability. Level 2 Data Flow Diagrams will normally have 4 to 8 processes. If too many processes are identified then some should be merged. Look at processes which are closely linked together in time or sequence, these are the most likely candidates for merger since they are most likely to be seen as one function by the users.

On a Level 1 Data Flow Diagram there should normally be a minimum of 6 or 7 processes. If there are too few processes on the diagram then there may have been a failure to achieve a similar level of detail in each process and one or two processes may require to be split. Achieving the correct level of detail in a Data Flow Diagram becomes easier the more the technique is used. Do not expect to draw a correct Data Flow Diagram of a system at the first attempt.

It is natural to draw an unbalanced Data Flow Diagram at the earlier attempts since the information gathered about the system will be more detailed for some parts of the system than for others. Attempting to draw the Data Flow Diagrams helps to identify where more detail information is required. The final set of Data Flow Diagrams require to be levelled so that a balanced view of the system can be achieved from the users' viewpoint of functionality. Levelling involves the processes in the Diagram. Each process on a level 1 Data Flow Diagram should correspond to the users' ideas of the functions of the system. Levelling is applied as the analyst revises the set of Data Flow Diagrams.

An example of unbalanced processes is shown in Figure 4.10. Process 8 is able to be expanded to a Level 2 Data Flow Diagram which shows the detailed data flows involved in Arrange Transport Authorization. Process 10, "check mileage total", could not be expanded to a Level 2 Data Flow Diagram since it involves one simple process which is only part of the function "pay claim".

Processes which can be examined for merger include those carried out in the same location which are closely connected in content, For instance processes 1 and 2 are both involved with authorizing car allowances and are both carried out in the Administration Department by the same person, they are part of the one function "authorize allowances". Other processes which can be merged might be very closely linked in sequence. For example processes 3,5,6 and 10 are carried out in a short period of time in the same department and would be viewed by the user as one function "pay claim".

The level one Data Flow Diagram has been redrawn in Figure 4.11, eliminating data stores which are not shared between processes and levelling processes into user functions. The system boundary can be indicated with a dotted line on a Level One Data Flow Diagram.

4.14.1 Explanation of the Levelled Data Flow Diagram

The diagram is consistent with the Context Diagram. There are the same four inputs and three outputs. If any new inputs or outputs are identified the Context Diagram should be amended to be consistent with the Level One Data Flow Diagram.

Notice that no error or exception data flows are shown on a Level One Data Flow Diagram. For instance in the Car Allowances System there may be occasions when an allowance is not authorized or a claim form is rejected. The resulting data flow is not shown on the Level 1 Data Flow Diagram or on the Context Diagram. Too much detail will obscure the main information flows in the system, error and exception conditions can be identified later on the lower level diagrams.

Do not expect to draw a perfect Data Flow Diagram at the first attempt. It will take several drafts before you achieve an acceptable diagram. Remember to keep External Entities to the outside of the diagram and avoid crossed flow lines by duplicating External Entities and data stores.

4.15 DFD Conventions

External Entities are normally kept to the outside edge of the diagram so that system interfaces can be clearly identified. To avoid long data flow lines an external entity can be shown more than once using a slanted line in the oval to indicate duplication. Processes should only be shown once. Note the numbering in the diagram. Process boxes are numbered, usually from top left to right, then down the page. It is important to note that the numbering does not imply sequence of processing, it is merely a convenient way of giving each process a unique identity and allows lower level diagrams to be easily cross-referenced to higher level diagrams.

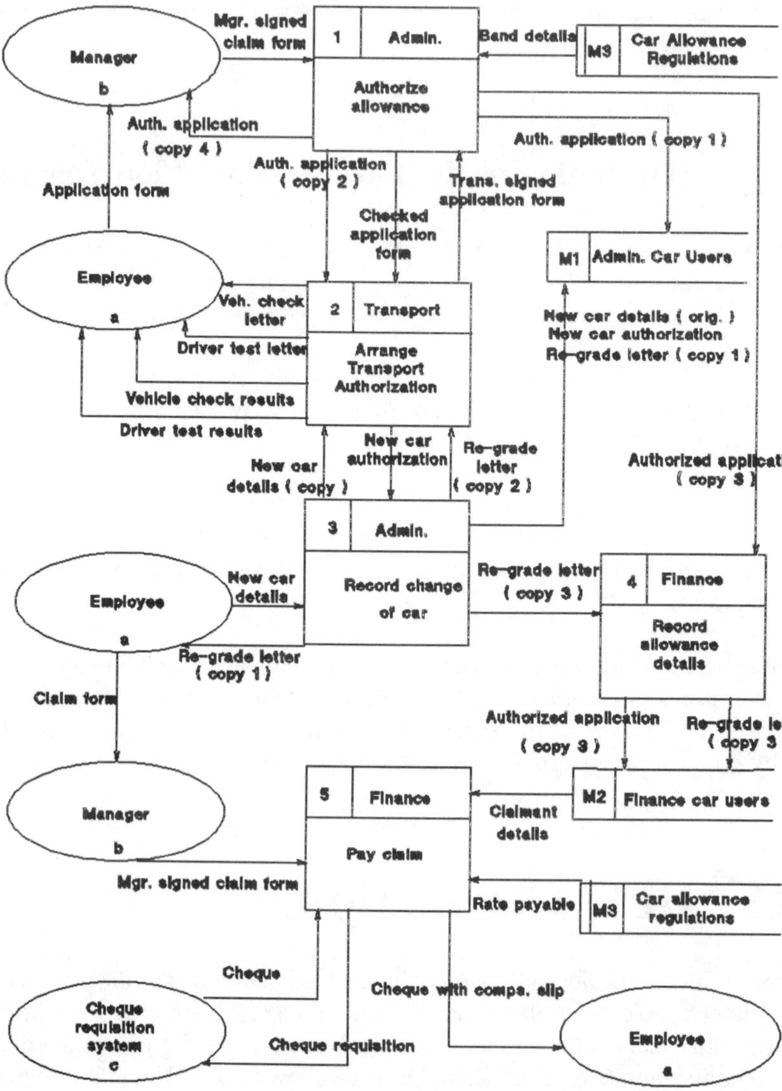

Figure 4.11 Level 1 Data Flow Diagram

Check the consistency of the diagram with the Context Diagram. There should be the same three input data flows and the same six outputs. The only changes are the expansion of the "process" box on the Context Diagram into five processes. Each input and output data flow goes to, or comes from one of these processes.

4.16 Exercises

1. Draw a Level 1 Data Flow Diagram for the Telephone Directory System described in Chapter 5, section 2.

2. Check the levelling of Data Flow Diagram you prepared for exercise 4.16.1 and amend it if necessary.

3. Draw a Level 1 Data Flow Diagram for the Student Administration System described in Appendix 2. (Do not expect your first attempt to be correct).

4.17 Level 2 Data Flow Diagrams

A level two Data Flow Diagram is an expansion of one process from the Level 1 Data Flow Diagram. Each Level 1 process and its inputs and outputs can be considered as a Context Diagram for a component part of the system. This is then expanded to show the detail of the information flows in that part of the system. To illustrate this the PAY CLAIM process is shown in Figure 4.12 with its inputs and outputs as indicated on the Level 1 Data Flow Diagram in Figure 4.11. The Level 1 process name and number is shown in the top of the large rectangle.

This process receives an input from one external entity and generates outputs to two different External Entities. The External Entities are shown outside the rectangle which represents the process boundary. The process also accesses a data store which is used by other Level One processes. Any data store which

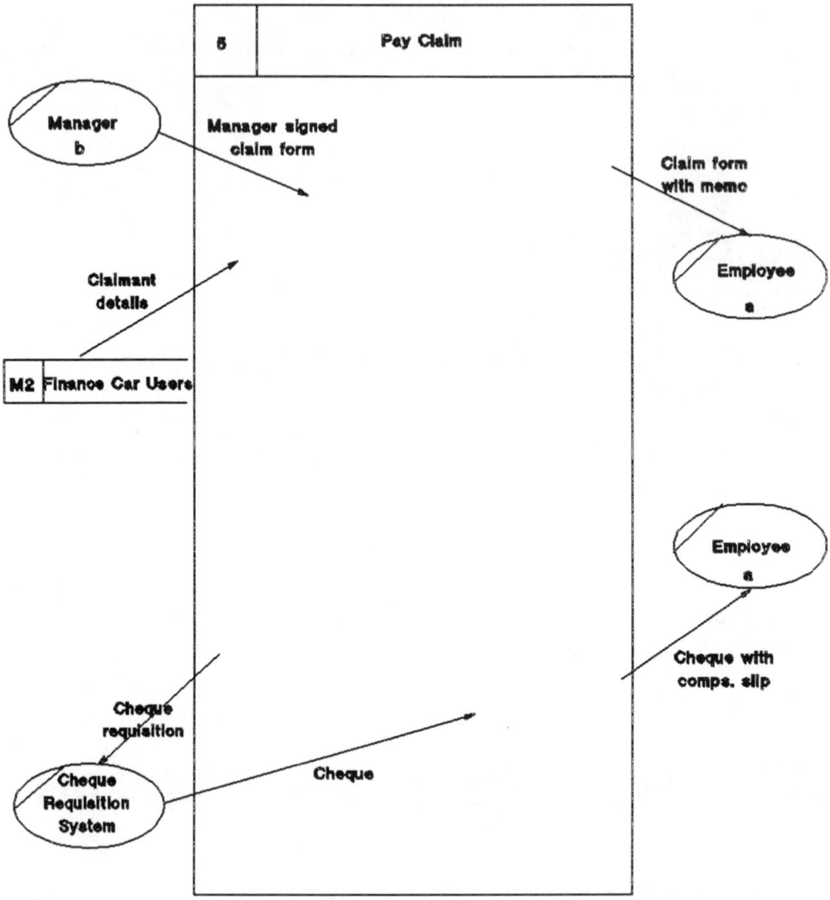

Figure 4.12 Outline Level 2 process box

appears on a Level 1 Data Flow Diagram appears outside the boundary line on a Level 2 Data Flow Diagram. Any data flows to other processes would also be indicated by a cross boundary data flow going to a labelled process symbol.

4.18 Drawing a Level 2 Data Flow Diagram

The detail of the processing required to pay claims is shown inside the boundary line of the Level 1 process. Any data stores used only by this process are shown inside the boundary line. The data stores identified on the Level 1 diagram as being required by more than one Level 1 process are shown outside the boundary line. Error and exception processing is shown in the bottom level Data Flow Diagram. The PAY CLAIMS process must have some rejected claims, since two checks are carried out on claims. They are first checked against the FINANCE CAR USERS data store and the mileage totals are checked. Both require a process which can deal with rejected claims. Most of the other information required for the Level 2 was included on the first draft Level 1 Data Flow Diagram in Figure 4.10.

The outline of the Level 2 Diagram can now be drawn. The processes are numbered using the identification number for the Level 1 process followed by a unique number for each process on this diagram. Any new data store identified is given the next available number. The source or destination of all data flows which cross the Level 2 system boundary are shown. Figure 4.12 shows the outline Level 2 Data Flow Diagram.

Figure 4.13 shows the completed Level 2 Data Flow Diagram including the process to deal with rejected claims.

4.19 Further Decomposition of Data Flow Diagrams

If required the processes on the Level 2 Data Flow Diagram can be decomposed in the same way to produce Level 3 diagrams,if there is sufficient detail in the process. In practice it is rarely necessary to go beyond Level 3 diagrams. When there is insufficient detail to model information flows further in a lower level Data Flow Diagram the process is marked with an asterisk in the bottom, right hand corner and further described in an Elementary Process Description. For every process on the lowest level Data Flow Diagram an Elementary

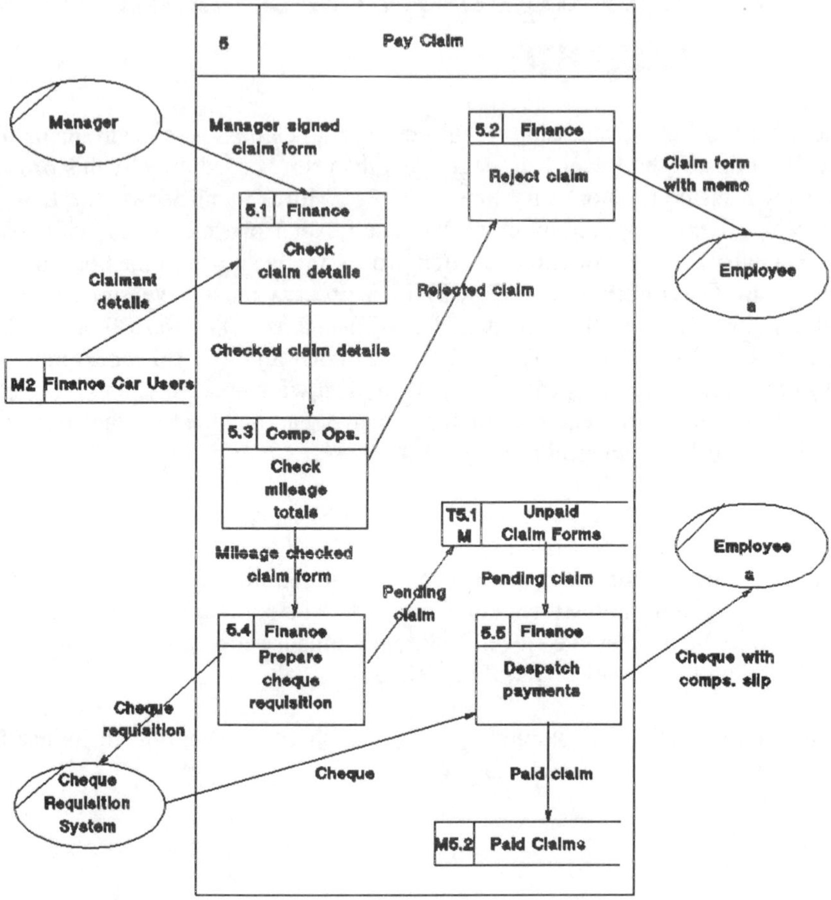

Figure 4.13 Completed Level 2 Data Flow Diagram

Process Description should be produced. See section 4.21 for a discussion of the supporting documentation for the Data Flow Model.

Data flows can also be expanded on the lower level diagrams. For instance, a Level One Data Flow Diagram may have the data flow "Customer Order". Customer orders may be handled differently depending on whether they are received by phone or by post. The Level One diagram may only show a process "Receive order" and does not require the data flow to be broken down any further. The Level Two expansion of the process "Receive order" may contain separate process boxes to deal with postal and telephone orders. The one data flow from the Level One diagram can be shown up to the boundary line where it then forks into two data flows "Customer Order (post)" and "Customer Order (phone). Using this process of decomposing data flows helps to remove unnecessary detail from the Level One diagram.

4.20 Checking A Data Flow Diagram

The following checks are useful when you are preparing the final draft of a set of Data Flow Diagrams:

i) Check that each process has at least one input and at least one output. If not, then some data flows are missing.

ii) The data flows into a single process should be clearly related to the data flows out. Check that you know where each document has come from and its final destination. Documents do not vanish when the processing is finished they are usually filed.

iii) Check the process names. If vague verbs such as "process" or "update" have been used replace them with a more descriptive verb.

iv) The Cross boundary flows on a lower level Data Flow Diagram should also appear on the higher level diagrams except for those resulting from error and exception processing.

v) The Level 1 processes should correspond to the users' view of the system functions. A pair of processes which have several data flows running between them should be carefully examined to see if they can be considered as one process.

vi) Requirements to produce ad-hoc or regular reports or to permit enquiries to be made of files, are best omitted from the Data Flow Model and specified in the Requirements Catalogue. In the Car Allowance System a report might be required to "print all regular car allowance holders in alphabetical order within department". Adding retrievals such as this to the Data Flow Model greatly increases its complexity. They should only be shown if the retrieval is a major part of the system's functionality and processing requirement. Retrievals will later be defined as enquiry functions which are supported by access paths through the Required System Logical Data Model..

4.21 Supporting Documentation

A Data Catalogue is created to describe all the items contained in I/O flows. The contents of the Data Catalogue are described below.

The Data Flow Model is a set of Data Flow Diagrams and supporting descriptive products:

- Elementary Process Descriptions
- Input/Output Descriptions
- External Entity Descriptions

This section discusses the content of these documents.

A further product, the Logical Data Store/Entity cross-reference, shows the correspondence between the data stores in the Data Flow Model and the entities in the Logical Data Model. This product is described in Chapter 5.

4.21.1 Data Catalogue

The Data Catalogue describes all the items contained in I/O flows. Information about default values and validation rules are recorded. A description is given of how any data items which are derived items are calculated, eg invoice gross total. It may be useful to give a character length for each item.

4.21.2 Elementary Process Descriptions

Every bottom level process on the Data Flow Model must be briefly described in narrative form as an Elementary Process Description. They should describe:

- the data accessed
- business constraints (eg credit levels governing acceptance of an order)

Where several external entities have inputs to a process, business constraints should be considered for each input.

Some bottom level processes may have processes that are common. These processes can be described in a common process Elementary Process Description but must be cross-referenced to and from the Elementary Process Descriptions of the using process.

4.21.3 Input/Output Descriptions

These are created for each data flow crossing the system boundary. They should list the data items contained in the data flow. The detailed description of each data item is contained in the Data Catalogue (see section 4.21.1). It is not necessary to record details of the structure of the data, eg repeating groups, since these will be defined during Function Definition.

4.21.4 External Entity Descriptions

Each external entity should be described. The data required includes relevant detail about the functions or responsibilities of the external entity and any constraints on its interface to the system.

4.22 Exercises

1. Draw the remaining level 2 Data Flow Diagrams for the Car Allowance Case Study. The following information has been gathered after interviewing Transport Department Staff:

   "All employees receiving car allowances must be company authorized drivers. The Transport Clerk checks to see if the applicant is new to the Car Allowance Scheme by checking with the Transport Car Users File. Any applicant who is new to the scheme is asked (by letter) to take part in a driving test to help them identify any bad driving habits which they have acquired. Each employee taking such a test is given a form at the end of the test stating any actions which they are recommended to take to improve their driving.

   Any applicant to the scheme, or any existing scheme member who changes their car must have their car checked by transport if the car is over 3 years old. Transport arranges the test by writing to the employee. At the end of the vehicle check the employee is given a form which outlines any repairs which are required or recommended before the employee can use the car on company business. Proof of compulsory repairs may be required, either by producing a garage bill confirming the repairs have been carried out, or by further inspection of the vehicle.

   While the checks are being carried out the Application Form 4 part set is held in a pending file. Once all the checks have been satisfactorily completed, the Application Form Set is signed by the Transport Manager and returned to the Senior Administration Officer. Copies of the driving and vehicle test results are retained in the Transport Car Users File.

2. Draw a complete set of Level 2 Data Flow Diagrams for the Student Administration System described in Appendix 2.

4.23 Summary

The Data Flow Model provides a clear pictorial model of the information flows in a system. The Level 1 Data Flow Diagram provides an overview of the major parts of the system and the inter-relationships between them. Information flows across the system boundary are also identified. Lower level Data Flow Diagrams provide a model of a component part of the system and clearly identify the interfaces with the rest of the system.

Do not expect to draw a Data Flow Diagram correctly at the first attempt. One of the benefits of this technique is that it identifies missing links in the analyst's understanding of the information flows in the system. Data Flow Diagrams are working for the analyst if they cause questions to be asked to clarify the workings of a system. Often revisions on a lower level diagram will cause alterations to be made to the appropriate level 2 diagram and to the Level 1 Diagram. Eventually a set of Data Flow Diagrams will be produced which the analyst and the user agree provide a good description of the information flows in the system.

Data Flow Diagrams are very easy to understand, both for analysts and users. In some installations the users draw the Data Flow Diagrams of existing systems since they have the necessary detailed knowledge of the system. A technique which users can apply themselves is a very useful aid in systems analysis and design. Data Flow Diagrams are used in several stages in SSADM. This chapter has described how to draw Data Flow Diagrams using SSADM symbols and conventions. Chapter 5 describes how SSADM uses Data Flow Diagrams.

4.24 Keywords

Context Diagram	External Entity
Physical Resource Flow	Process
Level 1 Data Flow Diagram	Data Store
Level 2 Data Flow Diagram	Data Flow
Data Flow Model	System Environment
Document Flow Diagram	System Boundary
Level 0 Data Flow Diagram	Data Catalogue
External Entity Description	Elementary Process Descriptions
Input/Output Descriptions	Logical Data Store/Entity Cross Ref.

4.25 Exercises

1. Explain the hierarchical structure of a set of Data Flow Diagrams.

2. What is the Data Flow Model?

3. Is a Document Flow Diagram essential when drawing a Data Flow Diagram?

4. How is a bottom level process indicated?

5. Is an external entity always external to the organisation?

CHAPTER 5

Using Data Flow Diagrams In SSADM

5.1 Introduction

Chapter 4 described how to draw Data Flow Diagrams. This chapter will explain how Data Flow Diagrams are used in SSADM. The reader should study Chapter 6, The Logical Data Model, before reading this chapter.

Data Flow Diagrams are used in the Feasibility Study, Requirements Analysis and Requirements Specification modules. They are developed from a description of the current physical system , the Current Physical Data Flow Model. This model is examined alongside the Current Environment Logical Data Model and a Current Logical Data Flow Model is established. The Requirements Catalogue is then examined and a Required Logical Data Flow Model is produced.

If there is no existing system then the Required Logical Data Flow Model is produced without any of the preceding models.

This chapter will use a simple example of a Telephone Directory System to explain the use of Data Flow Diagrams in SSADM. The Car Allowance System discussed in Chapter 4 will then be used to give a further example.

5.2 Case Study

The following description of a system to produce an internal telephone directory will be used as an example throughout this chapter.

A University has a manual system to keep its internal telephone directory up to date. The directory is re-issued twice a year and is maintained by the Central Services Department.

The directory gives the name, job title, department, building, room number and extension number of each member of staff. Some members of staff work part of the week in one location and part in another so they can have two building, room number and extension entries. An extension can be shared by more than one employee. There are two sections in the directory. One is in alphabetical order of surname, the second is in alphabetical order of surname within department. See Figure 5.1 for an extract from the directory. Note that on the very unusual chance of two people having the same name sharing an extension, the name entries for that extension would attempt to distinguish between them using initials or, if necessary, full names.

Changes in name at a particular extension are either phoned through to the company telephone exchange or notified on an internal memo to the Administration Officer. After recording the changes in their own directories, the telephone exchange make a note of changes on a telephone message form and pass these through to the Administration Officer. The Administration Officer leaves all these notification of changes in filing tray until the end of the week when a consolidated weekly list of amendments is prepared and a copy sent to the telephone exchange. This allows the operators to incorporate any changes sent direct to the Administration Officer on their directories. Once a month the Administration Officer uses the weekly lists to prepare a monthly amendment list which is circulated round the company using the Distribution List (discussed later). The weekly list is filed with the master copy of the current directory and replaced by the monthly amendment list when the changes have been consolidated.

The Administration Officer theoretically controls the allocation of additional extensions but, since the current system is overloaded, there are no additional extensions to allocate. Sometimes a departmental re-organisation means that telephone extensions are moved to different rooms. The Administration Officer maintains a typed list of extension numbers and their location. When a department sends notification of a change of location of extension numbers the list is updated using correction fluid to delete the old location and the new location is written in by hand. The list is retyped once the number of changes makes it difficult to use.

Twice a year the monthly amendment lists are consolidated to show all the changes since the last directory update, each item is numbered. The Administration Clerk takes the current directory and rules a line through any entries which have to be deleted. Inserts are marked with an arrow and the number from the amendment list. This is a lengthy process since the telephone directory has both an alphabetic listing and a departmental listing so each amendment causes two changes to the directory.

Before passing the directory to the typing pool the clerk has to work out where a new page starts (40 names/page). A red line is drawn on the current directory where a page break is required. The start of names under a new letter of the alphabet or new department requires extra spacing and care has to be taken that enough space is left at the end of a page to start a new section. The current typewriters do not allow much manipulation of text so this laborious process is essential.

The typing pool then types the whole directory from scratch. Once the directory has been typed it is carefully checked by the Administration Clerk and then the Directory is used to work out how many copies of the directory are required for each department. The Distribution List is updated where necessary and a copy sent to the Mail Room. The Distribution List is also used when sending out the monthly amendment lists. Once the Clerk is satisfied the directory is sent to the Print Room where it is printed and bound. The Print Room retains the print original and sends the finished directories to the Mail Room who distribute the directories according to the distribution list.

The University is about to purchase a new telephone exchange and, since all extensions will switch from a 3 digit number to a 4 digit number, it has been decided to investigate the computerisation of the internal telephone directory. It is intended that the new directory will be maintained by the Telephone Exchange staff.

Main alphabetical listing

NAME	JOB TITLE	DEPT	LOC	ROOM	EXT
Achmed, Dr A	Head of Department	BIS	AH	613	2157
Adams, Dr S	Lecturer	COMP	WHB	108	2278
Adams, Ms A	Admin. Assistant	PERS	OC	011	2789
Adamson, Mr T	Senior Lecturer	MS	AH	734	2187
Allan, Mrs R	Lecturer	CVENG	WHB	706	2134
Allen, Mr E	Technician	CMENG	WHB	311	2712
Andrews, Ms D	Senior Technician	BIS	AH	625	2456
			MHB	101	2135
Andrews, Mr T	Senior Lecturer	MS	AH	734	2187
Arnold, Mrs K	Senior Lecturer	LANG	JPB	203	2569
Ashton, Miss F	Lecturer	LING	JPB	204	2134
Bainbridge, Mr G	Financial Accountant	FIN	OC	045	2765
Barnaby, Mr H	Admin. Assistant	FIN	OC	024	2894
Beardsley, Dr S	Principal Lecturer	BIS	AH	606	2656

Departmental Listing

DEPARTMENT OF BUSINESS INFORMATION SYSTEMS

NAME	JOB TITLE	LOCATION	ROOM	EXT.
Achmed, Dr A	Head of Department	AH	613	2157
Andrews, Ms D	Senior Technician	AH	625	2456
Beardsley, Dr S	Principal Lecturer	AH	606	2656

Figure 5.1 Extracts from internal telephone directory

5.3 Current Physical Data Flow Model

The Data Flow Model describing the existing system is called the Current Physical Data Flow Model. This Data Flow Diagram, or set of diagrams, should show what actually happens in the existing system. It will require many drafts before a full understanding of the present system is gained.

In many systems investigations the existing system may be a mix of manual and computerised systems. The Case Study in section 5.2 describes a purely manual existing system. The system is small so enough detail can be contained on a Level One Data Flow Diagram. There are many manual stores of data in this system. For instance the Change Messages are held in a filing tray until the Weekly Amendment Lists are produced, so a data store called Pending Changes has been included. The Current Telephone Directory is a collection of data retained in a filing cabinet by the Administration Manager so it is shown as a data store.

Once the analyst and users are satisfied that the Data Flow Diagrams satisfactorily describe the information flows in the system then a System Boundary can be agreed. A Current Physical Data Flow Model for the Telephone Directory System is given in Figure 5.2. This model may be prepared during the Feasibility Study or Requirements Analysis Modules.

The documents supporting the Data Flow Model are also created at this time. They are the Elementary Process Descriptions, External Entity Descriptions and I/O Descriptions. In addition the Data Catalogue is also created. These supporting products are described in more detail in section 4.21.

5.4 Current Logical Data Flow Model

In Requirements Analysis, Stage 1 (Investigation of the Current Environment) the Data Flow Diagrams produced represent the current physical system. As a basis for identifying the problems inherent in the current system these Current Physical Data Flow Diagrams must be converted into Current Logical Data

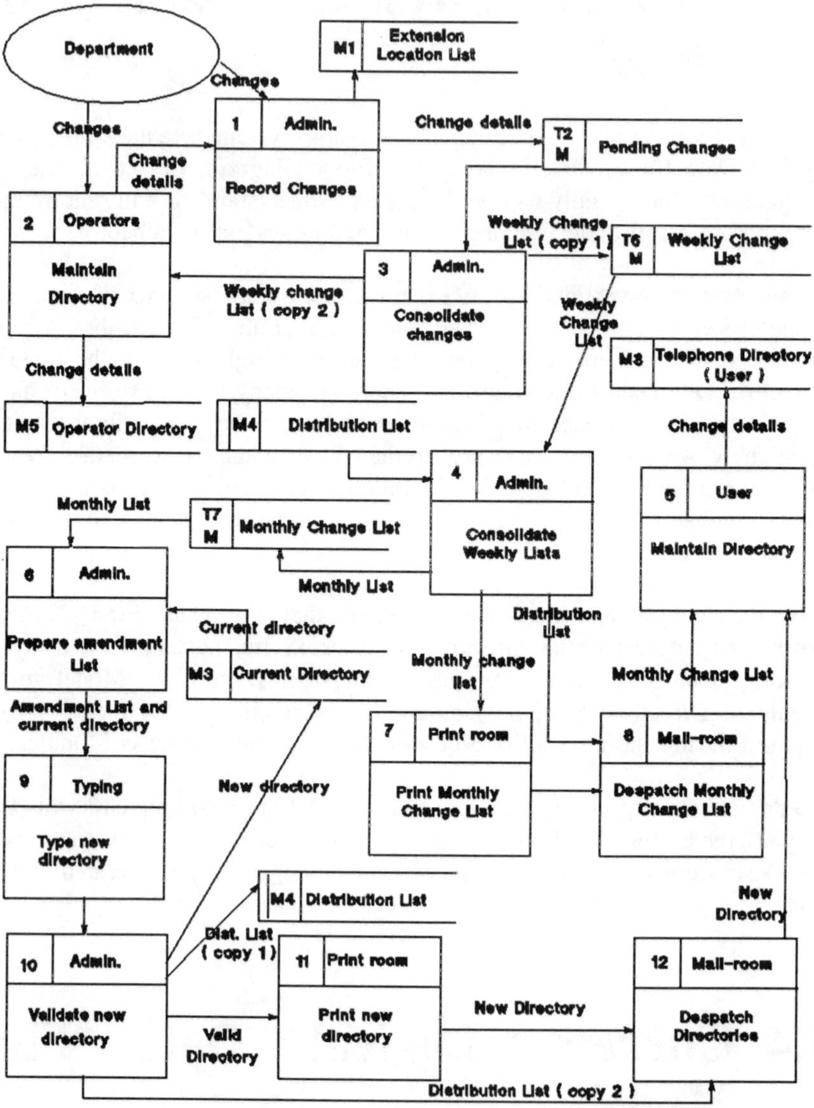

Figure 5.2 Current Physical Data Flow Diagram for Telephone Directory System

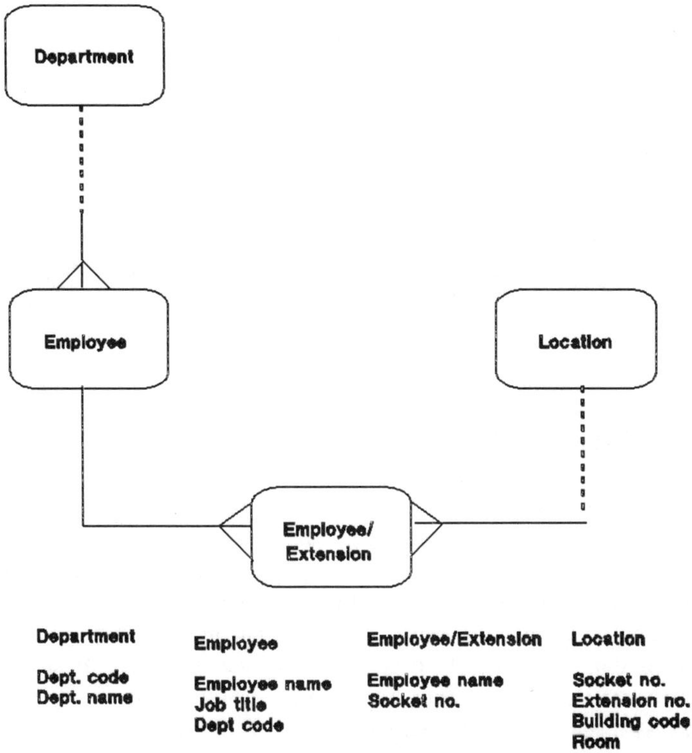

Figure 5.3 Current Environment Logical Data Model for Telephone Directory System

Flow Diagrams. The Current Physical Data Flow Diagrams show what is happening in the existing system and how it happens. Logicalisation removes any reference to the physical facilities and constraints of the existing system and helps to identify the underlying processing and the groups of data which are required to support this processing. This forms the basis for producing a model of the required system when considered alongside the Requirements Catalogue. Logicalisation is carried out at Stage 1 (02 if a Feasibility Study takes place) and from Stage 2 onwards all Data Flow Diagrams are logical.

There are four main tasks:

a) Rationalise data stores
b) Rationalise bottom level processes
c) Group bottom level processes into higher level processes
d) Check for consistency and completeness

The Current Physical Data Flow Diagram and the Current Environment Logical Data Model for the Telephone Directory example are shown in Figures 5.2 and 5.3.

5.4.1 Rationalise Data Stores

The Current Physical Data Flow Model and the Current Environment Logical Data Model of are examined together. The data stores in the Current Physical Data Flow Model indicate the way data is actually held, this may involve a lot of duplication of data items with a resulting duplication of processing to update all occurrences of each data item. The logicalisation process removes this duplication of data and its link to specific physical files and produces logical groupings of data items. The data stores on the Logical Data Flow Model must correspond with the entities on the Current Logical Data Model.

There are two main areas to examine:

- Main Logical Data Stores
- Transient Logical Data Stores

5.4.1.1 Main Logical Data Stores

Main data stores represent data held centrally in a system so that it can be used by a number of different processes. They are identified by the reference letter 'D' or 'M' (see section 4.3). A main logical data store on a Logical Data Flow Diagram must correspond to an entity or group of entities on the Logical Data Structure. An entity must be entirely within a single main logical data store. Groups of entities are often obvious but, if not, can be formed from entities which conform to one or more of the following:

a) They are part of the same major system input or output, eg 'Customer Order'
b) They can be described by one name, for example 'Customer Accounts' or 'Employee Details'.
c) They are created at the same time and/or have similar lives (this anticipates Entity Life Histories).
d) They are linked by relationships (as identified on the Logical Data Structure).

An examination of the entities on the Logical Data Model in Figure 5.3 shows that the two entities Employee and Employee/Extension can be grouped together since they are related to each other and can be described by one name "Telephone directory details". They are also all part of the major system output "Telephone Directory". The entity Department has a similar life to the other three entities since it is created, amended and deleted at the same time as the telephone directory entities so it can also be added to this logical grouping.

The entity Location could, in theory, exist without the other entities. The socket no. information is not required in the Telephone Directory. The main data stores on the Current Physical Data Flow Diagram are:

M1 Extension/Location List
M3 Current Directory
M4 Distribution List
M5 Operator Directory
M8 User Directory

There is some duplication of data in data stores in this system. This duplication is removed by identifying the logical data stores in correspondence with the Logical Data Model. Data stores M3, M5 and M8 are all duplicates of each other and can be merged. M4 maps onto the same group of entities which relate to the telephone directory so it can also be merged with the telephone directory data stores. The result is one logical main store which corresponds to the entity grouping 'Telephone Directory'. This logical main data store can be numbered D1 and also named 'Telephone Directory'. There is a second main store Extension Location which holds the socket no. details. Note that the reference number of a main logical data store is always prefixed by a 'D' since all reference to physical format of the data has been removed.

The Logical Data Store/Entity Cross Reference clearly identifies the mapping of entities to data stores. The Logical Data Store/Entity Cross Reference for the Telephone Directory System is given in Figure 5.4.

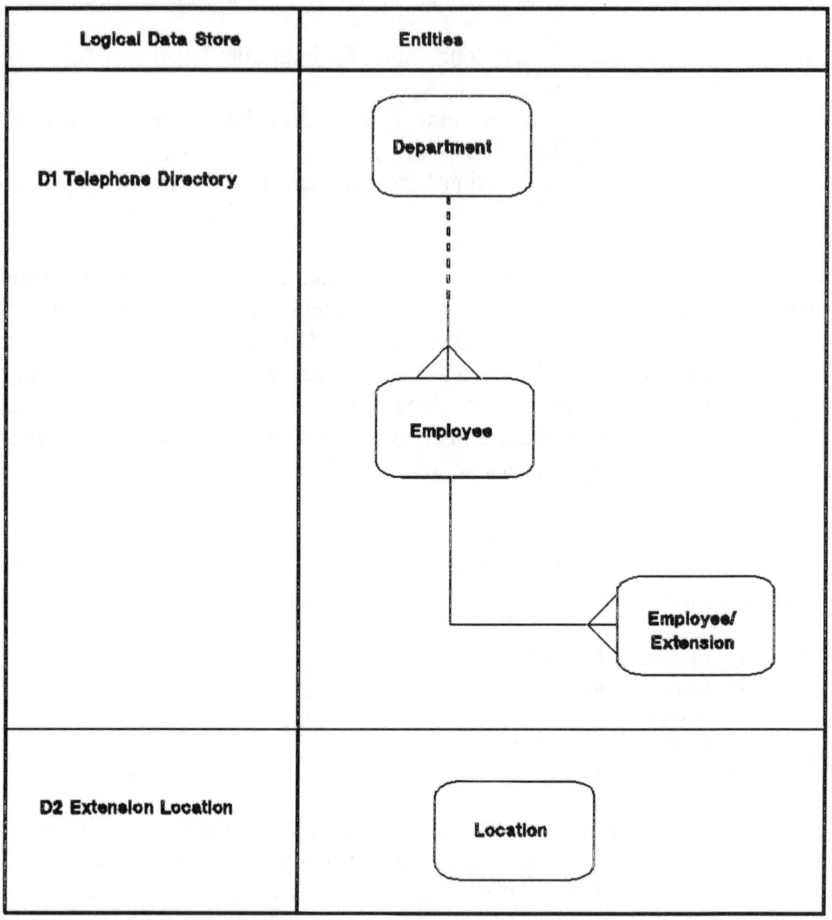

Figure 5.4 Logical Data Store/Entity Cross Reference

5.4.1.2 Transient Data Stores

Temporary data stores often arise because of some kind of constraint in the current system. For instance geographical constraints can arise in data such as sales figures being held for processing until the figures from all area offices arrive by post. Another reason for delay may be constraints produced by staffing restrictions for instance, requisition forms for internal stationery orders may be collected together and only processed on Tuesdays since that is the only day the Clerk responsible can be released from other duties. Constraints could also be caused by machines which only process data in batch mode thus causing temporary collections of data, for example a current computer system. Such data stores are not required logically. There is no logical reason why an order cannot be filled as soon as it is received.

A main data store corresponds to entities on the Logical Data Model, a transient data store does not. A transient data store may temporarily contain a copy of instances of data which are being held until a main data store can be updated. Transient data stores have the following characteristics:

i) a read deletes data from the data store so that data in the store can be used only once, eg T2(M), Pending Changes, in the Telephone Directory Example is a filing tray which holds pieces of paper until a weekly update process. The process removes the data from the filing tray and does not replace it.

ii) a single process will extract data although more than one process may add data, eg T2(M), T6(M) and T7(M) in the telephone directory example all transient stores have the data extracted by a single process.

iii) data cannot be updated although further instances of the data may be written to store, eg in data store T6(M) in the Telephone Directory Example, a new weekly change list is added every week. The existing weekly change lists are not amended in any way. They are merely held until extracted to compile the monthly change list.

A transient data store which is to be removed from the Current Logical Data Flow Diagram can be replaced by either:

- merging the two processes which use the data store
- a process to process data flow

A transient data store may sometimes appear in a Logical Data Flow Diagram. A situation where this might be necessary is when a batch of data such as cheque requisitions has to be held until the arrival of the separate input 'Authorization'. This input is the trigger to run the process Produce Payment'. This situation is shown in Figure 5.5.

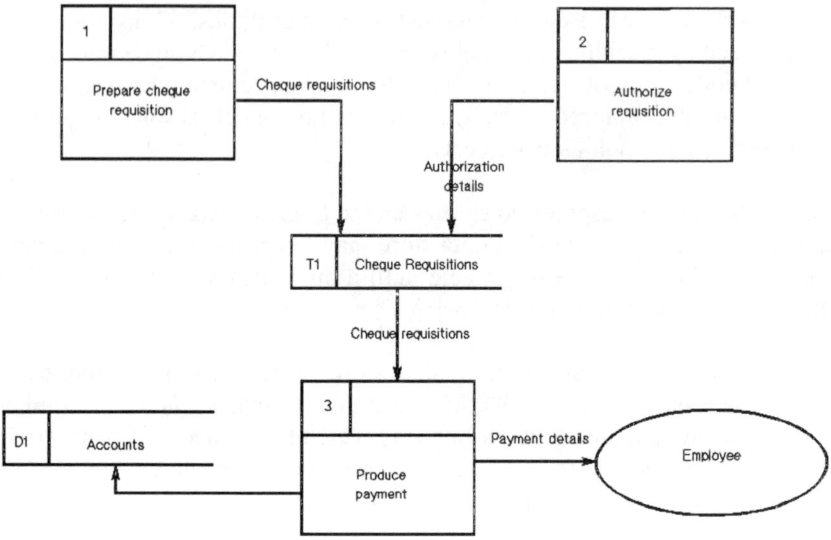

Figure 5.5 Transient data store.

The transient data store 'Cheque Requisitions' is logically necessary in this situation. Note that a logical transient data store is indicated by the letter 'T' before the reference number, the '(M)' suffix is not used on a logical data flow diagram since this indicates the physical form of the data store. You should think very carefully before using transient data stores on a logical data flow diagram since they have the following implications:

- an enquiry will delete the data, see characteristic i) above.

- the main data store related to the transient data store is not up-to-date eg in the example in Figure 5.5 the main data store which is updated by the cheque requisition information cannot be up to date until the authorization trigger allows process 3 to operate.

- recovery procedures for main data stores may not cover transient data stores. Complex security audit and control procedures must exist where transient data stores exist. In the example in Figure 5.5 the main data store 'Accounts' may have very rigorous back-up and recovery procedures. Similar procedures will be required for the data in the transient store T1.

The transient data stores in the Telephone Directory Example are:

T2(M) Pending Changes
T6(M) Weekly Change List
T7(M) Monthly Change List

Data store T2(M) holds change data temporarily until the Weekly Change Lists can be compiled. New data is added by placing another change memo in the filing tray. The update process results in the removal of the change data from the filing tray, it is presumably placed in the bin once the Weekly Change List has been compiled. This transient data store is not logically necessary and is omitted from the Current Logical Data Flow Diagram. It can be replaced by merging processes 1 and 2 on the Current Physical Data Flow Diagram. Data store T6(M) Weekly Change List is required until the monthly change list is compiled, the weekly change list can then be destroyed. Data store T7(M) also holds data which is discarded during process 6 Prepare Amendment List. The data on the monthly list is never updated once it has been created. The monthly and weekly change lists also hold data which duplicates the Current Directory, if changes are applied immediately to the current directory. Data stores T6(M) and T7(M) are not logically necessary and can be omitted. The logicalisation process removes all the transient data stores in this example.

5.4.1.3 Decomposed Data Stores

Where a data store has been decomposed on the Current Physical Data Flow Model it may remain on the Current Logical Data Flow Model if it has not been removed by logicalisation. For example decomposition may occur because of a mutually exclusive relationship between a master entity and two or more detail entities. An example would be in a Car Allowance System where one set of details was kept about all employees claiming allowance and then different information was required for regular and casual car users. This situation would result in a master entity 'Employee' with the mutually exclusive detail entities 'Regular User' and 'Casual User'. It is useful in this instance to break the rule that an entity should only appear against one main data store on the Logical Data Store/Entity Cross Reference.

5.4.1.4 Logical/Physical Data Store Cross Reference

It is useful to record the relationship of the new main logical data stores to the physical data stores since this will help in the rationalisation of the processes.

It will also help to ensure that no data described in the Current Physical Data Flow Model has been missed. The Logical/Physical Data Store Cross Reference is a working document which can be used for this purpose. The relationship between the physical and logical main data stores in the Telephone Directory Example is shown in Figure 5.6.

Physical data store	Logical data store
M1 Extension Location List	**D1 Telephone Directory**
M3 Current Directory	
M4 Distribution List	
M5 Operator Directory	
M8 User Directory	

Figure 5.6 Logical/Physical Data Store Cross Reference for Telephone Directory Example

5.4.2 Rationalise Bottom Level Processes

The following areas should be examined for all bottom level processes, these processes are indicated by an * on the Current Physical Data Flow Model:

5.4.2.1 Location

All references to location or person should be omitted from a logical process. The location reference stripe at the top, right of the process box is left blank. A logical process should not indicate where or by whom a process is carried out.

5.4.2.2 Serial processes

If two processes are always performed together as a series they should be merged. Examples might be where one department validates data and then passes it to another department for further validation. Once references to location have been removed there is no logical need to retain the division and the two processes can be merged.

5.4.2.3 Data transformation

A logical process is normally required only where input data is being transformed into output data in a manner which alters the data in some way eg calculations, merging two inputs or updating a logical main store. A process which re-organises data, such as a sort, is not logically necessary and should be removed.

Any enquiries or retrievals for display or print which do not alter data stores should be removed and placed in the Requirements Catalogue. They should only be retained in the Logical Data Flow Diagram if they are a major part of the system's functionality.

In the Telephone Directory Example, processes 2, 4, 5, 6, 7, 8, 10 and 11, all fall into this category and can therefore be removed. The Requirements Catalogue should be updated to show that a printed version of the Telephone Directory is needed. Process 9 is only required because of tedious re-typing of data to prepare the new Telephone Directory. It is not logically necessary and can be omitted.

5.4.2.4 Tasks requiring to be carried out by a person

Remove subjective decisions from a process. A subjective decision is the type of decision which cannot be computerised since the decision maker uses factors such as intuition in arriving at a result, and the decision cannot be reduced to a number of predetermined factors. An example could be choosing a candidate after a series of job interviews. In such cases the decision maker should be removed from the process and become an external entity. The automatable part of the process remains.

Where a process requires a person to carry out a process for legal or security reasons, then the task should be removed and treated as an external entity.

5.4.2.5 Duplicate processes

Remove identical low level processes. Low level processes may often be performing identical functions in different parts of the system. This can arise because the processes are maintaining duplicate copies of the data. The data duplication is removed during logicalisation, so there is no need for the duplicate processes. Duplicated processes should be examined carefully to see if the removal of duplication will result in the introduction of any ambiguity into the system.

In the Telephone Directory Example, processes 1, 3 and 12 all maintain duplicate copies of the Telephone Directory, only 1 such process is required in the logical Data Flow Diagram.

5.4.2.6 Changes to bottom level processes

To summarize, in the Telephone Directory example the processes on the Level 1 Current Physical Data Flow Diagram are the bottom level processes and are affected as follows:

Process	Logicalisation
1 Record changes	Remove location reference
2 Consolidate changes	Data stores T2(M) and T6(M) have been removed. Logically there is no need to send a weekly list to the operators since only one main data store remains containing the current version of the telephone directory. This process is now redundant.
3 Record changes	This process duplicates another low level process, process 1 and maintains a duplicate copy of the telephone directory data. It is logically redundant.
4 Consolidate weekly lists	Data store T7(M) no longer exists so this process is logically redundant
5 Despatch change list	This process is directly connected to process 4 and so is no longer required.
6 Prepare amendment list	Processes 6 to 11 are not required since they re-organise data or print it, without changing the data.
8 Type new directory	

9 Validate new directory

10 Print new directory

11 Despatch directories

12 Maintain User Directory This process duplicates processes 1 and 3, it is logically redundant.

5.4.3 Group Bottom-Level Processes

The remaining logical bottom-level processes should now be grouped into higher-level processes to produce the Current Logical Data Flow Model. The objective of this exercise is to group processes which have most in common functionally and to minimise the number of data flows between processes.

5.4.3.1 Guidelines for grouping

The high-level processes are based on the following:

i) Functions

A function is a user view of the system and the users should be closely consulted during this process. The bottom-level processes should be grouped so that a level one process covers a single function. A function should not span more than a single level one process. The users view of functions may well be related to the structure of the organisation. It is likely that some of the process groupings on the Physical Data Flow Diagrams will be retained on the Logical Data Flow Diagrams.

When grouping the bottom level processes remember that functions should be easy to identify. A useful way to think of this is that these level one processes would probably correspond to the choices on a top level menu if this was a model of a computer-based system.

This is the most important basis for grouping bottom-level processes.

ii) Similarity of process type

Another guideline for grouping is to look for processes which are of a similar type. There are two main types:

- processes which support the business of a system
- processes which maintain reference data and carry out housekeeping tasks

It is unlikely that the two types of process will be grouped together. In a payroll system the processes involved with collecting time sheet and absenteeism data might be one group. A second group of processes might be concerned with the production of payslips and payments. A third group of processes might be housekeeping tasks such as updating the pay grades reference file with new rates of pay for each grade at annual review time or updating the tax tables when the Government changes income tax bands and rates.

iii) Grouping processes which access the same data

Processes which update the same data store are likely to be grouped together. For example in a payroll system all the processes which could change the details held about an employee might be grouped together eg.change of personal details (name, address etc), change of job, change of grade in present job etc.

A useful aid to identifying such process groupings is to use the Process/Entity matrix. This is a working document which shows bottom-level processes down one side and entities along the other side. Mark on the Matrix which processes access which data stores distinguishing between read, write and read + write. Look at the Matrix carefully and group those processes which access the same data stores, writes taking precedence over reads. A sample matrix for the Telephone Directory System is shown in Figure 5.7.

Normally the completed Logical Data Flow Diagram should only have one external entity linked to a process. The data flow from this external entity providing the trigger to the process. Sometimes a process will require more than one trigger because the process contains a complicated series of actions but the norm is one trigger for each process. A process may be linked to any number of data stores but should not be directly linked to any other process.

Processes \ Entities	D1 Telephone Directory	D2 Extension Location
Record changes	R/U	R/U
Extract details	R	R

Figure 5.7 Process/Entity Matrix

A useful principle to apply is to group the bottom-level processes on the basis of the maximum cohesion with the minimum coupling. Cohesion refers to the independence of one process from another. A process is highly cohesive if it requires little interaction with other procedures. Coupling is a measure of the interconnection between processes. It is desirable to reduce coupling between processes to a minimum. Direct connections between level one processes on a Logical Data Flow Diagram indicate a failure to group processes in an optimum way. Processes should be linked through data stores.

A completed Logical Data Flow Diagram for the Telephone Directory Example is shown in Figure 5.8. Note that only one process remains. All that is required is a process which allows the Telephone Directory and Extension Locations to be changed.

5.4.4 Check For Consistency And Completeness

Check the Logical Data Flow Diagram to ensure that all the data flows, processes and data stores in the current physical system have been considered and their absence or presence in the Logical Data Flow Diagram can be justified. The processes and data stores on the new Current Logical Data Flow Model will require to be numbered.

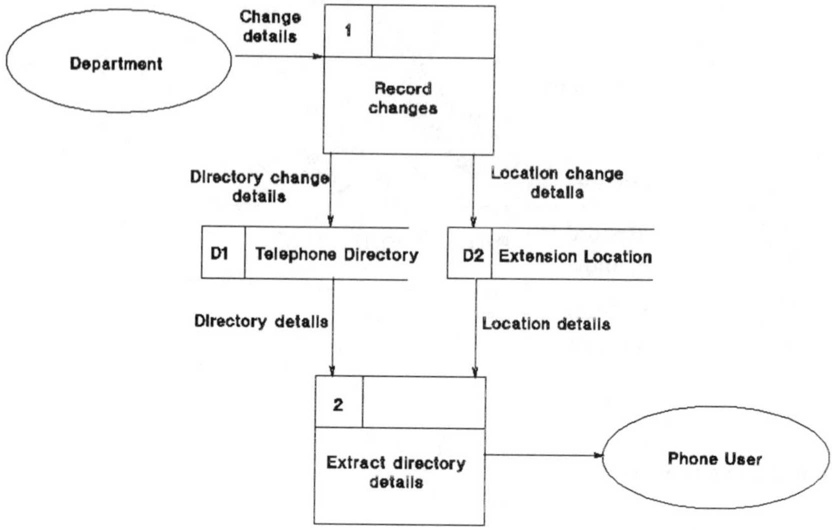

Figure 5.8 Logical Data Flow Diagram for Telephone Directory System.

The location section on the process box should remain blank. It is probably easier to number the new model without reference to the old so that the logical view of the system is seen as completely separate from the physical view.

5.5 A More Complex Worked Example

The Telephone Directory Example is relatively simple to logicalise since it has only a level one Data Flow Diagram and it is a logically simple system. The Car Allowance System discussed in Chapter 4 is a little more complex. For convenience the complete Current Environment Data Flow Model for the Car Allowance System is given in Figure 5.9. The Logical Data Model is shown in Figure 5.10.

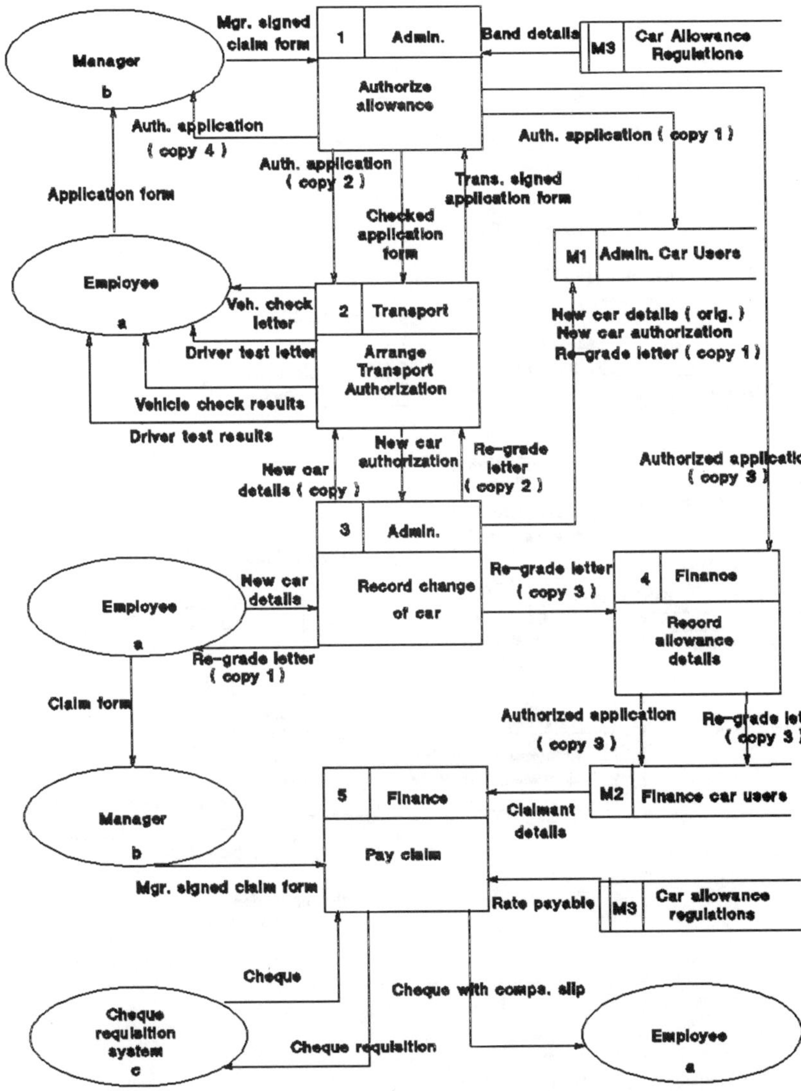

Figure 5.9(a) Current Environment Level 1 Data Flow Diagram for Car Allowance System

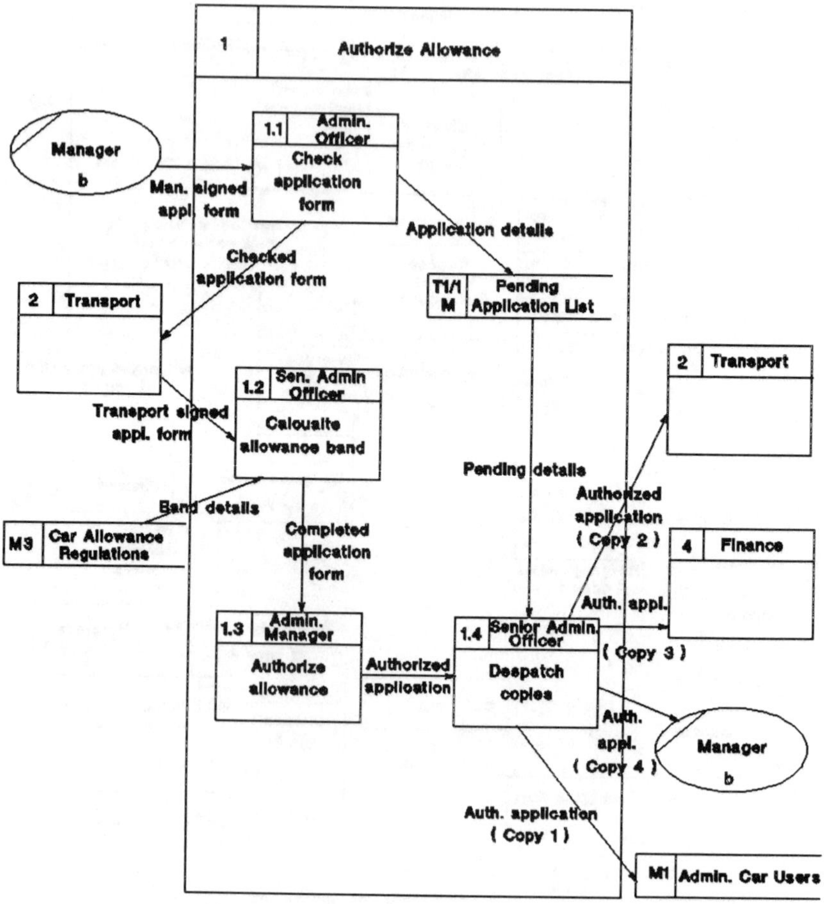

Figure 5.9(b) Process 1, 'Authorize allowance', Level 2 DFD

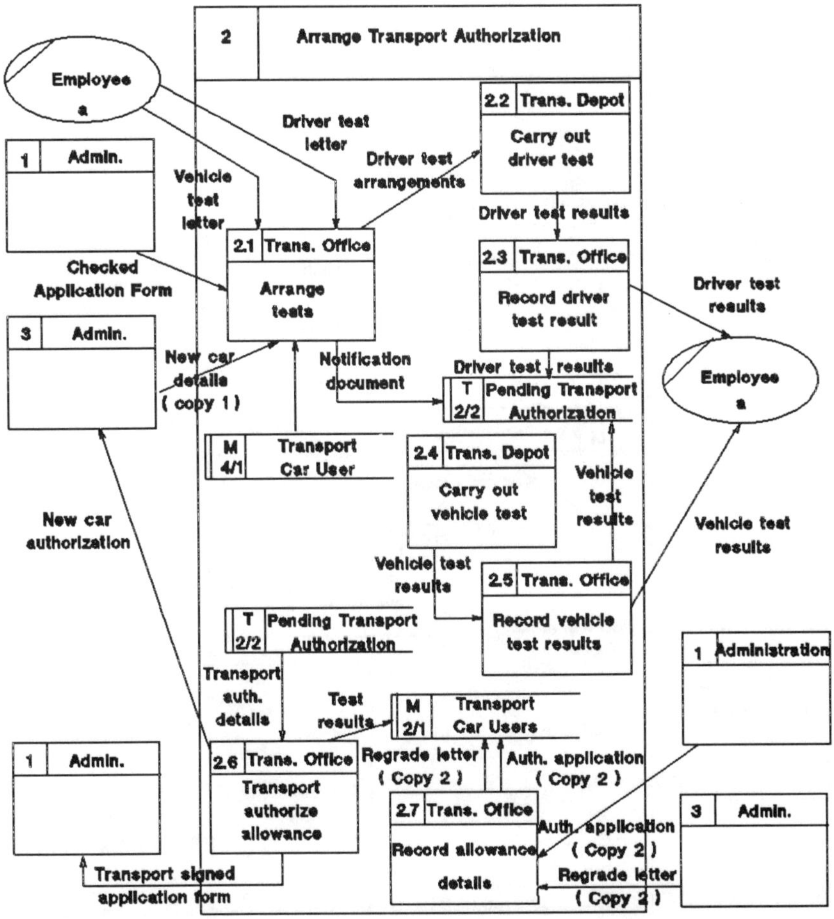

Figure 5.9(c) Process 2, 'Arrange Tramsport authorization', Level 2 DFD.

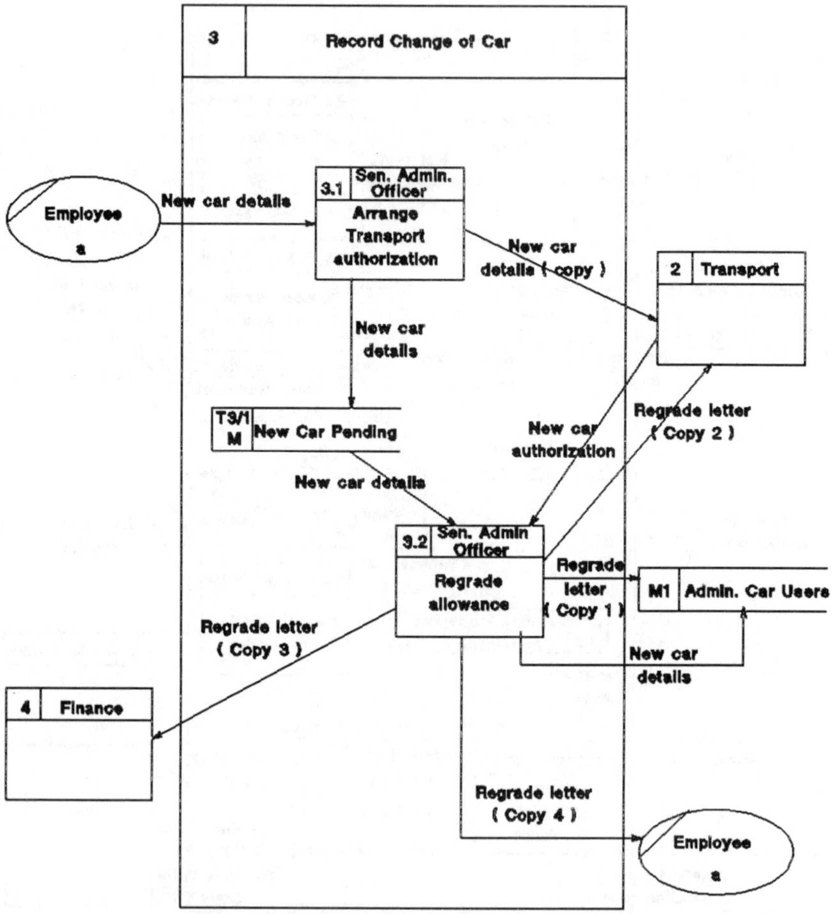

Figure 5.9(d) Process 3, 'Record change of car', Level 2 DFD.

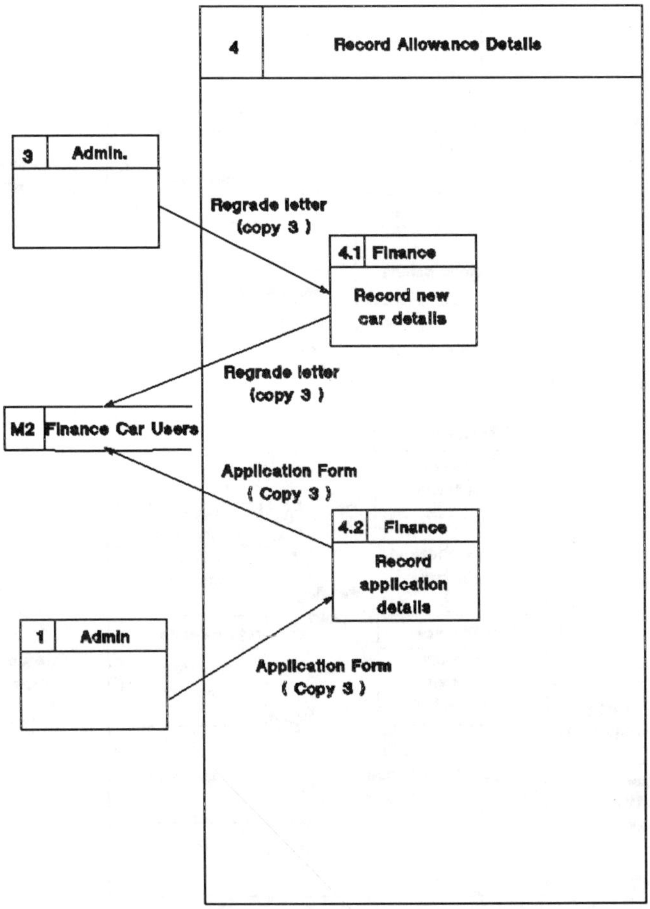

Figure 5.9(e) Process 4, 'Record allowance details', Level 2 DFD.

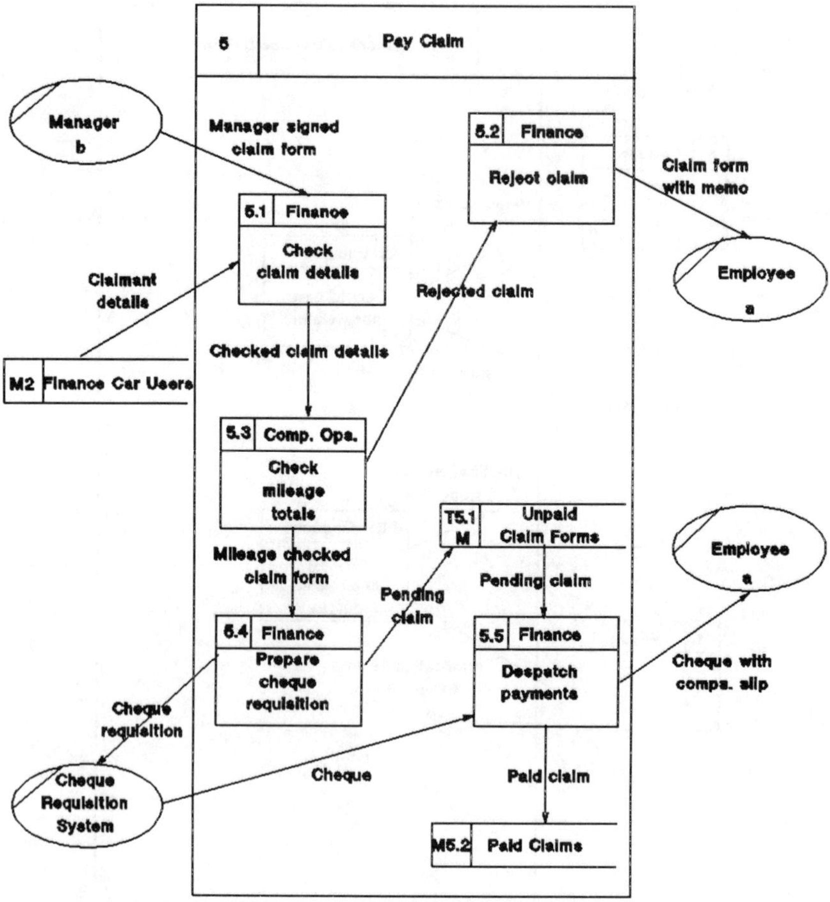

Figur~ 5.9(f) Process 5, 'Pay claim', Level 2 DFD.

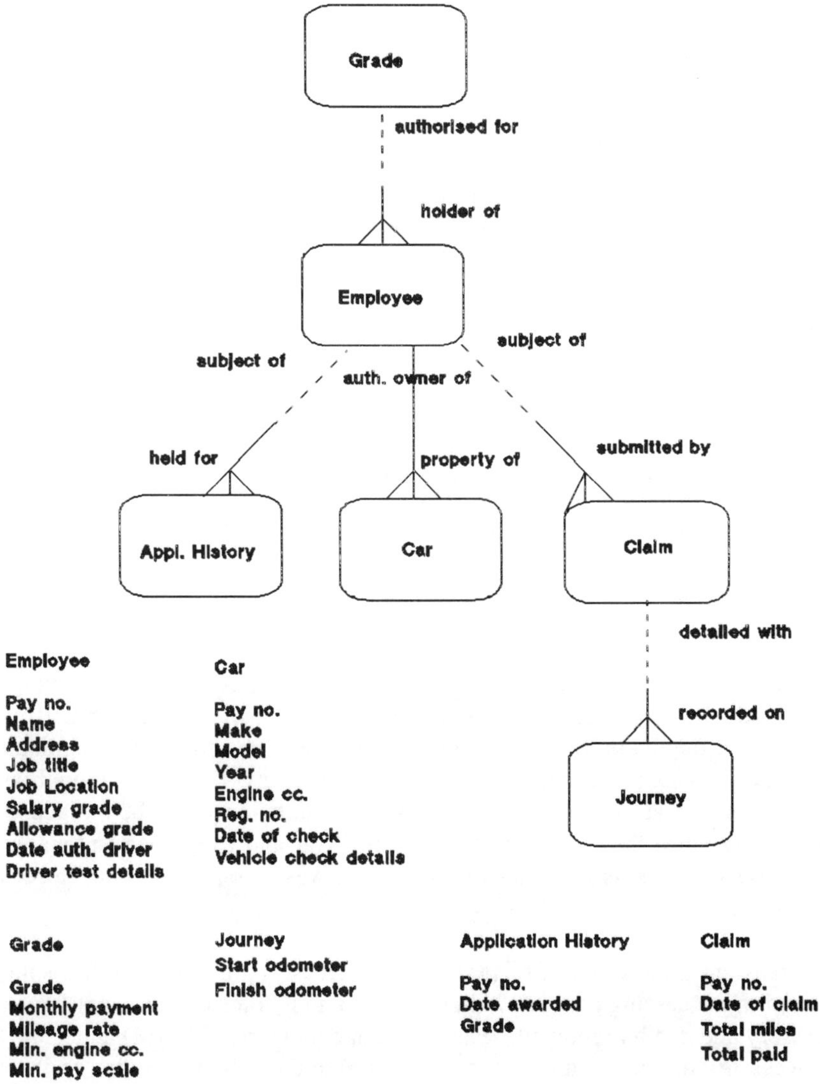

Figure 5.10 Current Environment Logical Data Model for Car Allowance System

5.5.1 Rationalise data stores

The data stores in the Current Environment Data Flow Model are as follows:

Main data stores

M1	**Admin. Car Users**
M2	**Finance Car Users**
M3	**Car Allowance Regulations**
M2/1	**Transport Car Users**
M5/2	**Paid Claims**

Transient data stores

T1/1(M)	**Pending Application List**
T2/2(M)	**Pending Transport Authority**
T3/1(M)	**New Car Pending**
T5/1(M)	**Unpaid Claim Forms**

Main data stores M1 and M2 are complete duplicates and can be merged. M2/1 holds the same data as M1 and M2 plus the vehicle and driver test result sheets. The duplicate data can be merged with M1 and M2. An examination of the Logical Data Model and accompanying Entity Descriptions in Figure 5.10 shows us that the vehicle and driver test results must also be merged with M1 and M2 since they are part of the entities Car and Employee and an entity can not be split across two data stores. This gives us one main data store, D1 Car Users.

The transient data stores T1/1(M) is only necessary because of the split in location of processing between Administration and Transport, it is not logically necessary and can be removed. The transient data stores T2/2(M) and T3/1(M) are necessary to hold data until the result of both the vehicle and driver checks have been carried out, they can be merged but must be retained. The transient data store T5/1(M) is not necessary since the examination of the processes in the next section removes the need for this temporary store.

The Logical/Physical Data Store Cross Reference is shown in Figure 5.11.The resulting Logical Data Store/Entity Cross Reference is shown in Figure 5.12.

Physical data store		**Logical data store**	
M1	**Admin Car Users**	**D1**	**Car Users**
M2	**Finance Car Users**		
M2/1	**Transport Car Users**		
M3	**Car Allowance Regulations**	**D2**	**Grades**
M5/2	**Paid Claims**	**D3**	**Claims**
T2/2(M)	**Pending Transport**	**T4**	**Pending Applications**
T3/1(M)	**New Car Pending**		
T5/1(M)	**Unpaid Claim Forms**		

Figure 5.11 Logical/Physical Data Store Cross Reference for Car Allowance System

5.5.2 Rationalise bottom level processes

The bottom level processes are those indicated by a * on the Current Physical Data Flow Diagrams. In the Car Allowance example, all the level two processes are bottom level processes. The following list describes the decision for each process:

Process	Decision
1.1 Check application form	Retain but merge with 2.1 since they are performed in sequence.
1.2 Calculate allowance band	Keep but merge with 1.1, there is no logical reason why the grade cannot be calculated before Transport authorization.

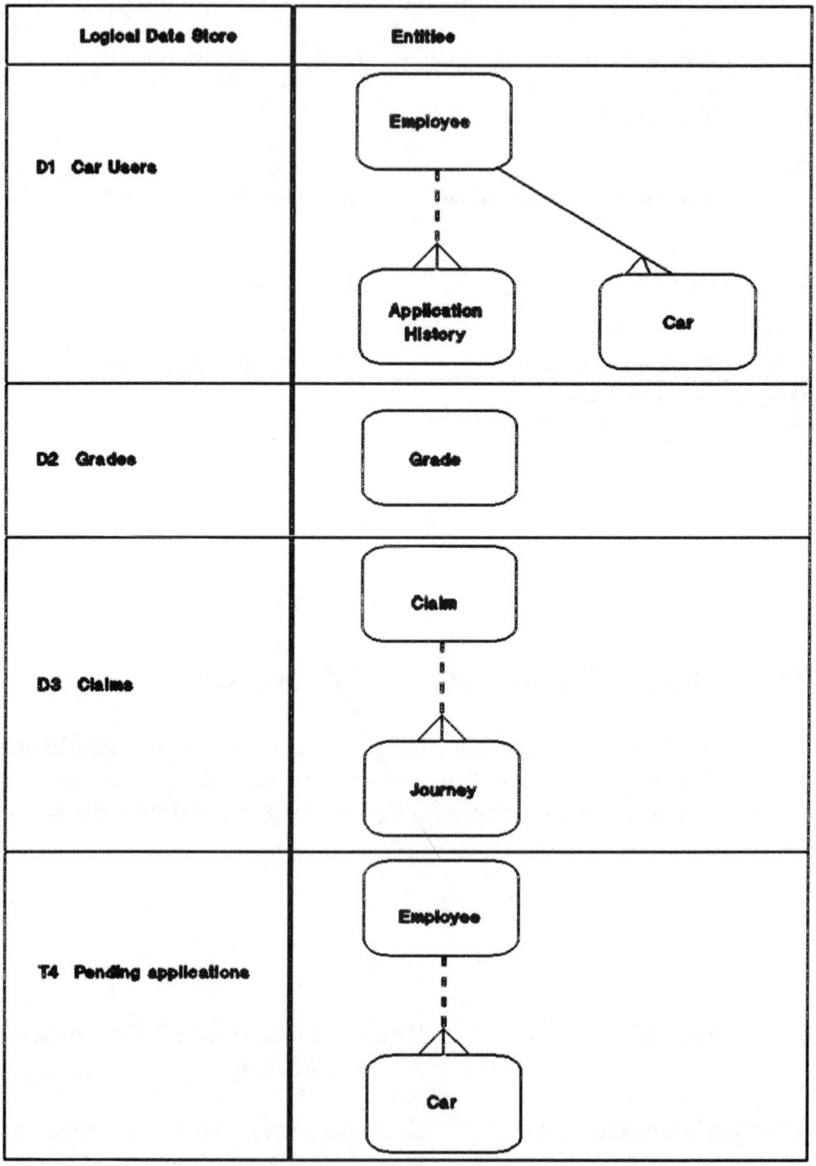

Figure 5.12 Logical Data Store/Entity Cross Reference

1.3 Authorize allowance	This process requires a signature, ie a person must carry this out. The Admin. Manager should become an external entity. The remaining element of the process involves sending the application to the Administration Manager for signature, this happens in sequence with processes 2.3, 2.5 and 2.6 and can be merged with them.
1.4 Despatch copies	The elements of this process which sends out duplicate application forms is no longer necessary with the removal of the duplicate data stores, except for the despatch of an allowance authorization notification to the employee's manager. The element which records the authorization of the allowance is necessary and should be retained.
2.1 Arrange tests	This is carried out in sequence with 1.1 and should be merged with that process.
2.2 Carry out driver test	This is a subjective process and should be carried out by an external entity - Tester.
2.3 Record driver test result	Keep, but combine with 2.5 since they are duplicate processes which only differ in the data items they update in the Car Users data store.
2.4 Carry out vehicle test	See 2.2 above
2.5 Record vehicle test results	Merge with 2.3

2.6 Transport authorize allowance	This requires a signature and should be carried out by an external entity. The despatch to the Administration Manager for authorization could logically be handled by the Transport Manager, since no change to the application details would be required between the two signatures.
2.7 Record allowance details	This can be removed since it retains a duplicate file.
3.1 Arrange Transport authorization	This process duplicates many of the elements of allowance authorization and can be merged with 1.1.
3.2 Regrade allowance	See 3.2 above.
4.1 Record new car details	Maintains duplicate file. Omit
4.2 Record application details	Maintains duplicate file. Omit.
5.1 Check claim details	Performed sequentially with 5.3 and 5.4, merge.
5.2 Reject claim	Retain, as part of 'Pay claim'.
5.3 Check mileage totals	See 5.1 above.
5.4 Prepare cheque requisition	See 5.1 above.
5.5 Despatch payments	For security reasons the cheques must be manually checked before despatch. This process is therefore carried out by a person and should be removed.

5.5.3 Constructing the Logical Data Flow Model

The users' view of the Car Allowance System sees two separate functions:

- **authorization of allowances**
- **payment of claims**

The change of car details is part of the authorization function since it can affect the grade authorized. Processes which access the same data should be grouped with updates having priority over reads. A Process/Entity Matrix for the Car Allowance System is shown in Figure 5.13. This suggests the same two logical groupings of processes. The process 'Pay claim' is the only process updating D3 and should be grouped separately. The other 4 processes use the same data stores. Note that the transient data store, T4, is a duplicate of the main data store D1.

Entities / Processes	D1 Car Users	D2 Grades	D3 Paid Claims	T1/1 Pending Application
Arrange tests		R		U
Record test results				U
Notify authorization	U			U
Pay claim	R	R	R/U	
Record change of car		R		U

Figure 5.13 Process/Entity Matrix

If the process which maintained data store D2 Grades was included, then it would have been separated from all the other processes because it maintains reference data and all the other processes support the business of the system. This would have given us a third process group, "housekeeping".

The resulting Logical Data Flow Diagrams are shown in Figure 5.14. Note that there are no process to process data flows, and there are additional external entities. The diagrams should be carefully checked against the Current Physical Data Flow Diagrams to ensure that no necessary functionality has been omitted from the Logical Data Flow Diagrams.

The other elements of the Data Flow Model, such as Elementary Process Descriptions, should be amended to support the Current Logical Data Flow Diagrams.

5.6 Required System Data Flow Model

The Required System Data Flow Model is built using the Current Logical Data Flow Model as a basis and then it is tailored to suit the Selected Business System Option. The Requirements Catalogue is annotated to show if, and how, requirements have been met. The Required Logical Data Model is developed simultaneously.

The Required System Data Flow Model is input to function definition and is also used to help identify events for Entity-event Modelling.

The Required System Data Flow Model for the Car Allowance System has the same functionality as the current system. The additional requirements are discussed in Chapter 2, section 2. Many additional requirements are for printouts of data from files without any further processing, these are logged in the Requirements Catalogue but are not shown on a Data Flow Model. Some requirements should be added to the Current Environment Logical Data Model as follows:

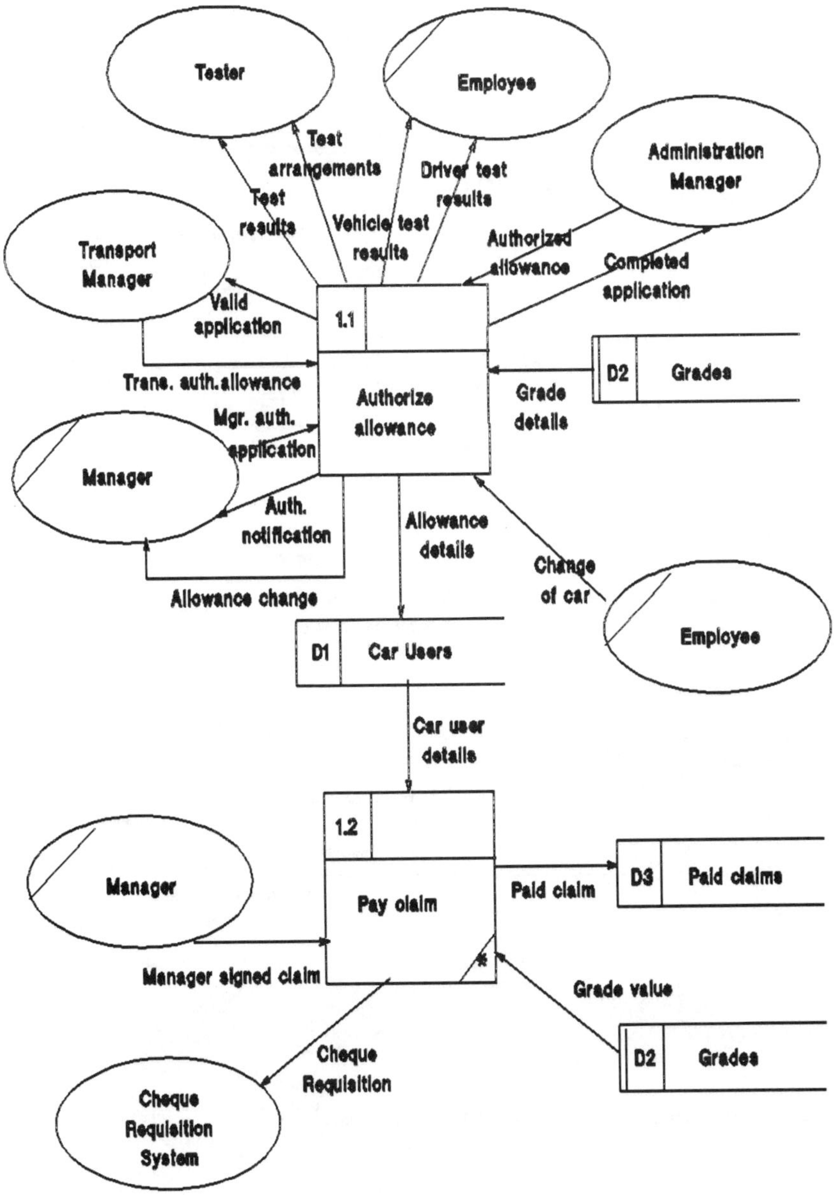

Figure 5.14(a) Current Environment Logical Data Flow Diagram, Level 1

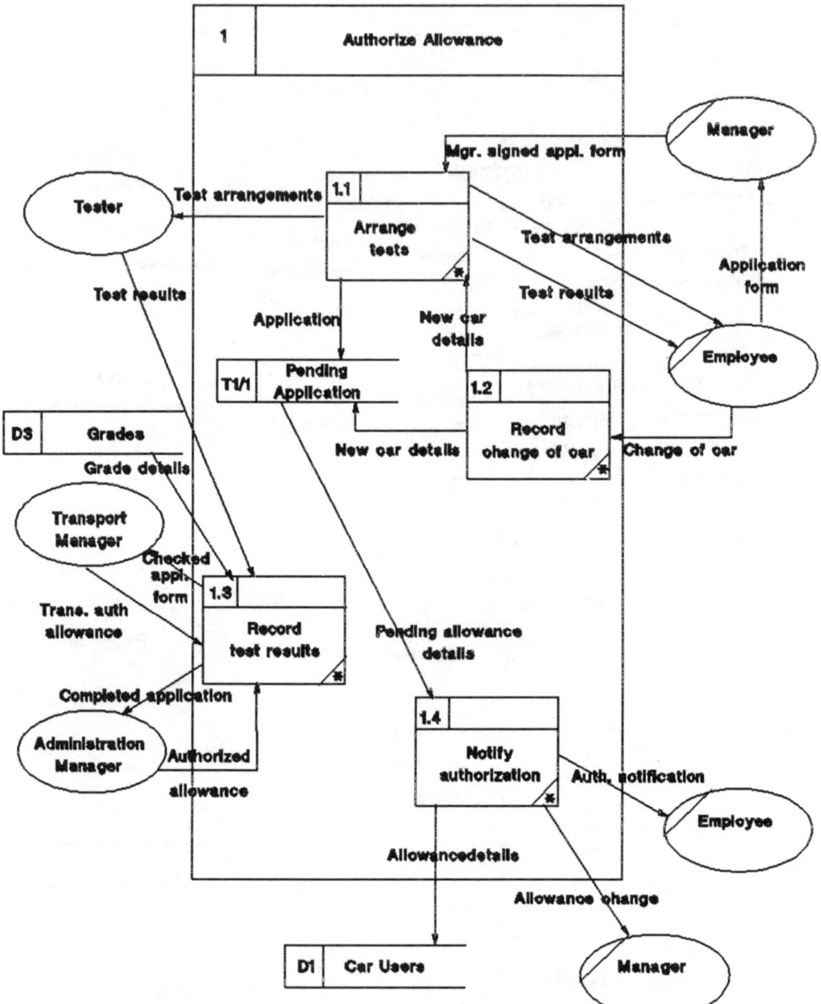

Figure 5.14 (b) Process 1, 'Authorize allowance', Level 2 DFD.

Requirement	Action
Employees' monthly statement	**Show as data flow from pay claim and amend elementary process description of process 2.1.**
Managers' monthly statement	**Show as data flow from pay claim and add a level 2 process "Produce monthly statements"**
Managers' annual statement	**Add new process group - and show new data flow.**
Print cheques	**Remove external entity Cheque Requisition System and add new level 2 process to Pay Claims to produce cheques and despatch payment.**

The Business Systems Options in Chapter 7 will discuss some of these requirements.

5.7 Use of Data Flow Diagrams in the stages of SSADM

This section discusses in detail the production and use of Data Flow Diagrams during the various Stages of an SSADM project. Associated documents and techniques are mentioned where relevant. This section does not provide a complete description of all the activities in the earlier Stages of SSADM, only those involving Data Flow Diagrams.

5.7.1 Feasibility Study Module

5.7.1.1 Step 010 Prepare for the Study

Initially a level one Data Flow Diagram is created to establish the boundaries of the system under investigation and to identify the major system inputs, outputs and interfaces with other systems and the outside world. Since this diagram is describing the current system it is called the Current Physical Data Flow Diagram. In parallel with this an initial Logical Data Model is prepared. The initial Level 1 Data Flow Diagram can be used to identify the system users and the system interfaces and these will become the main areas for investigation.

5.7.1.2 Step 020 Define the Problem

The current and required environments are described using Data Flow Diagrams and the Logical Data Model to support narrative description. The Requirements Catalogue is used to record problems and requirements. The User Catalogue is created to record intended users of the new system. Interviews and other fact finding activities will result in expansion of the initial Data Flow Diagram from Step 010 with reference to the initial Logical Data Structure. The expansion of the Data Flow Diagram can be limited to those processes which can be usefully expanded to aid discussion with the users. The decomposition need go no further than Level Two Diagrams.

5.7.1.3 Step 030 Select Feasibility Options

Business System and Technical System Options are assessed. The Data Flow Model is amended to show the agreed scope of the project.

5.7.1.4 Step 040 Assemble Feasibility Report

The Data Flow Model is used as part of the Outline Current Environment Description and the Outline Required Environment Description.

5.7.2 Requirements Analysis Module

5.7.2.1 Step 110 Establish Analysis Framework

Some or all of the Data Flow Diagramming required at this stage may have been done within a preceding Feasibility Study. Initially the current physical system is documented using a Level One Current Physical Data Flow Diagram. An outline Logical Data Structure is constructed alongside the Data Flow

Diagram. The Data Flow Diagrams can be used as a basis for identifying users and areas and techniques to be used for further investigation. The Requirements Catalogue is also created at this stage.

5.7.2.2 Step 130 Investigate Current Processing

The Level one Current Physical Data Flow Diagram is reviewed and revised in parallel with Step 120 Investigate and Define Requirements and Step 140 Investigate Current Data. Level two and three Current Physical Data Flow Diagrams can be developed as necessary. The process of decomposing Data Flow Diagrams can result in amendments to the higher level Data Flow Diagrams.

Elementary Process Descriptions for the bottom level Data Flow Diagram processes can now be developed. The Input/Output Descriptions and External Entity Descriptions should be created to complete the Current Physical Data Flow Model. The Data Catalogue is also created at this point.

5.7.2.3 Step 150 Derive Logical View of Current Services

The Current Physical Data Flow Diagrams are converted into a logical view and the Current Logical Data Flow Model is derived. The documentation supporting the Data Flow Diagrams, such as the Input/Output Descriptions must be updated to support the logical model. The Data Catalogue is also updated. The Requirements Catalogue will be updated with enquiry and retrievals which have been omitted from the Logical Data Flow Model. The Logical Data Store/Entity Cross Reference is produced.

5.7.2.4 Step 210 Define Business System Options
Step 220 Select Business System Option

The production of Business System Options in Step 210 starts to shape the new system. Business System Options are discussed in more detail in Chapter 7.

Any requirements for the new system must now be identified from the Requirements Catalogue and the Current Logical Data Flow Diagrams. Narrative descriptions of possible options which meet the requirements are drawn up. Data Flow Diagrams can be used to support the narrative for each option but this is not mandatory.

5.7.3 Requirements Specification Module

5.7.3.1 Step 310 Define Required System Processing

The Logical Data Flow Diagrams and the Requirements Catalogue are adjusted to take account of the Selected Business System Option. Additional processes may be included and other processes excluded within the Business System Option boundary. Lower level processes may need to be adjusted, particularly to maintain new data in the Required System Data Model which is being defined in parallel. Elementary Process Descriptions, External Entity Descriptions and Input/Output Descriptions should be added or amended as necessary.

5.7.3.2 Step 330 Derive System Functions

The Required System Data Flow Diagrams and Requirements Catalogue are used to identify update and enquiry functions. This provides an initial list of events and the entities they act upon which can then be input to Entity-event modelling. Subsequently further functions are defined as new events are identified. Every bottom-level process should be assigned at least one function. The Required System Data Flow Model may require amendment as a result of this analysis. The Input/Output Descriptions which support the Data Flow Model are used to identify the user interface for each update function and these are specified as Input/Output Structures. The users help to identify the enquiry interface. Chapter 8 describes Function Definition. Chapter 11 describes Entity-event modelling.

5.7.3.3 Step 350 Develop Specification Prototypes

Specification prototyping demonstrates selected parts of the Requirements Specification in an animated form for demonstration to users. The Required System Data Flow Model may be used for reference when developing the prototypes. Prototyping is discussed in Chapter 10.

5.7.3.4 Step 360 Develop Processing Specification

This Step involves the production of Entity Life Histories and Effect Correspondence Diagrams. The Required System Data Flow Model may be used as a reference point for this process although the Required System Logical Data Model provides the main source of input to these techniques. See Chapter 11.

5.7.4 Logical System Specification

5.7.4.1 Step 410 Define Technical System Options
Step 420 Select Technical System Option

Up to six Technical Options are considered, Data Flow Diagrams may be used as part of the outline documentation provided for each option. Two or three Skeleton Options are developed for further consideration. These are then expanded to a more detailed Technical Option Specification. The Technical Option Specifications must be presented to the Users and the Data Flow Diagrams can be used as part of the presentation material. The chosen option must then be fully documented in the Required System Specification with the Data Flow Diagrams being adjusted as necessary to reflect the chosen Technical Option. The Required System Specification is then formally reviewed and this may require some amendments to the Data Flow Diagrams.

5.8 Summary

Data Flow Diagrams provide a view of the information flow through a system and this is cross checked with the other views of the system through the various stages of SSADM. The first Data Flow Model produced is the Current Physical Data Flow Model which describes how the current system actually works. This set of diagrams is then logicalised to become the Current Logical Data Flow Model which shows the processing which is currently carried out without the physical, staffing and timing constraints. This set of diagrams is used as the basis for developing the Required System Specification. Any new requirements for the system are added and the result is a set of Required Logical Data Flow Diagrams. Many SSADM documents are associated with or derived from these Data Flow Diagrams.

5.9 Keywords

Current Physical Data Flow Model
Current Logical Data Flow Model
Required System Data Flow Model
Current Environment Logical Data Model
Logical Data Store/Entity Cross Reference
Logical/Physical Data Store Cross Reference
Logicalisation
Requirements Catalogue
Process/Entity Matrix
Main data store
Transient data store

5.10 Exercises

1. Describe the different types of data flow diagram and how they are related to each other.

2. Describe the use of the Requirements Catalogue when drawing Data Flow Diagrams in SSADM.

3. Describe the characteristics of a transient data store.

4. Describe the relationship of main logical data stores and entities.

5. What are the four main tasks when converting Current Physical Data Flow Diagrams into Logical Data Flow Diagrams?

6. Can an entity appear against more than one data store on the Logical Data Store/Entity Cross Reference?

7. Outline how bottom-level processes are re-grouped after rationalisation.

8. Describe the relationship of the Data Flow Models to the following techniques:

   Logical Data Modelling
   Dialogue Design
   Function Definition
   Technical System Options
   Requirements Specification
   Business System Options
   Entity Event Modelling

9. Prepare a Current Logical Data Flow Model for the Student Administration System described in Appendix 2.

10. There are some necessary processes missing from the Car Allowance System Logical Data Flow Diagrams in Figure 5.14. Can you identify them.

11. Prepare a Data Catalogue and Elementary Process Descriptions for the Car Allowance System.

12. Prepare a Required System Data Flow Model for the Car Allowance System.

CHAPTER 6

Logical Data Modelling.

6.1 Introduction

Data Flow Diagrams are used to provide a structured set of pictures of the movement of data within an information system. In isolation they do not provide an adequate description of the system. The Logical Data Model provides another view of the system, that of the data structures. The Logical Data Model is constructed in parallel with the Data Flow Model, the two techniques support one another and cannot be developed in isolation.

6.2 The Need For a Logical Data Model

A Logical Data Model shows the relationships between the data groups within a processing system. It consists of a Logical Data Structure and supporting documentation. The aim of the technique is to provide a firm foundation for file or database design. 'Data Modelling', 'Entity Modelling' and 'Bachman Diagramming' are almost identical techniques which have been in use for almost 20 years since the introduction of database implementations produced a requirement for new data design tools.

In the early stages of data modelling the analyst is not usually aware of all the data items (fields) that will eventually be included in the data model. The analyst is more likely to know that there will be data items held about eg customers, parts and suppliers than to know exactly what all the data items will be. In most situations there will be a large number of data items, the number growing as the analyst's understanding of the system develops. A technique which allows a top down view of the data structure by looking at groups of data items is a useful tool for the analyst. For instance, the analyst knows that data is kept about customers. The customer's name and address and account number are some data items which can be grouped together as 'customer' in the model, other data items belonging to this group will be identified as the system investigation continues.

The data structure of a system does not consist of isolated groups of data items. The relationships between data items must also be identified. For instance it is important to know the relationship between customer and order in the system under examination. Can a customer have only one order in the system at a time or can there be several orders for each customer?. Both of these relationships are possible and depend on the situation. The analyst must have a clear idea of the time span under which relationships are being considered since time may alter the nature of the relationship.

The Logical Data Model provides a top down view of the data structure of a system. It identifies data groups and examines the relationships between them. It is not necessary to identify all the data items which belong to a particular data group but it is a starting point for this process. As the understanding of the system develops, the data items that belong to a particular data group are identified and descriptions of each data group can be built up and formally recorded on an Entity Description Form.

The Logical Data Model consists of the following:

- Logical Data Structure
- Entity Descriptions
- Relationship Descriptions
- Attribute Descriptions (in Data Catalogue)
- Grouped Domain Descriptions (in Data Catalogue)

Enquiry access paths are defined in the Enquiry Function Description.

6.3 Logical Data Structures - Definitions.

A Logical Data Structure is based on ENTITIES, ATTRIBUTES AND RELATIONSHIPS.

6.3.1 Entity

A group of data items in a Logical Data Structure is called an entity. An entity is a thing about which data is kept, this corresponds to the logical groups of data items, discussed in section 2, above such as Customer, Order, Part, Supplier. An entity is represented on the model by a soft box (rectangle with rounded edges) containing a meaningful name which identifies the entity. An entity name should be singular, for example Employee not Employees. An entity may, in addition, be identified by a unique number which should be allocated in a non-significant way.

6.3.2 Attributes

The data items which belong to an entity are known as attributes of that entity. The entity Customer may have the attributes 'Customer-number', 'customer-name', 'customer-address', 'sales-to date'. As soon as the analyst starts identifying entities an Entity Description Form should be started for each entity. As attributes are identified they are added to the description. In later stages of the study volume and format information can be added to the form.

Some attributes are optional and will not apply to all occurrences of an entity. For example 'Date of Last Order' will only apply to customers who have previously placed an order. Such optional attributes can have a null value for some occurrences of the entity. A mandatory attribute must have a value for every entity occurrence. Mandatory attributes can have a default value, for instance, the default value for a new customer's 'Credit limit' might be £100. Such default values are automatically set but can be changed if required.

Each occurrence of an entity has a unique set of attribute values. Values for the attribute 'Customer' might be 'Jones & Sons', 'Bain Ltd' etc. It may be helpful to think of an entity as a file, an entity occurrence being the equivalent of a record. Since an entity occurrence is unique there must be at least one unique identifier for each entity occurrence which distinguishes it from all other occurrences of that entity. The unique identifier may be:

- one or more mandatory attributes
- a combination of one or more mandatory attributes and the entity's participation in one or more mandatory, non-transferable relationships (see sections 6.4.2 and 6.10)
- the entities participation in two or more mandatory, non-transferable relationships see sections 6.4.2 and 6.10).

Often a group of attributes might have the same format, range of values, validation rules and/or permitted classes. An example might be date attributes eg 'Date of order', 'Date delivery required', 'Date of last order'. These attributes share the same format and validation rules (eg no 31st of November). They can be said to be based on the same grouped domain, 'Date'. A Grouped Domain Description can be used to record common attribute details to save effort.

6.3.3 Entity Relationship

Relationships are represented by a line joining two entities, or an entity to itself. The line may annotated in a number of ways. All occurrences of the entity must conform to the relationship.

6.4 Characteristics of Entity Relationships

Relationships have the following characteristics:

- degree
- optionality
- relationship link phrase

These are discussed in detail below.

6.4.1 Degree

There are three classifications of degree:

- one-to-many relationship (1:M or M:1)
- one-to-one relationship (1:1)
- many-to-many relationship (M:N)

6.4.1.1 One-to-many relationship

A 'crow's foot' symbol is used at the many end of the relationship. The 'crow's foot' allows for a zero relationship. The relationship should be read in both directions. The example in Figure 6.1 shows that a Customer may have none, one or several Orders, but that an Order must belong to one and only one Customer.

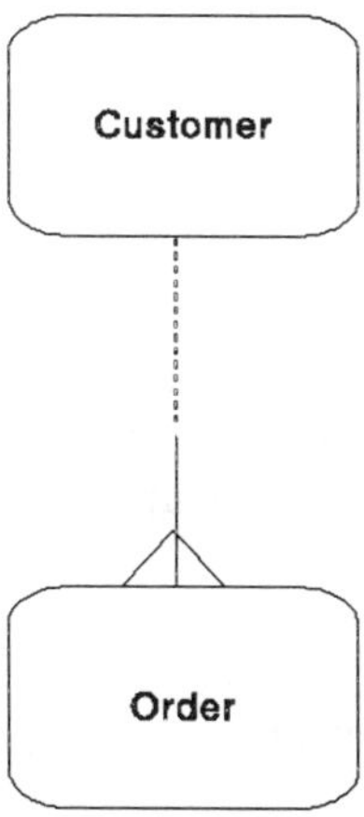

Figure 6.1 One to many relationship

The one side of the relationship is considered the master, and the many side the detail. The detail in one relationship can become the master in another. In Figure 6.2 'Order' is the master of 'Order item' and the detail of 'Customer'. Entity relationships are based on this hierarchical concept of Master/Detail.

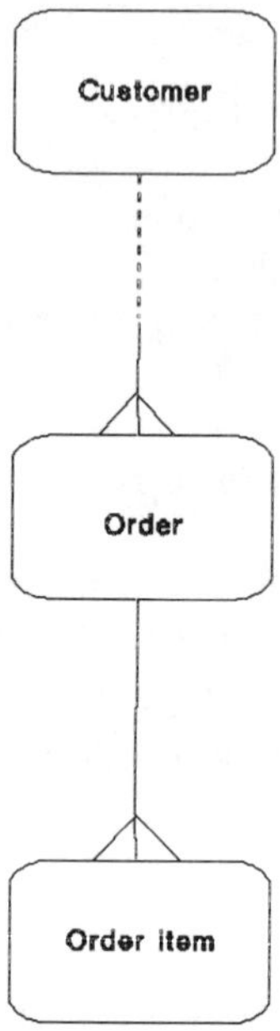

Figure 6.2 Master-detail concept

The Logical Data Structure should be drawn to emphasise this hierarchy with the master entities appearing at the top of the diagram and the details beneath them. If you have 'dead crows' on your diagram then you have not followed this principle, see Figure 6.3.

6.4.1.2 One-to-one relationship

In most cases a one-to-one relationship is not allowed in SSADM. If a one-to-one relationship is identified it should be examined closely to see if the two entities can be combined. There are a very few cases where a one-to-one relationship can exist if the two entities have different keys, different lives and are governed by different time periods.

The one-to-one relation in Figure 6.4 shows a customer having only one order in the system at a time and an order only belonging to one customer. This could happen, for instance, in a domestic kitchen fitting company. However if the customer can have only one order then the customer reference number

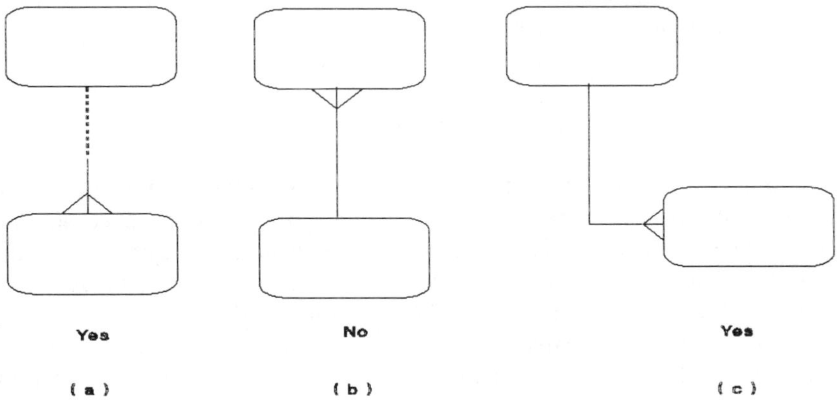

Figure 6.3 Master-detail concept (layout of diagram)

could also be used to identify the order, there is no need to have a separate key for each entity. The order in such a system may be created at the same time as the customer details. In such circumstances it would be desirable to merge the two entities into one called 'Customer order'.

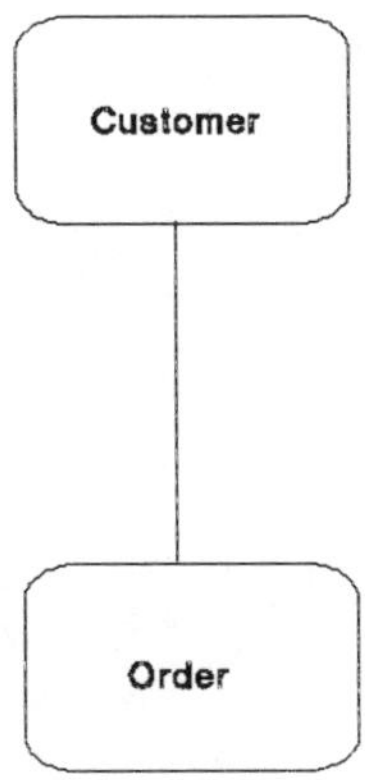

Figure 6.4 One to one relationship

If a true one-to-one relationship does exist then it is best treated as a special occurrence of a one-to-many relationship.

6.4.1.3 Many-to-many relationship

Many-to-many relationships are not permitted in SSADM, they contradict the Master/Detail concept. For any given relationship a detail can have only one master. The existence of such a relationship indicates a missing link entity. For instance in the relationship in Figure 6.5(a) a 'Film' can have many 'Actors' and an 'Actor' can appear in many films. A link entity is needed to identify which actors appeared in which films, typically such a link entity will contain the key field of each of the entities it is linking. The new 'Actor/Film' entity called 'Role' is shown in Figure 6.5(b). The attributes of 'Actor' might be (actor-name, address, sex, age). The attributes of 'Film' could be (film-title, year, director, producer, film company). The attributes of 'Role' might then be (film-title, actor-name, part-name). Note that this has resulted in two master entities sharing a detail entity.

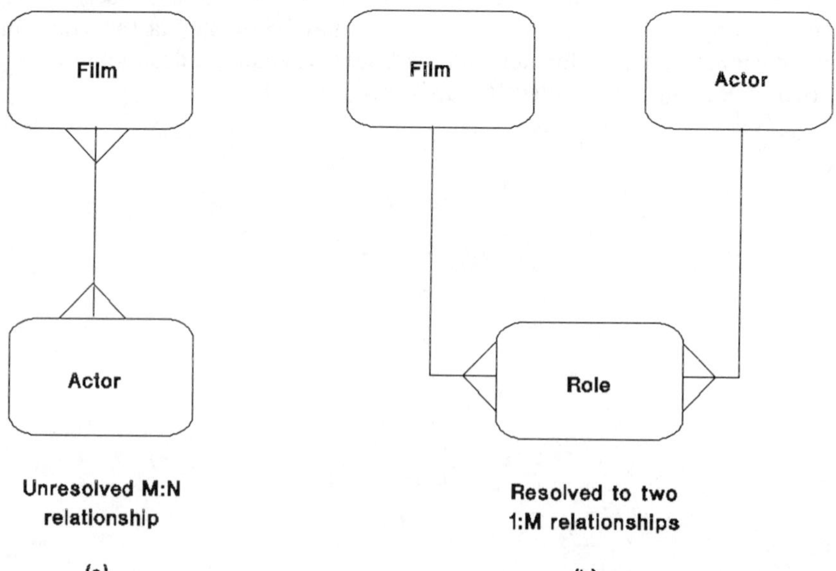

Figure 6.5 Many to many relationships

6.4.2 Multiple Relationships

The following situations can occur:

i) Detail belonging to two Masters

A Detail can belong to two masters. For instance any link entity is sandwiched between two 'crow's feet' and is automatically the detail of two masters as in Figure 6.5(b).

ii) Master having more than one detail

A Master can have more than one detail. If we take the situation in Figure 6.6, a 'Department' has many 'Employees' and a 'Department' also has many items of 'Equipment'.

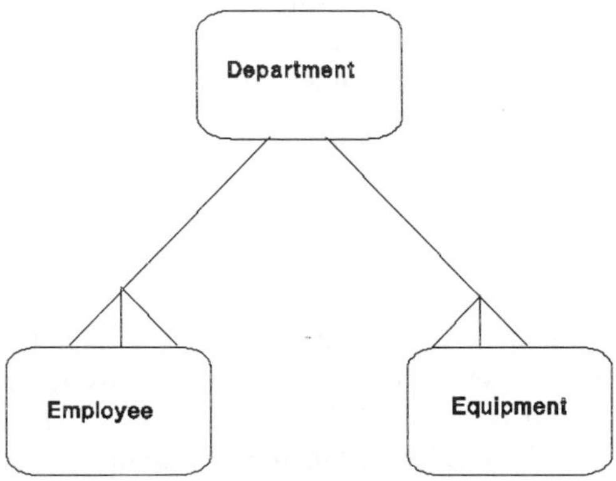

Figure 6.6 Master having more than one detail

iii) Multiple relationships between entities

It is possible for more than one relationship to exist between two entities. The example in Figure 6.7 shows two relationships between the entities Lecturer and Project. One relationship shows the Lecturer who has sponsored a Project, the other relationship shows the Lecturer who is

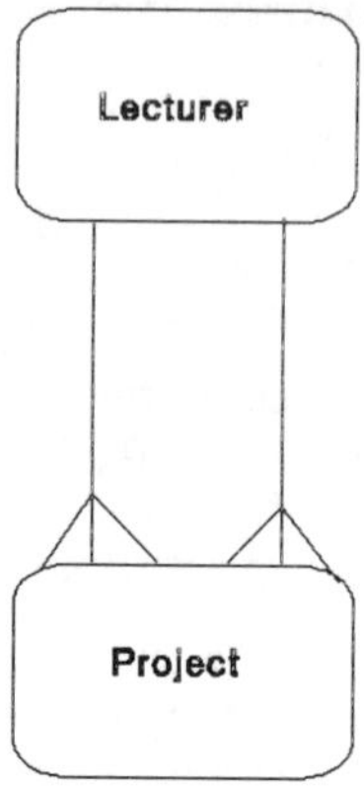

Figure 6.7 Multiple relationships between two entities

supervisor of a Project. A single occurrence of Project could be connected to two different occurrences of Lecturer. Each relationship will be named, as discussed in section 6.4.3.

6.4.2 Optionality

A relationship is mandatory if an entity occurrence cannot exist without being a member of the relationship. A mandatory relationship is shown by a solid line. This is illustrated in Figure 6.8 a), an entity occurrence of 'Order item' can only exist if it is in a relationship with an entity occurrence of 'Order'. Similarly an entity occurrence of 'Order' can only exist if it is in a relationship with at least one entity occurrence of 'Order item'. The master and detail must be created at the same time.

In some situations it is possible for the detail in a relationship to exist before the master, or the master to exist without the detail. This is an optional relationship and is indicated by a using a dashed line. The dashed line shows that entities at the dashed line end of the relationship need not be associated with entities at the other end. Figure 6.8 b) shows such a situation. The Master entity 'Book' can have many 'Reservations' but a book may not necessarily have a 'Reservation' so the relationship is optional. This means that an occurrence of the entity 'Book' can exist without any occurrence of the entity

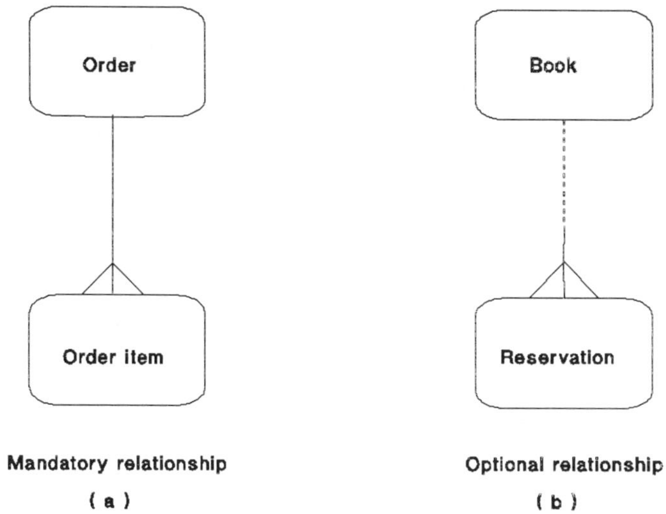

Figure 6.8 Optionality

'Reservation'. This means that the master and detail are created at different times. It is important to identify such situations since they may be important in the Physical Design.

6.4.3 Relationship Link Phrase

A relationship must have a unique identifier with the following structure:

<subject entity name> <relationship link phrase> <object entity name>

The relationship link phrase describes the entity from the perspective of the subject entity. Each relationship must have two relationship link phrases since it must be described with each entity, in turn, being the subject entity.

The link phrase should consist of a past participle and phrases for the relationships in Figure 6.8 are shown in Figure 6.9. Link phrases should read correctly when preceded by the phrases:

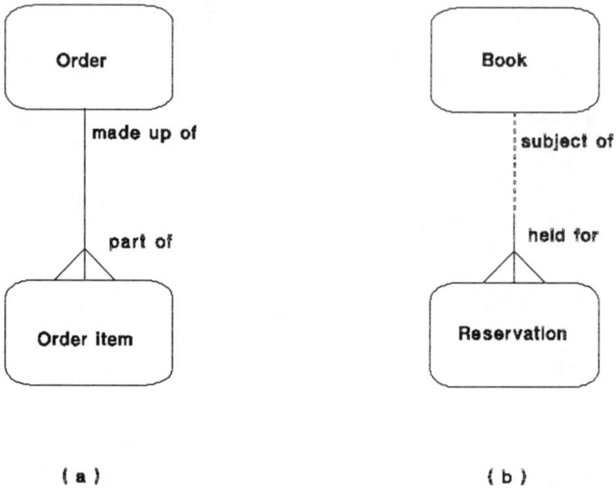

Figure 6.9 Link phrases.

i) 'must be' if the relationship end is mandatory
ii) 'may be' if the relationship end is optional

To avoid ambiguity do not use the words 'a' or 'the' in a link phrase. The link phrase should change when the perspective changes from one end of the relationship to another.

The relationship link phrases for Figure 6.8 are shown in Figure 6.9.

6.5 Relationship Statements

A relationship line must be able to be read from either end without any ambiguity. It is formulated as a plain English 'Relationship Statement', quoting optionality, meaning and degree, as follows:

Each	**<subject entity>**	**must be/ may be**	**<link phrase>**	**one or more/ one and only one**	**<object entity>**

For instance the relationship statements for Figure 6.9 a) read:

Each Order must be made up of one or more Order items.

and

Each Order item must be part of one and only one Order.

The Relationship Statements for Figure 6.9 b) read:

Each Book may be subject of one or more Reservation.

and

Each Reservation must be held for one and only one Book.

Note that the plural of the entity name is used where the degree of a relationship is many. The degree of a relationship is expressed as 'one and only one' at the one end, and 'one or more' at the many end of a relationship.

In some situations two or more different relationships may exist between a pair of entities. Where more than one relationship exists between any two entities

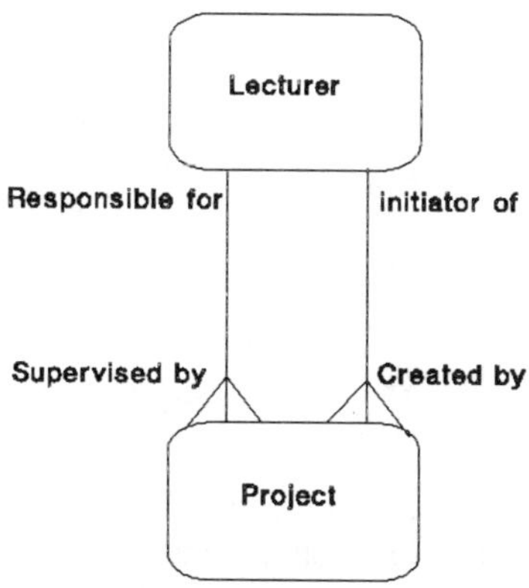

Figure 6.10 Link phrases for multiple relationships

they are distinguished by the relationship link phrases. Figure 6.10 shows such a situation between the two entities 'Project' and 'Lecturer'. A 'Lecturer' can be supervisor of one or more 'Projects', a 'Lecturer' can also be initiator of one or more 'Projects', but does not necessarily supervise and initiate the same 'Projects'. The Relationship Statements for the relationships are:

Each Lecturer may be responsible for one or more Projects.
Each Project must be supervised by one and only one Lecturer.

Each Lecturer may be initiator of one or more Projects.
Each Project is created by one and only one Lecturer.

6.6 Exclusive Relationship Groups

It is possible for a master entity to have detail entities which are mutually exclusive. An arc is used to indicate an exclusive group relationship.

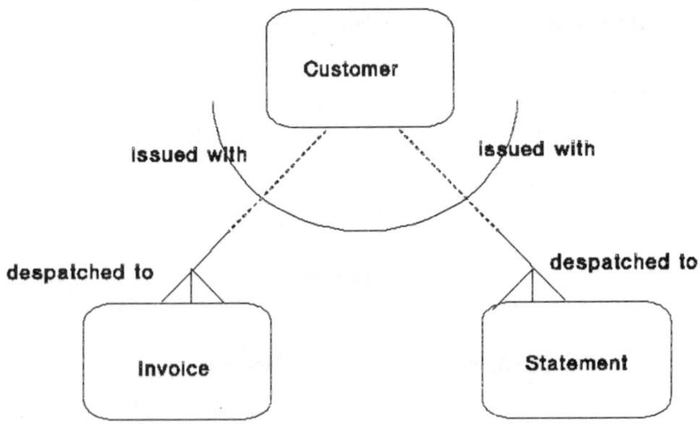

Figure 6.11 Optional exclusive group

Consider the situation indicated in Figure 6.11. A Customer is either issued Invoices for each transaction or a Statement at the end of each month. The existence of an Invoice for a Customer automatically excludes the possibility of data being held about a Statement for that Customer. The relationships are exclusive, only one can exist for a particular Customer.

Figure 6.11 is an example of an optional exclusive group. This means that a Customer may be issued with either a Statement or an Invoice or neither of these. This could occur where Statements or Invoices are only sent out when transactions have occurred for a customer account.

Figure 6.12 shows an example of a mandatory exclusive group. This means that one, but only one, of the relationships in the exclusive group must exist.

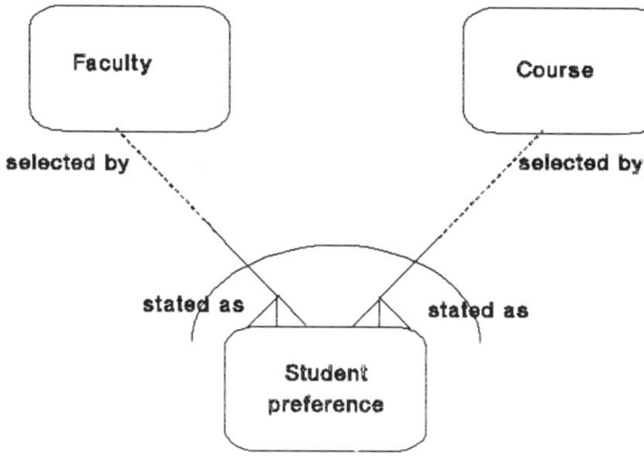

Figure 6.12 Mandatory exclusive group

6.7 Recursive Relationships

An entity may be recursively related to itself. The classic situation is when dealing with a Bill of Materials. A part can consist of other parts stocked by the same company. This situation is shown in Figure 6.13(a). Since the 'pig's ear' notation indicates a many-to-many relationship, a link entity must be introduced as shown in Figure 6.13(b). The Relationship Statements for this read:

> Each Part may be used as one or more Components.
> Each Component must be for the use of one and only one Part.
>
> Each Part may be made up of one or more Components.
> Each Component must be on the assembly list of one and only one Part.

A one-to-many recursive relationship can also occur. A typical situation is shown in Figure 6.14(a) This shows a hierarchical structure where the grade of Officer has no logical significance and could be made an attribute of the

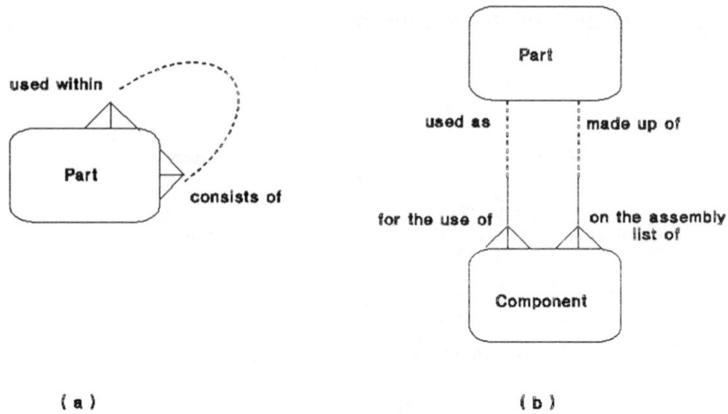

Figure 6.13 Recursive relationship

Officer entity. This can be redrawn as an optional, recursive relationship as shown in Figure 6.14(b). The relationship is optional at both ends since there may be no person holding a particular officer grade due to resignation, death etc. This solution also allows the most senior officer not to report to another officer and the most junior officer not to be in charge of any other officers. A better representation is shown in Figure 6.14(c) , it can be described as follows:

> Each Officer must be responsible to one and only one Manager or responsible to one and only one Officer.

6.8 Exercises

1. Identify possible link phrases and then write out the Relationship Statements for the relationships shown in Figures 6.1, 6.2, 6.5(b), 6.6 and 6.8.

2. Draw a Logical Data Structure for each of the following situations showing the relationships between Customer, Order and Item. Write out the Relationship Statements for each relationship.

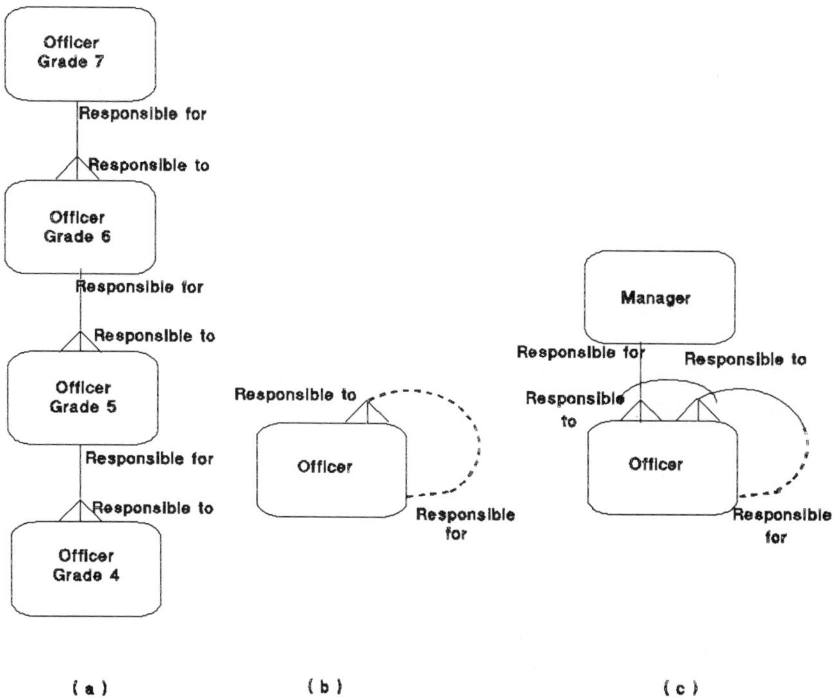

Figure 6.14 One to many recursive relationship

i) A Department Store has several thousand account customers. A customer can order as many items as they wish at one time. Orders can be placed with different departments.

ii) A customer's order can either be a credit order or a cash order. Different information is held about credit and cash orders. An order can be for more than one item. A customer may have both cash and credit orders.

iii) A travel agent takes orders for holidays. A customer order can consist of only one holiday. A customer may book more than 1 holiday in a year so the customer records may hold more than one order at a time for each customer.

iv) A company sells pianos to domestic customers. A customer never orders more than one piano in a lifetime.

v) A Department store allows new customers to order goods before a customer record is created. An order can be for more than one item. Several orders may be held for each customer.

6.9 Keys

It is convenient for design purposes to record keys during Logical Data Modelling as follows:

- a primary key for each entity, using one of its unique identifiers
- one or more foreign key attributes to represent each relationship from a detail to a master. This involves copying the primary key of the master into the detail.

Entities which are not the detail of any other entities are reference entities and are identified by one or more of their attributes.

The following definition of keys may be useful:

candidate key — any set of one or more attributes which will uniquely identify one occurrence of an entity. There may be more than one candidate key for any one entity. For instance the Course entity could have the candidate keys 'Course code' and 'Course name'

Course
Course code
Course name
Duration
Course type

primary key — A candidate key which has been selected to be **the** unique identifier for the entity. The candidate key 'Course code' is most likely to be the primary key since it is always likely to remain unique, two courses of the same name could exist at some time but would have different codes. The code is also shorter than the name, this is an advantage when processing data.

foreign key — An attribute, or group of attributes in one entity that corresponds to a candidate key in another entity.

Student
Student no.
*Course no.
Student name
Student Address
Personal tutor employment no.

The attribute 'Course no.' in the Student entity identifies an occurrence of the entity Course since it matches the candidate key 'Course no.' in the Course entity. 'Course no' in the entity Student is an example of a foreign key. An * before the attribute name designates a foreign key.

simple key — When a candidate key consists of only one attribute is known as a simple key. An example is the entity Module which has the simple key 'Module code'.

Module
Module code
Module name
Duration

compound key — When a candidate key consists of two or more foreign keys it is known as a compound key. The entity Course Unit has the compound key 'Course code, Module code'. 'Course code' is a foreign key since it is the primary key of the entity Course. 'Module code' is a foreign key since it is the primary key of the entity Module.

Course Unit
***Course code**
***Module code**
Employment no.
Assessment type

composite key — When a key consists of a foreign key and a non-foreign key it is known as a hierarchic key or a composite key. The key to the entity assignment is made up of the primary keys to the entity Course ('Course code') and the entity Module ('Module code'), these are therefore foreign keys. This is combined with an attribute of Course Unit ('Assignment No.') to give the composite key 'Course code, Module code, Assignment No.'.

Assignment
***Course code**
***Module code**
Assignment No.

Primary and foreign and candidate keys are Relational Data Analysis concepts and are explained in more detail in Chapter 9. Normalised relations and entity models are two ways of representing similar information. An entity is equivalent to a relation and a relationship is equivalent to a candidate/foreign key.

6.10 Transferable Relationships

In the example in Figure 6.15 the Relationship Statements are as follows:

A Course may be taken by one or more Students
A Student must be registered on one and only one Course

It is not unusual for a student to swap to a different course at the institution they are attending. This would mean that an occurrence of the entity Student

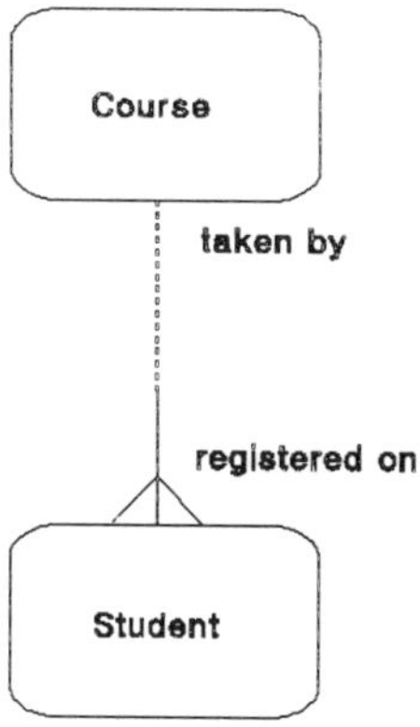

Figure 6.15 Transferable relations.

could transfer from one occurrence of the entity Course, to another occurrence of the entity Course. The object entity, Course, is said to be transferable.

In most mandatory relationships, the object entity is non-transferable. In every optional relationship, the object entity is potentially a transferable one. If a master entity has a foreign key which is part of the primary key of a detail entity, then the master entity is not transferable since this would change the key of the detail entity.

6.11 Partitioning

A Large Logical Data Structure can be difficult to understand. It is often clearer to users and analysts to create sub-diagrams which show a portion of the main diagram. A way of doing this is to use the following concepts:

- the incomplete entity
- the incomplete exclusive relationship group

These concepts are illustrated in Figure 6.16

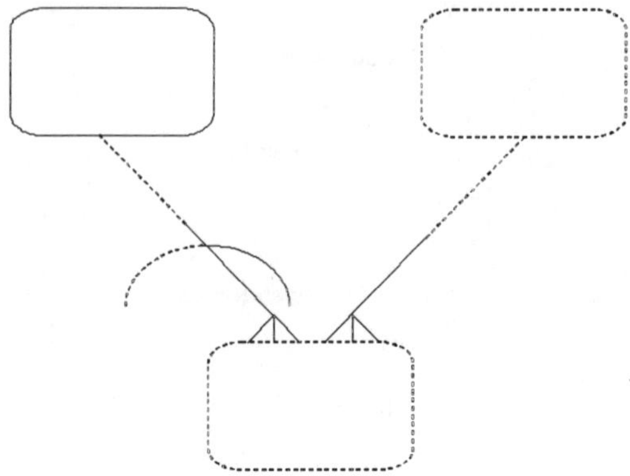

Figure 6.16 Notation for partitioning

i) The incomplete entity

This is an entity which has relationships and connected entities not shown on the sub-diagram. An incomplete entity is shown as a dotted box. Relationships are only shown if both participating entities are on the sub-diagram.

ii) The incomplete exclusive relationship group

This is an exclusive relationship group which has relationships not shown on the sub-diagram. Incomplete exclusive groups are shown by exclusion arcs with dotted edges.

6.12 Drawing a Logical Data Structure

There are a number of tasks involved in the Logical Data Modelling technique. The tasks below may be carried out in parallel or in a different sequence or even omitted.

1. Identify the entities.
2. Identify the relationships.
3. Draw the Logical Data Structure.
4. Normalise the Logical Data Model
5. Validate the Logical Data Model against functional requirements.
6. Remove redundant relationships from the Logical Data Structure.
7. Define Enquiry Access Paths

A variety of fact finding techniques are used to identify entities, relationships and attributes. The most productive is probably interviewing but other techniques may provide useful information.

The following example will be used to work through each of these tasks:

A student is registered on a degree course. Each degree consists of a number of modules but a student has no choice in the modules taken. Each module on a particular course has one lecturer teaching on it. A module may be offered on more than one course. A lecturer may be assigned to more than one course and more than one module. In addition, within two months of starting the course, each student is assigned a lecturer as a personal counsellor. Students are assessed on each module either by a series of assignments or by a set of exams, never a mixture of the two. Different data is held about assignments and exams.

6.12.1 Identify the entities.

It is not always easy to identify entities but the following hints may help.

a) Look in the system for data items which are likely to be key fields. For example, the existence of a data item 'Employee Number' would suggest an entity 'Employee'. A entity which consists only of its key attribute(s) is not strictly an entity, but 'key only' entities may be introduced to aid processing requirements. The following gives some further examples:

Possible key	Entity
Student Matriculation Number	Student
Stock Item Number	Stock Item
Purchase Order Number	Purchase Order
Membership Number	Member
Booking Reference Number	Booking

b) Avoid using dates as entities except in applications such as statistical systems where the calendar may be an important part of the data structure.

c) Use your knowledge of the application area and the data flow diagrams to help identify entities. There should be at least one entity for each data store on your data flow diagrams.

d) Look for nouns which might identify a group of data items.

In the example we can identify several things in the system about which we might like to keep data, as indicated in Figure 6.17.

Entity	**Possible attributes**
Student	**Matriculation number, name, home address, term address**
Lecturer	**Employment No, Name, Department, Courses**
Course	**Course reference number, Course name, Duration, Course type, Lecturers**
Module	**Module reference no, module name, courses**
Assignment	**Assignment No, Title, module, date completed**
Exam	**Exam Title, Exam date, module**

Fig. 6.17 Entities and attributes for student/course example

6.12.2 Identify the relationships

Each pair of entities (or an entity and itself) must be checked for the possibility of the existence of a relationship. It can be useful to draw up a matrix chart showing entity against entity. Relationships between a pair of entities are marked by a cross on the grid. Only direct relationships should be marked. If a relationship between two entities can be described in terms of another entity on the grid, it may be an indirect relationship and should not be shown.

The matrix is not a SSADM product but is a convenient means of checking that all possible relationships have been considered. It can be a useful tool for beginners to this technique but many analysts choose not to use it since it postpones naming the relationships. Writing out the Relationship Statements for each relationship identified can be very helpful in understanding the nature of the relationship and can often identify the existence of further entities and relationships.

The following relationships can be identified for the Student/Course Example:

Student/Lecturer
Student/Course
Student/Assignment
Student/Exam
Lecturer/Course
Lecturer/Student
Lecturer/Module
Course/Module
Module/Assignment
Module/Exam

Student to Module is not a direct link. A student takes a Course, a Course consists of one or more Modules, so from this we can derive that a Student takes one or more modules. The other relationship from Student to Module is that a Student gains either Exam or Assignment records for each module taken. This link to Module is not a direct link but can be derived through the Assignment or Exam entities. The link from Lecturer to Assignment and Exam is not a direct link. Since only one Lecturer takes each module on a particular course, we can derive the link from Lecturer to Assignment and Exam through the Module entity. Course is linked to Exam and Assignment through Module.

An entity/entity matrix for the Student/Course Example has been drawn up and is shown in Figure 6.18.

Entity \ Entity	Student	Lecturer	Course	Module	Assignment	Exam
Student		M:1	M:1		M:N	M:N
Lecturer	1:M		M:N	1:M		
Course	1:M	M:N		M:N		
Module		M:1	M:N		1:M	1:M
Assignment	M:N			M:1		
Exam	M:N			M:1		

Figure 6.18 Entity/Entity Matrix.

At this stage the analyst should identify the following:

i) exclusive groups
ii) degree
iii) link phrases
iv) multiple relationships
v) optionality.

The Student/Course Example can be analyzed as follows:

i) Exclusive groups

An exclusive group can be identified for the method of assessment. A student can be either assessed by exam or by assignment, but not both.

ii) Degree

When a relationship has been identified, the degree of the relationship should be established. Most relationships will be one-to-many (1:M) or many-to-one (M:1). One-to-one (1:1) and many-to-many (N:M) relationships may appear at this stage, they can be resolved later.

In our Student/Course Example the relationships can be identified as follows:

Student/Lecturer	M:1
Student/Course	M:1
Student/Assignment	M:N
Student/Exam	M:N
Lecturer/Module	1:M
Lecturer/Student	1:M
Lecturer/Course	M:N
Course/Module	M:N
Module/Assignment	1:M
Module/Exam	1:M

iii) Link Phrases

The link phrases can be identified on the Relationship Statement as follows:

Each Lecturer...........**counsellor for** one or more Students.
Each Student............**personal tutee of** one and only one Lecturer.

Each Course.............**taken by** one or more Students.
Each Student............**on the classlist of** one and only one course.

Each Student...........:
either **assessed on** one or more Assignments.
or **assessed on** one or more Exams.

Each Assignment.........**completed by** one or more Students.
Each Exam..............**taken by** one or more Students.

Each Lecturer...........**teaching on** one or more Modules.
Each Module............**delivered by** one and only one Lecturer.

Each Course............**made up of** one or more Modules.
A Module...............**part of** one or more Courses.

Each Module...........:
either **assessed by** one or more Assignments.
or **assessed by** one or more exams.
Each Assignment.........**required for** one and only one Module
An Exam................**required for** one and only one Module.

iv) Multiple relationships

Any multiple relationships between two entities should be identified and appropriate link phrases created. In the Student/Course Example there are no multiple relationships. There is a potential multiple relationship between Student and Lecturer, since a Lecturer can teach a Student or be a personal counsellor. However if we know the Course a Student is taking and the Modules on that Course then we can identify the Lecturer.

v) Optionality

The Relationship Statements can be completed by the addition of 'may be' for optional relationships and 'must be' for mandatory relationships, as follows:

Each Lecturer **may be** responsible for one or more Students.
Each Student **must be** personal tutee of one and only one Lecturer.

Each Course **may be** taken by one or more Students.
Each Student **must be** on the classlist of one and only one course.

Each Student **must be**:
either assessed on one or more Assignments.
or assessed on one or more Exams.
Each Assignment **may be** completed by one or more Students.
Each Exam **may be** taken by one or more Students.

Each Lecturer **may be** teaching on one or more Modules.
Each Module **must be** delivered by one and only one Lecturer.

Each Course **must be** made up of one or more Modules.
A Module **must be** part of one or more Courses.

Each Module **may be**:
either assessed by one or more Assignments.
or assessed by one or more exams.
Each Assignment **must be** required for one and only one Module
Each Exam **must be** required for one and only one Module.

6.12.3 Draw the Logical Data Structure

The analyst has probably drawn sections of the Logical Data Structure during the process of identifying entities and relationships. Rough versions of the Logical Data Structure may be drawn as analysis progresses. The level of detail should correspond to the Data Flow Diagram which is being drawn in parallel. The Current Environment Logical Data Structure will be less detailed than the Required Logical Data Structure and more detailed than the Overview Logical Data Structure. If the diagram is too large it can be partitioned, as discussed in section 6.11.

The diagram should be drawn so that masters are above details, with the reference entities appearing along the top of the diagram. Neatness and layout are important and crossing lines should be avoided if possible. Avoid the use of abbreviations, they can cause confusion to users and other analysts. All relationship ends should be named.

The Logical Data Structure for the Student/Course Example is shown in Figure 6.19.

The three many-to-many relationships have been resolved in this diagram by the addition of link entities. It can be useful in the early stages of analysis to leave the M:N relationships on the diagram. Eventually they will have to be resolved since they obscure the concept of master/detail and camouflage access paths through the model.

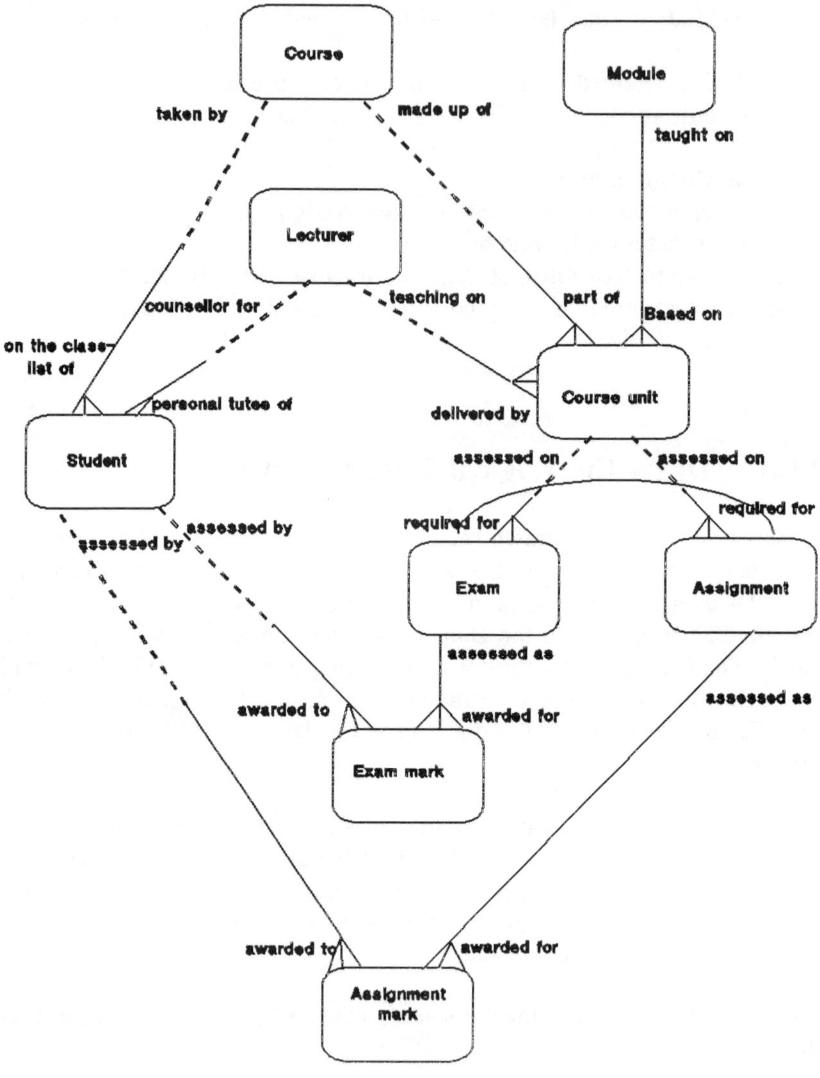

Figure 6.19 Logical Data Structure for Student/Course example.

There are no one-to-one relationships shown in this diagram. Again it can be useful in the early stages of analysis to leave one-to-one relationships on the diagram. All the relationships in the final Logical Data Structure must have master and detail so each one-to-one relationship must be resolved, either by merging the two entities together, or by representing the relationship as a one-to-many relationship.

6.12.4 Normalising the Logical Data Model

The entities should be examined to see if they are in Third Normal Form. This means considering each entity as a relation and applying the rules of Relational Data Analysis. In fact most of the entities will already be in at least Third Normal Form but this is a useful check for missing entities and relationships.

i) First Normal Form

No attribute should have more than one value per entity occurrence. A repeating group is an entity in its own right and is the many end of a 1:m relationship with the original entity.

ii) Second Normal Form

Where an entity has a compound identifier, then any set of one or more attributes which are only dependent on part of the identifier should become a separate entity.

iii) Third Normal Form

Where an entity has a set of one or more non-identifier attributes which are dependant on another non-identifier attribute, then that set of attributes should become a separate entity.

The entities in the Student/Course Example can be expressed as relations as follows:

Course
Course code
Course name
Duration
Course type

Module
Module code
Module name
Duration

Lecturer
Employment no.
Lecturer Name
Department
Room no.

Course Unit
Course code
Module code
Employment no.
Assessment type

Student
Student no.
Course no.
Student name
Student Address
Personal tutor employment no.

Exam
Course code
Module code
Exam date

Assignment
Course code
Module code
Assignment No.

Exam mark
Course code
Module code
Exam date
Student no.
mark

Assignment mark
Course code
Module code
Assignment No.
Student no.
grade

The key fields are shown in bold type. All of these relations are in Third Normal Form. Note that the keys become bigger as the relations progress down the hierarchy of the diagram. Often detail entities form a key based on the identifier of the master entity plus one or more of their own attributes, this is a composite key. Link entities, such as Exam Mark, are thus likely to have an identifier from each of the master entities plus one or more of their own attributes. In a situation where the identifier is several attributes long, it may be useful, after discussions with users, to create an artificial identifier. An attribute 'Exam reference number' would simplify access to the Exam Mark entity. Although Student is a link entity, it has only a single identifier since one of its own attributes, 'Student no.' is sufficient to uniquely identify each occurrence of the entity.

6.12.5 Validate the Logical Data Structure

A Logical Data Model must be consistent with the corresponding Data Flow Model. The following aspects should be checked:

- processes
- data stores
- access paths

i) Processes

For each entity identify at least one process in the corresponding Data Flow Model which can create and delete the entity. It may be useful to use a Process/Entity Matrix to assist with this validation check. Processes should be added to the Data Flow Model if necessary. Chapter 5 describes this in more detail.

ii) Data Stores

Each entity on the Logical Data Model must be contained within one and only one data store on the corresponding Logical Data Flow Model. If necessary the two models must be adjusted to ensure this is possible. The Logical data Store/Entity Cross Reference is used to record this association. Chapter 5 describes this in more detail.

iii) Access Paths

The proposed model must now be checked to see if it meets the processing requirements of the system. The validation should cause questions to be asked about the adequacy of access paths. The Logical Data Model must supply an access path for each Elementary Process Description defined in the corresponding Data Flow Model. All the update and major enquiry processes in the model must be supported. The procedure may show up new relationships or new entities and will result in the revision of the Logical Data Model, Elementary Process Descriptions or both. This is an informal examination of access paths, they are fully defined in a later step and this is explained in more detail in section 6.12.7.

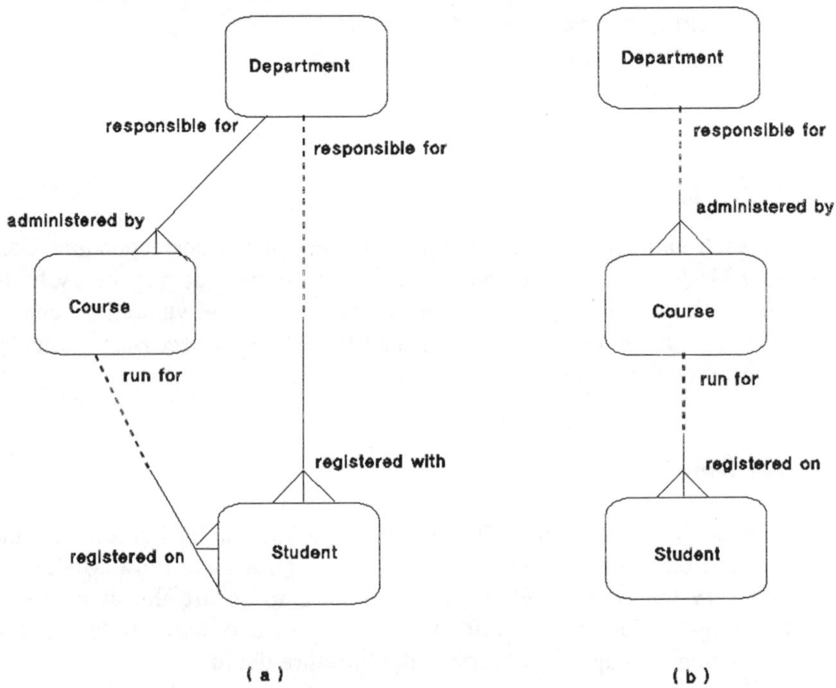

Figure 6.20 Closed loop redundant relationship.

6.12.6 Remove redundant relationships

The relationships on a Logical Data Structure may not all be functionally necessary. Redundant relationships should be identified and removed from the Logical Data Structure.

Redundant relationships can occur in closed loops as shown in Figure 6.20a). The link from Department directly to Student is not required since the relationship from Department to Course and then from Course to Student provides the same information. The redundant relationship can be removed and the diagram redrawn as in Figure 6.20b). The link phrase of the relationships are very similar, this can provide a clue to possible closed loop redundant relationships. Great care must be taken that the entity Department is linked to the same occurrence of Student no matter which relationship is used, looking at the diagram is not sufficient, the occurrences of the entity must be understood. If the relationships in a closed loop produce different entity occurrences of Student then both are necessary. The illustration given is a simple closed loop, more complicated structures should also be carefully examined to see if there are any closed loop redundant relationships

Redundant relationships may also occur in a 'double V' structure, as shown in Figure 6.21, this is a section of the diagram shown in Figure 6.19. This occurs when two entities have relationships through two or more link entities. After careful examination of the occurrences of the link entities it may be possible to redraw the structure by removing the relationships from the entities to one of the link entities and adding a relationship between the two link entities. In Figure 6.21 the entities Student and Course Unit are involved in this type of structure with the two link entities Exam Mark and Assignment Mark. These links can not be removed because of the existence of the exclusive group from Course Unit to Exam or Assignment. Figure 6.22 shows how a duplicate link entity can be removed.

The rigour of the validation will depend on the stage of the system development process. A Logical Data Structure prepared during the Feasibility Study is an overview document and requires to be validated much less rigorously than in Stage 5 when the Logical System Design is reviewed and validated. The benefit of the validation in the earlier Stages is that it causes questions to be asked which improve the understanding of the present system and of the required data structure.

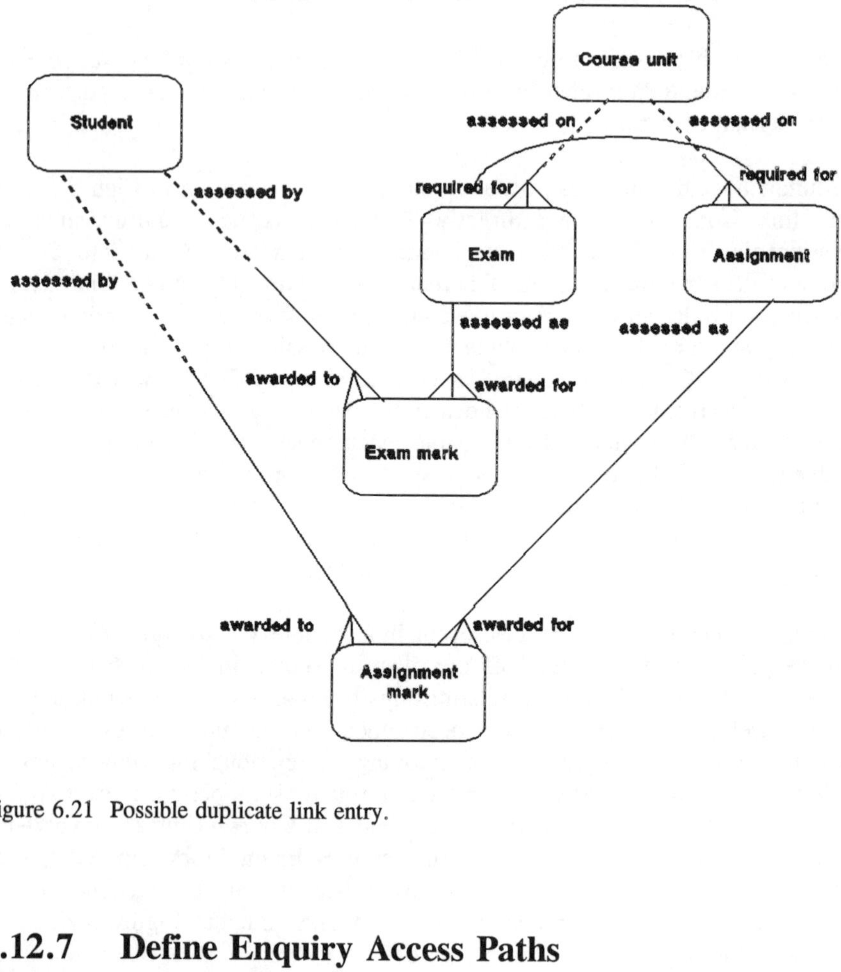

Figure 6.21 Possible duplicate link entry.

6.12.7 Define Enquiry Access Paths

The definition of Enquiry Access Paths is important for validating the Logical Data Model. The specification of the enquiry name, enquiry trigger and Enquiry Access Path are completed in Step 360. The remainder of the procedure is completed by Step 530. An Enquiry Access Path is produced for each enquiry, except the ad-hoc enquiries which have not been predefined. Chapter 8 on Function Definition describes how functions are identified and documented to provide Function Definition Descriptions and I/O Descriptions. Each enquiry must eventually be documented as an Enquiry Process, this procedure is described in Chapter 13 on Logical Database Process Design.

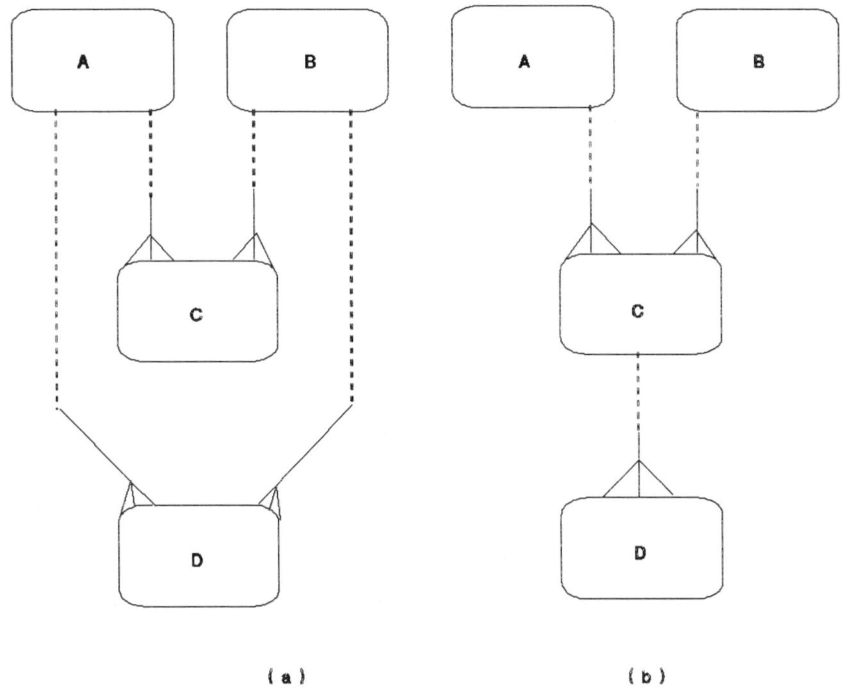

Figure 6.22 Removing a duplicate link entity.

6.12.7.1 Specify enquiry name

Each enquiry should have a unique name which has been defined in Function Definition. The name of the enquiry can be used as the name of the access path.

6.12.7.2 Specify enquiry trigger

An enquiry trigger is made up of the data items input to the enquiry and, optionally, selection criteria for the retrieval of detail entities. The data items input are normally the key of the entity which provides the entry point to the Logical Data Model. The data items are listed on the Enquiry Access Path and are indented to show repeating groups, where necessary. Input data items will appear as input elements in the I/O Structures and Descriptions associated with each Function Definition. Selection criteria are defined in the Function Definition Description. Each enquiry may be listed on more than one Function Definition since it may be input through more than one function.

6.12.7.3 Specify Enquiry Access Path

Enquiry Access Paths are identified by using the following procedures:

i) Select the entity which will be the entry point for the enquiry and identify all the entities which contain the data identified on the I/O structures.

ii) Redraw the section of the Logical Data Structure containing the chosen entities using the following principles:

   a) access from a master to a detail should be shown vertically
   b) access from a detail to a master should be shown horizontally

   An enquiry requires 'For a given Department, list all Students'. Department is master of Course, Course is master of Student. The enquiry access path is from Department, through Course to Student. The section of the diagram drawn in Figure 6.23a) reflects rule a), since access is always down the structure from master to detail.

   Another enquiry might be 'Find all the Lecturers who counsel Students on a particular Course'. Course and Lecturer are both masters of Student. The diagram is therefore drawn as in Figure 6.23b). Access is through Course to the detail Student so Course is vertically above Student, following rule a). Access is then from the detail Student to the master Lecturer so, following rule b), Lecturer is shown horizontally across from Student.

iii) The required view should be redrawn as entity (Jackson) structures linked by access correspondence arrows. The arrows show the direction of access.

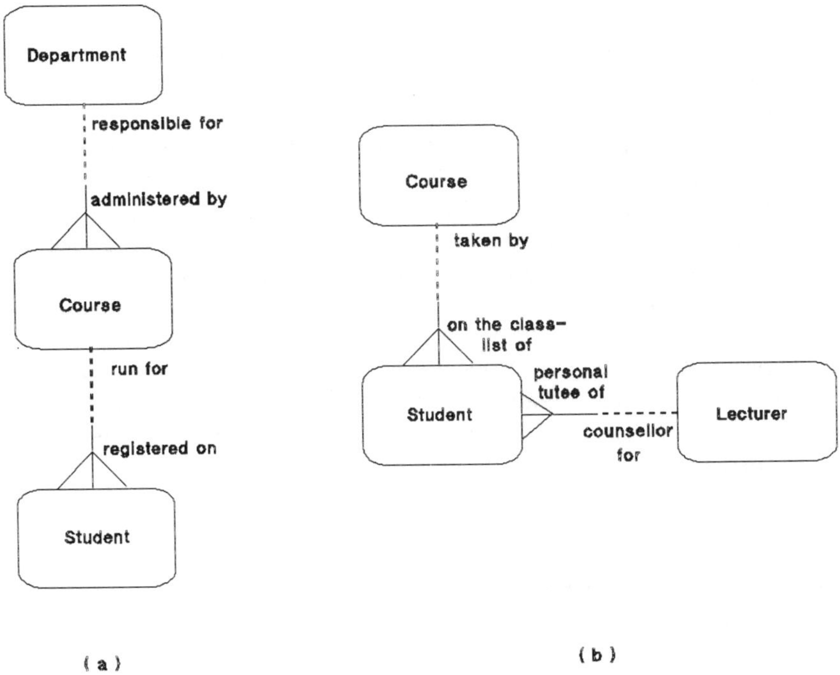

Figure 6.23 Access up and down relationships.

Structure diagrams are used in several other SSADM techniques, namely:

- Entity event modelling
- Function definition (I/O structures)
- Logical Database Process Design
- Dialogue design (dialogue structure)

They are described in more detail in the Chapter 11, Entity Event Modelling.

Examples of Enquiry Access Paths using the iteration and select concepts are described below.

Iteration

Downward accesses mean that we have accessed down to the many end of a relationship, for instance from Department to Course in Figure 6.23a). We will have to look at all the occurrences of Course to match our enquiry criteria of finding all Students on all Courses in a particular Department. Reading more than one entity occurrence requires an iterative structure and this is indicated by placing a * in the top right of the entity box and placing above it a box containing 'Set of' and the entity name. This is shown in Figure 6.24. In Figure 6.24a) the entities Course and Student are both at the many end of the relationship and are read more than once. They are both shown as iterative structures. In Figure 6.24b), the entity Student is at the many end of a relationship and so it is shown as an iterative structure. The entity Lecturer is at the one end of the relationship. For each occurrence of Student there is only one occurrence of Lecturer so no iteration is required.

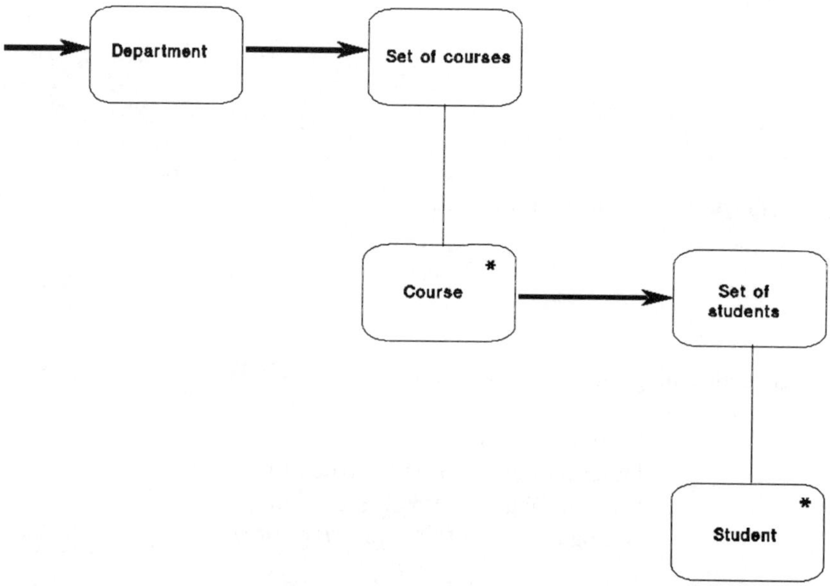

Figure 6.24(a) Enquiry Access Paths - iteration.

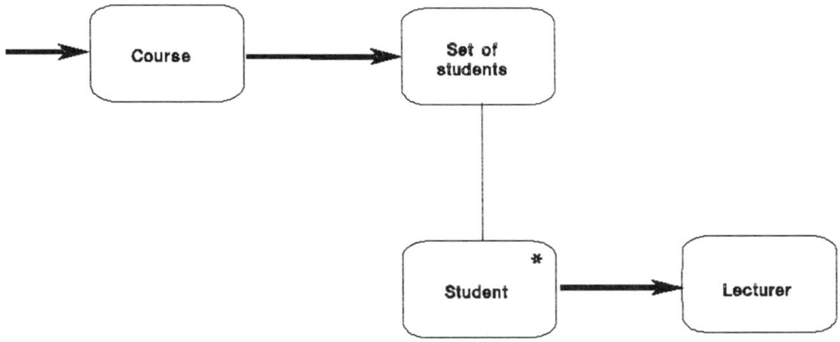

Figure 6.24(b) Enquiry Access Paths

Selection

Where selection is required the box below the selection box consists of boxes containing the ° symbol. An example might be the enquiry 'For a given course, list all the course units, assessment details and the name of the lecturer leading the course'. This requires the view of the entity model shown in Figure 6.25a). Figure 6.25b) shows the required view as Jackson structures. The addition of selection and enquiry triggers is shown in Figure 6.25c).

iv) Annotate the access correspondence arrow to the entry point entity with the attributes used for entry. There are three types of entry point:

- via the primary key of an entity
- via non-key attributes of an entity
- to all occurrences of a given entity (do not label the access correspondence arrow)

Figure 6.25c) shows the attributes required for entry to the Course entity as Course No which is the key field for that entity. Entry points should never be made through a foreign key. An entry point through a foreign key should be documented as an entry point on the relevant master entity.

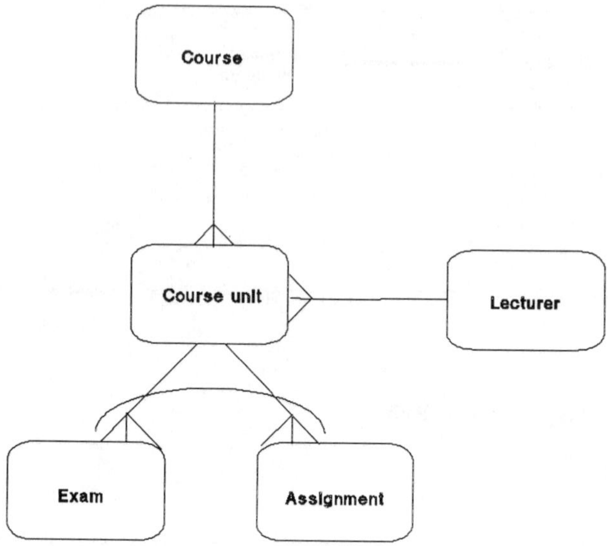

Figure 6.25(a) Required view of Entity Model

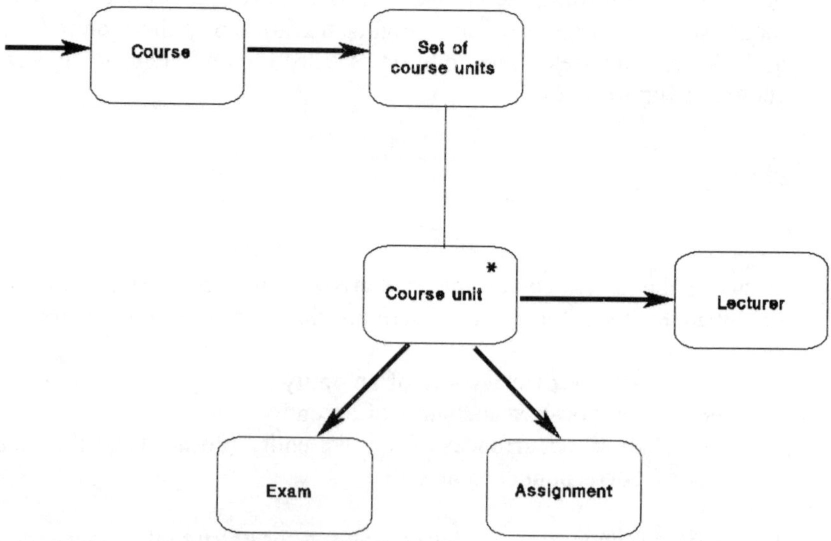

Figure 6.25(b) Required view of Entity Model shown as Jackson structures.

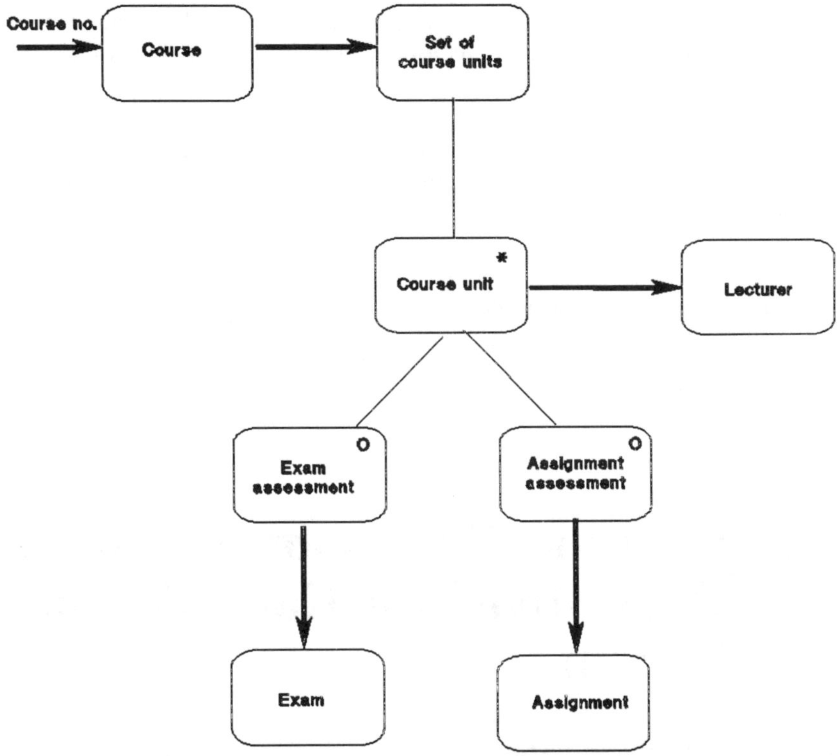

Figure 6.25(c) Addition of selection and enquiry triggers.

v) Check that all the required data can be obtained using the following:

- read entity directly using key
- read next detail of a master entity
- read master entity of detail entity

If the all the data required by an enquiry cannot be obtained by one of these operations then either:

- the Logical Data Structure should be modified to match the enquiry requirement, or
- document a process-based solution, such as a sort.

An modification of the Logical Data Structure might involve the introduction of a new entry point. Another option is the addition of new entities and relationships if important business requirements have been overlooked.

The Entity and Attribute Descriptions should be checked to ensure that the defined access rights are consistent with the access required by the enquiry.

vi) All entry points must be documented in one copy of the Logical Data Structure, this may show more than one entry point for each entity.

6.13 Current Environment Logical Data Model for Car Allowance System

6.13.1 Identifying the entities

A good starting point for drawing up a Logical Data Structure for the Car Allowance System is to look at the documents in the system, these are listed in Chapter 4, Figure 4.5. Many of the documents are duplicate copies and close examination shows that the following documents exist:

- Application Form
- New Car Details
- Claim Form
- Cheque Requisition
- Cheque

The final version of the Current Physical Data Flow Diagrams are shown in Chapter 5, Figure 5.9. Some additional major documents can be identified from this:

- Regrade Letter
- Vehicle Check Results
- Driver Test Results

There are additional minor documents which do not result in any stored data. The Logical Data Structure is drawn up to determine the data which is required to support the existing system. The next stage is to consider the degree of relationship between these documents.

Claim Form has a one-to-one relationship with Cheque Requisition, Cheque Requisition has a one-to-one relationship with Cheque, so these three can be combined as one entity Claim. A Claim Form consists of header information about the employee claiming, information about a claim such as date, total mileage, amount claimed etc, and a repeating group of details about each journey. A Claim Form therefore has three entities Employee (an employee submits one or more claims over the year), Claim (date, amount claimed etc) and Journey (a claim consists of more than one journey).

An Application Form contains information about the employee and their job, authorisation information such as date of authorization and grade, details of one or two cars which the employee is permitted to use on company business. This can be considered as two entities Employee and Car with Car being at the many end of a one-to-many relationship with Employee. The details about an employee on the Claim Form overlap with the Application Form so they can be considered to be part of the same entity.

An examination of the current files shows that information is normally only kept about the currently authorised cars. New Car Details contains information which substitutes the information in the Car entity identified from the Application Form.

Vehicle Check Results have a one-to-one relationship with the Car entity so any additional data items contained on this document could become attributes of the Car entity.

An employee only has to sit the driver test once during their employment with the company so the details on the Driver Test Results Form have a one-to-one relationship with Employee and can become attributes of the Employee entity.

An examination of the files in Administration shows that information is retained on changes to the car allowance grade of an employee, job changes etc. The data that is important is the date of a grade change and the new grade. This requires an entity Application History.

The Regrade Letter contains data held either in the Employee or Application History entities.

The data stores on the Current Physical Data Flow Diagrams should also be checked to identify any missing goups of data. Most of the data stores are related to application details and claim details and are covered by the entities already identified. The data store M3, Car Allowance Regulations, contains data which does not belong to any of the entities identified. Each car allowance grade has criteria of minimum job grades and minimum engine capacity which determine the mileage amount paid. In addition some grades give a standing monthly payment to employees in addition to the rate paid for miles covered. A new entity Grade is required to store this information.

6.13.2 Identifying the Relationships

The entities identified in section 6.13.1 were:

- Employee
- Application History
- Car
- Claim
- Journey
- Grade

An Entity/Entity Matrix can now be drawn up to help identify the relationships between entities. This is shown in Figure 6.26.

The next step is to identify link phrase for each relationship. The relationship statements for the Car Allowance System are listed below:

Each Grade may be authorised for one or more Employees.
Each Employee must be holder of one and only one Grade.

Each Employee may be subject of one or more Application History.
Each Application History must be held for one and only one Employee.

Entity \ Entity	Employee	Appl. History	Car	Claim	Journey	Grade
Employee		1:M	1:M	1:M		M:1
Appl. History	M:1					
Car	M:1					
Claim	M:1				1:M	
Journey				M:1		
Grade	1:M					

Figure 6.26 Entity/Entity Matrix for Car Allowance system.

Each Employee must be authorized owner of one or more Cars.
Each Car must be property of one and only one Employee.

Each Employee may be subject of one or more Claims.
Each Claim must be submitted by one and only one Employee.

Each Claim may be detailed with one or more Journeys.
Each Journey must be recorded on one and only one Claim.

6.13.3 Draw the Logical Data Structure

The Logical Data Structure should now be drawn and then validated. Figure 6.27 shows a Logical Data Structure for the Current Environment Car Allowance System with skeleton Entity Descriptions. Note that a Claim could consist of a request for a standing monthly payment (some grades only) and no journeys.

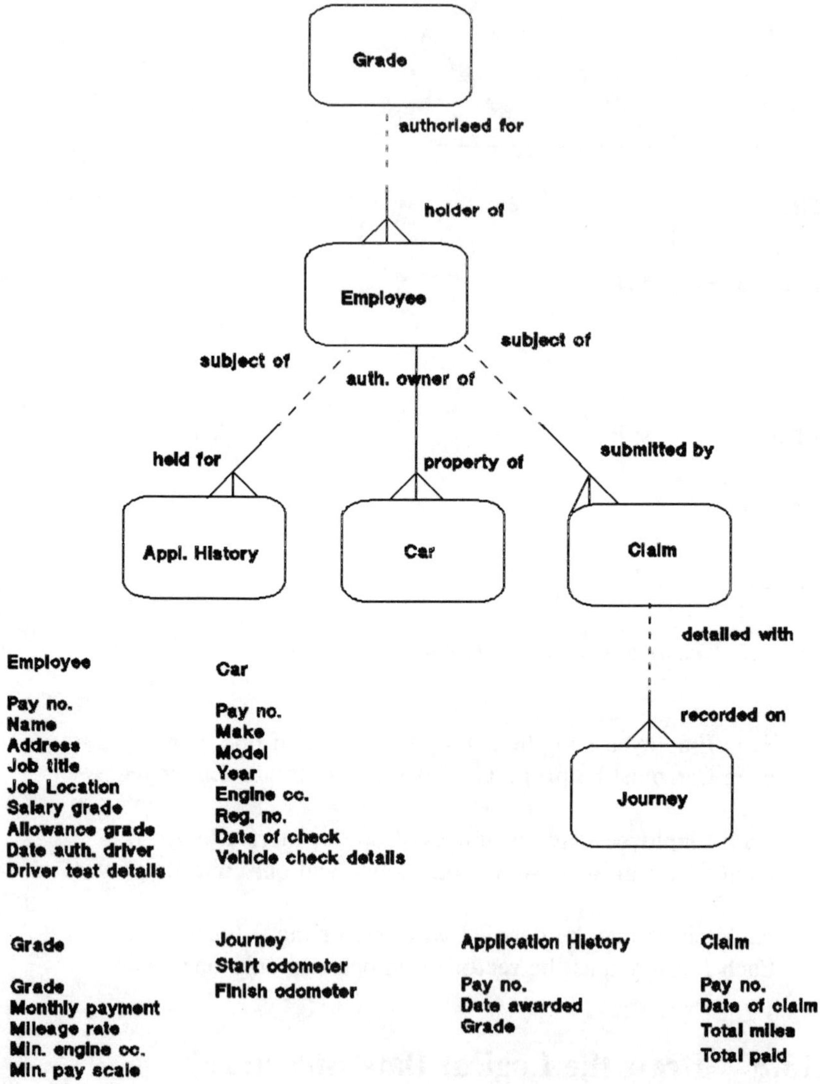

Figure 6.27 Logical Data Model for Current Environment Car Allowance System

6.14 Exercises

1. Draw Structure Diagrams showing the Enquiry Access Paths for the following enquiries based on the Logical Data Structure shown in Figure 6.18:

    i) For a particular course, find the name of the lecturers leading each course unit.

    ii) For a particular course, find the name of the lecturer leading a particular course unit.

    iii) For a particular course, find the name of all the students.

    iv) For a particular course, find the exam marks for all students on that course.

2. Use the Logical Data Model of the Car Allowance System described in section 6.13 to draw the Enquiry Access Paths for the following enquiries:

    i) For a particular grade, find all the employees who can claim.

    ii) For a particular employee, find details of all claims.

6.15 Documenting the Logical Data Model

The Logical Data Model consists of the Logical Data Structure and the following set of supporting documentation:

(i) Attribute Descriptions (part of Data Catalogue)
(ii) Entity Descriptions
(iii) Grouped Domain Descriptions (part of Data Catalogue)
(iv) Logical Data Structure
(v) Relationship Descriptions

6.15.1 Attribute Descriptions

An Attribute Description should include the attribute name, synonyms,an optional description,validation details, derivation rules eg if a calculated field), the format (numeric/character etc), length, unit of measure. Additional information might be: whether the attribute is mandatory and, if so, any default values it might take; the user roles which will have access and their access rights (Insert, Read, Modify, etc); standard messages (help, error messages etc).

6.15.2 Entity Descriptions

An Entity Description should give the entity name followed by a list of attributes of that entity. Each attribute should be ticked if it is a primary key. Foreign keys should be indicated by the number of the relationship(s). Relationships in which the entity takes part should be numbered and listed, giving the full relationship statement. The number of occurrences of the entity should be recorded.

In addition for each entity the following information should be documented: the user roles which will have access to occurrences of the entity; access rights for each user; the person responsible for deciding which access rights will be permitted; growth rate of entity occurrences; archiving details; security measures; valid state indicator values and their meanings.

6.15.3 Grouped Domain Descriptions

Grouped Domain Descriptions are used where validation rules, formatting rules, permitted classes and ranges of values are common to more than one value. Examples are date and price attributes. The grouped domain would be given an appropriate name, such as Date or Price. Use of a Grouped Domain Description should save duplication of information in several Attribute/Data Item Descriptions.

6.15.4 Logical Data Structure

The documented Logical Data Structure changes as the systems investigation proceeds. The final version should support the Required System. When the required system Logical Data Model has been completed in Step 360, a copy can be produced and annotated with entity and relationship volumes.

6.15.5 Relationship Descriptions

Relationships are documented for each end of a relationship and should include the following details: the name of the subject entity; an indication if the relationship end is mandatory or optional; % of occurrences of the subject entity not participating in the relationship; link phrase; object entity name; an indication whether the entity is at the one or many end of a relationship; growth rates etc.

6.16 Place of Logical Data Structure in SSADM

6.16.1 Module FS, Feasibility Study

6.16.1.1 Step 010 Prepare for the Study

An overview Logical Data Structure is produced along with the Requirements Catalogue, the Context Diagram and the Current Physical Data Flow Diagram Level 1.

6.16.1.2 Step 020 Define the Problem

The Logical Data Structure is used as part of the description of the current and required environments. The model is fairly high level, but is more detailed than in Step 010. Data Flow Diagrams and narrative description are also used and the Requirements Catalogue is updated.

6.16.1.3 Step 030 Select Feasibility Options

The Logical Data Structure is an input to the process of drawing up Business System Options and Technical System Options. When the shortlist of Feasibility Options is prepared, subsets of the Logical Data Structure and the Data Flow Diagram are produced as part of the Outline Required Environment Description. They are used to estimate system complexity and size.

6.16.1.4 Step 040 Assemble Feasibility Report

The Logical Data Structure is included as part of the Outline Current Environment Description and the Outline Required Environment Description.

6.16.2 Module RA, Requirements Analysis

6.16.2.1 Step 110 Establish Analysis Framework

An Overview Logical Data Structure is developed alongside the Current Physical Data Flow Diagram and Context Diagram. Specific System Requirements are recorded in the Requirements Catalogue.

6.16.2.2 Step 120 Investigate and Define Requirements

The Requirements Catalogue is expanded as more detailed investigation is undertaken. The development of the Current Environment Logical Data Model in Step 140 may result in the identification of further requirements.

6.16.2.3 Step 130 Investigate Current Processing

This step identifies the information flows in the current environment and documents them in the form of Data Flow Diagrams. Step 140 Investigate Current Data is being carried out in parallel and the Current Environment Logical Data Model may be used for reference during this activity.

6.16.2.4 Step 140 Investigate Current Data

A model of the data that supports the current services is produced during this Step. It is carried out in parallel with Step 130 Investigate Current Processing and uses information gathered for Step 120 Investigate and Define Requirements. The model only shows data required in the current system, the additional data requirements of the new system are not included. The Elementary Processing Descriptions supporting the Current Physical Data Flow Diagrams are used to validate that the data model does support the processing in the current environment. Only the most significant attributes associated with each entity need to be defined at this time. Relational Data Analysis is also used to help validate the Logical Data Model.

6.16.2.5 Step 150 Derive Logical View of Current Services

The Current Physical Data Flow Model is converted into the Current Logical Data Flow by removing the physical aspects of current processing. The data stores are rationalised against the Logical Data Model so that each data store consists of one or more related entity types. Once the Data Flow Model has been logicalised, the Logical Data Model must be validated to ensure that it supports the Elementary Process Descriptions. Access paths are only documented informally at this point. The Logical Data Store/Entity Cross Reference is produced during the logicalisation process and the Logical Data Model is amended as necessary.

6.16.2.6 Step 160 Assemble Investigation Results

This step involves checking the consistency and completeness of the products of Stage 1, the Current Environment Logical Data Model is one of the products checked.

6.16.2.7 Stage 2, Business System Options

The Business System Options are optionally supported by the Logical Data Model and Logical Data Flow Model.

6.16.3 Module RS, Requirements Specification

6.16.3.1 Step 320 Develop Required Data Model

This is carried out in parallel with Step 310 Develop Required System Processing. The objectives are to develop a Logical Data Model which can support the processing in the required system and to define the non-functional requirements associated with the Logical Data Model. The Current Environment Logical Data Model is reduced so that it reflects only the entities and relationships which support the chosen Business System Option. It is then extended to support any additional requirements of the new system. All the remaining attributes for each entity must be defined during this step. The next task is to verify that the Elementary Process Descriptions can be supported by the Logical Data Model, the access paths are not formally documented. The Logical Data Model must now be updated with non-functional requirements identified in the Requirements Catalogue, such as security and archiving requirements. The Required System Logical Data Model is output from this Step.

6.16.3.2 Step 330 Derive System Functions

This is carried out in parallel to steps 310 and 320. The Logical Data Model is used as a reference during the process of defining system functions. Enquiry functions, Input/Output Structures and Input/Output Descriptions are defined.

6.16.3.3 Step 340 Enhance Required Data Model

The Required System Logical Data Model produced in Step 320 is validated using Relational Data Analysis techniques. A selection is made of the system functions and the input/output specifications have Relational Data Analysis applied to develop a set of normalised relations for each function. The normalised relations are then converted into individual data submodels which are compared to the existing Logical Data Model. Any differences are resolved by reference to the users and the processing requirements. The Required System Logical Data Model is updated with new entities and relationships as necessary. Chapter 9 describes Relational Data Analysis in more detail.

6.16.3.4 Step 350 Develop Specification Prototypes

This step is the development of selected parts of the Requirements Specification in animated form. The Required System Logical Data Model is an essential input to this technique. Chapter 10 describes prototyping in more detail.

6.16.3.5 Step 360 Develop Processing Specification

The Logical Data Model is used to identify events which update entities. Entity Life Histories are created and then an Effect Correspondence Diagram for each event. This technique may identify new or redefined entities. The Logical Data Model must be amended to reflect such changes. An Enquiry Access Path must be developed for each enquiry function and the Required System Logical Data Structure updated with entity and relationship volumes. Entity-event Modelling is described in more detail in Chapter 11.

6.16.3.6 Step 370 Confirm System Objectives

The Requirements Catalogue, Function Definitions, and the Required System Logical Data Model must be checked to ensure they provide a full and complete set of documentation expressing system requirements. The functional requirements must be documented using the appropriate specification products. Outstanding non-functional requirements , such as security and archiving, must be identified and defined, this may involve updating the Required System Logical Data Model.

6.16.3.7 Step 380 Assemble Requirements Specification

The Required System Logical Data Model is one of the outputs of this module as part of the Requirements Specification and must be cross-checked with other products of the module to ensure consistency and completeness.

6.16.4 Module LS, Logical System Specification

6.16.4.1 Stage 4, Technical System Options

The Logical Data Model, as part of the Requirements Specification, is used as an input and reference during the technique of Technical System Options. The technique is discussed in more detail in Chapter 12.

6.16.4.2 Step 520 Define Update Processing

The logical specification of update functions is completed. State indicator values are allocated to Entity Life Histories and the meaning of the values is documented in the Entity Description (part of the Logical Data Model).

6.16.4.3 Step 530 Define Enquiry Processes

The Enquiry Access Paths developed in Stage 3 and the Input/Output Structure are used to develop a single processing structure for each enquiry. The Enquiry Access Path is seen as the input data structure and the Input/Output Structure is used to derive the output data structure. The two data structures are merged to produce an Enquiry Process Model.

6.16.4.4 Step 540 Assemble Logical Design

The Required System Logical Data Model, Data Catalogue and Enquiry Access Paths form part of the Logical Design products and must be checked for consistency and completeness with the other Logical Design products.

6.16.5 Module PD, Physical Design

6.16.5.1 Step 620 Create Physical Data Design

The Physical Data Design (first cut) is produced. The starting point is the identification of the features of the Required System Logical Data Model that are required for physical data design. Chapter 14 describes Physical Data Design in more detail.

6.16.5.2 Step 640 Optimise Physical Data Design

This Step allows the development of a Physical Data Design which meets the space and timing objectives. The Required System Logical Data Model is used as a reference during this process.

6.16.5.3 Step 660 Consolidate Process Data Interface

This Step examines the mapping between the Physical Data Design and the logical view of the data. It examines any mismatches between a function component that handles data access according to the Required System Logical Data Design and the Optimised Physical Data Design.

6.16.5.4 Step 670 Assemble Physical Design

The completeness and consistency of the Physical Design is examined by reviewing all the Physical Design products and related products such as the Required Logical Data Model and the Requirements Catalogue.

6.17 Summary

The Logical Data Model consists of the Logical Data Structure, Attribute Descriptions, Entity Descriptions, Grouped Domain Descriptions, Relationship Descriptions.

A Logical Data Structure provides a view of the relationships between the data groups in a system. The technique examines these data groups, or entities, and derives a hierarchical data structure based on the master/detail concept. Relationships can all be expressed as a one-to-many relationship. The relationship can be further refined to be an optional or mandatory. Relationships can also be part of an exclusive group. Once a Logical Data Structure has been defined then Enquiry Access paths can be defined.

Logical Data Structures are developed alongside Data Flow Diagrams and develop through the stages of SSADM from the Overview Logical Data Model to the Current Environment Logical Data Model and then to the Required System Logical Data Model.

6.18 Keywords

Entity	Attribute
Relationship	Logical Data Model
Recursive relationship	1:1 relationship
Optional relationship	1:M relationship
Mandatory relationship	N:M relationship
Exclusive relationship group	Logical Data Structure
Master/detail concept	Entity Description
Link phrase	Attribute Description
Relationship Statement	Relationship Description
Transferable relationship	Grouped Domain Description
Key attribute(s)	Primary key
Compound key	Foreign key
Composite key	Simple key
Enquiry Access Path	Candidate key
Structure Diagram	Enquiry trigger
Current Environment Logical Data Model	Entity/Entity Matrix
Required System Logical Data Model	Jackson Structure

6.19 Exercises

1. Prepare a Current Physical Logical Data Structure for the Car Allowance System described in section 2.6 and Figure 2.11. Assume access is required through Employee Name to Allowance Details and Claim Details.

2. Prepare a Logical Data Structure for the existing Telephone Directory System described in section 3.2 and Figure 3.3. Develop your Logical Data Structure to a Required Logical Data Structure.

3. Prepare a Current Physical Logical Data Structure for the Student Administration System described in Appendix 2.

CHAPTER SEVEN

Business System Options

7.1 Introduction

Each Business System Option describes a required system. The system is described in terms of its boundary, inputs, outputs and processes. The Business System Option outlines what the system should do by describing:

- the functionality of the system
- the requirements dealt with
- the probable effect on the organization.

A Business System Option does not describe how the selected sets of features should be implemented.

Several Business System Options are drawn up, each meeting a different set of the requirements described in the Requirements Catalogue. The users can compare solutions which provide different levels of functionality and then use this as the basis for deciding which solution, if any, best meets their needs within the constraints of cost and time.

The selected Business System Option becomes one of the major inputs to the Requirements Specification Module.

7.2 Preparing a set of Skeleton Business System Options

Business System Options are developed from the Requirements Catalogue, User Catalogue, Current Services Description and the Project Initiation Document. Each Business System Option describes one possible solution for a proposed information system.

A useful way to draw up a set of Business System Options is to put all the mandatory requirements in a single Business System Option (the minimum option). A maximum option is then prepared by putting all the features possible in another Business System Option. Having examined the two extremes of possible solutions, some further options can be prepared which satisfy the mandatory requirements and a selection of additional features. The priority rating given for each Requirements Catalogue entry can be used to help determine possible options.

If too many Business System Options are prepared it can become difficult for the users to select an option. It is better to let the users select from a maximum of six options and make minor modifications to their preferred option, than to try and cover every possible set of solutions. For instance the minimum option may be selected with some additional features which change the system boundary slightly.

Each Business System Option is described in narrative form which may be supported by a Data Flow Model and a Logical Data Model. At the stage of drawing up the initial set of options for selection, only skeleton Business System Options are required.

The following information should be contained in each Skeleton Business System Option:

i) A statement of the importance of the different functional areas of the system to the business as a whole.

ii) An indication of the size of the system in terms of data storage, processing timetable and workload.

iii) An indication of the practicality of the proposed solution. This should include technical considerations such as possible impact on existing facilities and constraints posed by company technical policies. The ease of integration of the different functional areas should also be considered.

iv) Costs

v) Timescale for development and implementation

vi) Training requirements

7.3 Preparing the final set of Business System Options

Once the set of skeleton options has been prepared they must be examined with the users to reduce the number of options to two or three. These options must then be more fully documented. The issues addressed should include constraints, costs, benefits and impact on existing systems. The descriptions should still be narrative but can be supported by data and process models.

A possible structure is:

i) A statement of how the proposed option meets the requirements in the Requirements Catalogue

ii) An outline of the features provided by the system, including those which meet both functional and non-functional requirements

iii) Cost/benefit impact analysis

7.4 Selecting a Business System Option

Once these Business System Options have been produced they should be presented for formal selection. The analysts will present the options to the Project Board or its designated Review Board.

The analysts will require to prepare and make a presentation for each option. The Review Board should not be swamped with detail but the analysts should be prepared to provide further information if required. The analysts should explain the strengths and weaknesses of each option, facilitate the decision making and ensure that agreement is reached. The final solution may be based on one of the options presented but with enhancements generated by the decision-making process. This solution should be formally recorded in the same way as the Business System Options which were input to the final selection process.

Once agreement has been reached it must be documented. The reasons for the selection of the required option and rejection of the other solutions should be included. The description of the selected Business System Option and the documentation from the selection process is then used as an input to Stage 3, Definition of Requirements.

7.5 Worked example using Car Allowance Case Study

A list of some of the functional and non-functional requirements for the Car Allowance Case Study is given. A minimum and a maximum Business System Option are then outlined using these requirements as a basis. The descriptions are not complete but give an indication of the level of detail required at this stage.

7.5.1 Functional requirements

7.5.1.1 Mandatory functional requirements

The following are mandatory functional requirements:

i) Maintain the split in authorization tasks between Administration, Finance and Transport.

ii) One central set of records to be maintained rather than the current duplication of files in each department.

vi) Administration to be permitted on-line enquiry and update of the system.

vii) Finance to be permitted on-line enquiry of the system.

7.5.1.2 Non-mandatory functional requirements

The following are some of the non-mandatory functional requirements:

i) Produce Cheque Requisitions (electronic form) plus listing for authorization signature.

ii) Provide a random check of claims processed by Finance. 15% of claims each month should have the details of individual journeys examined in detail, the other claims need only have the total miles claimed entered.

iii) Provide monthly and annual printed reports of claims analyzed by department.

iv) Print cheques and control documentation.

v) Print monthly and annual statements for claimants.

vi) Link to Payroll System to pay car allowance claims with salary.

7.5.2 Non-functional requirements

7.5.2.1 Mandatory non-functional requirements

i) Passwords to be provided for all access to the system. The passwords should be unique to each department and to each system function.

ii) On-line access required during normal working hours.

7.5.2.2 Non-mandatory non-functional requirements

i) Control listings to be provided for cheque requisitions and changes to/addition of authorized user details.

ii) Electronic cheque requisitions to be produced weekly to fit with schedule of the central system which produces all of the company's cheques.

7.5.3 Business System Options

Two examples of Business System Options are given, the first specifies the minimum option and incorporates only the mandatory requirements. The second is a maximum option and incorporates all of the mandatory and non-mandatory requirements given above.

7.5.3.1 Minimum Option

Description

This option satisfies all of the mandatory requirements in the Requirements Catalogue, none of the non-mandatory requirements have been considered. This system would remain basically the same as the current system with the authorization procedure for new users or changes to users remaining substantially as at present. It has the following features:

- A central database of authorised car users and cars so that all information is held only once.
- Update of the central database is to be restricted to Administration Department. Finance and Transport Departments will have enquiry facilities.
- A user number will be allocated to each user.
- Passwords will be allocated to each system function.
- On-line access to the central database will be available to all departments during normal working hours. Terminals will be provided on appropriate desks.
- Existing hardware and software can be utilized.

Benefits

This option has the following benefits:

- The central database will ensure that data is entered once only and will eliminate the problem of conflicting data being held by different departments.
- Reduced costs and time delays in producing ad-hoc reports on authorised users and cars.
- Substantial reduction in physical storage space required in each department. Note that one paper copy of each authorization and change to authorization will still be held.
- No major outlay on hardware or software required.
- Very little difference to procedures for employees claiming car allowance.

Costs

This option has the following costs:

- Terminals will be required on desks in the three departments. Some rewiring will be required. Appropriate furniture will be required for staff not currently using computer equipment.

- In-house development using existing software would be relatively inexpensive.

- Training costs will be fairly low.

- File conversion costs will be relatively high but essential if any computerised version of the system is implemented.

7.5.3.2 Maximum Option

Description

This option satisfies all of the mandatory requirements and also all the non-mandatory requirements. The authorization of car allowance users and cars is still carried out as at present. Note that some of the non-mandatory requirements are self-exclusive. For instance there is no need for the required system to print cheques if car allowance is paid with salaries. The system involves a central database of authorised users and cars. The processing of claims is also automated. Links are provided to the Payroll System.

The following features are provided:

- A central database of authorised car users and cars so that all information is held only once.

- Authorization of car users and cars is carried out using substantially the same procedures as at present. Details are only entered on the system when the authorization process is complete.

- Update of the central database is restricted to Administration and Finance Departments. Administration creates details of authorised users and cars. Finance enters details of claims. All three departments have enquiry and reporting facilities.

- Automatic processing of claims.

- 15% of claims will be randomly checked for full journey details by the system.

- Allowances will be paid through the Payroll System.

- Claimants will receive monthly and annual statements of claims.

- Monthly and annual printed reports of claims by department will be provided.

- User numbers will be allocated to each user.

- Passwords will be allocated to each system function.

- On-line access to the central database will be available to all departments during normal working hours. Terminal provided on appropriate desks.

- Existing hardware and software can be utilized.

Benefits

This option has the following benefits:

- The central database will ensure that data is entered once only and will eliminate the problem of conflicting data being held by different departments.

- On-line access to relevant information for each department.

- Reduced costs and time delay in producing claims.

- Reduced costs and time delays in producing ad-hoc reports on authorised users and cars.

- Substantial reduction in physical storage space required in each department. Note that one paper copy of each authorization and change to authorization will still be held.

- Better management information.

- Better information for claimants which should reduce the level of enquiries to both Finance and Administration Departments.

- Comptometer (adding machine) operators no longer required to check journey details on claim forms.

Costs

This option has the following costs:

- Existing computers have sufficient capacity to cope with the required system. Some expenditure may be required on peripherals.

- Terminals will be required on desks in the three departments. Some rewiring will be required. Appropriate furniture will be required for staff not currently using computer equipment.

- Existing software facilities can be used to develop the system but development costs will be relatively high.

- Training costs will be fairly low.

- File conversion costs will be relatively high but essential if any computerised version of the system is implemented.

7.6 The place of Business System Options in SSADM

7.6.1 Feasibility Module

7.6.1.1 Step 030 Select Feasibility Options

Up to 6 outline Business Systems Options are prepared. Possible technical solutions are identified for each option. The Business System Option and Technical System Option together provide a Feasibility Option. These composite options are described in less detail than in the Full Study. The Project Board selects an option for further study.

7.6.1.2 Step 040 Assemble the Feasibility Report

The Feasibility Options and the results of the Project Board's deliberations are described in the Feasibility Report.

7.6.2 Requirements Analysis Module

7.6.2.1 Step 210 Define Business System Options

The Business System Options are created during this Step. Up to 6 skeleton options are produced and these are then reduced to two or three options after discussion with the users. The remaining options are described more fully, including a cost benefit analysis.

7.6.2.2 Step 220 Select Business System Option

The Business System Options are presented to the Project Board. An option is selected which may be an enhanced or reduced version of one of the presented options.

7.6.3 Requirements Specification Module

7.6.3.1 Step 310 Define Required System Processing

The Requirements Catalogue and the Logical Data Flow Diagrams are adjusted to reflect the selected Business System Option.

7.6.3.2 Step 320 Develop Required Data Model

The Logical Data Model of the current environment is adjusted to reflect the selected Business System Option.

7.6.3.3 Step 380 Assemble Requirements Specification

The selected Business System Option is used as a reference point when checking the consistency and completeness of the products of the Requirements Specification Module.

7.6.4 Logical System Specification Module

7.6.4.1 Step 410 Define Technical System Options

The Technical System Options are developed to provide possible approaches to the physical implementation of the required system. They may include some variations on the system functionality specified in the Selected Business System Option as a result of further analysis or new possibilities opened by the technical investigation.

7.7 Summary

The production of Business System Options allows the analyst and users to explore the boundaries and functionality of the required system. The main aim is to provide the users with sufficient detail for them to decide that the option chosen provides a satisfactory level of functionality. This then provides a firm basis for the next phase in the development of the system.

7.8 Keywords

Skeleton Business System Option
Business System Option
Requirements Catalogue
Functional requirements
Non-functional requirements
Project Initiation Document
Selected Business System Option
Minimum option
Maximum option
User Catalogue
Project Board
Cost/Benefit Analysis
Current Services Description

7.9 Exercises

1. Describe the progression from Skeleton Business System Option to the Selected Business System Option.

2. Who selects the Business System Option?

3. What SSADM documents are used to help create the Skeleton Business System Options.

4. Which SSADM techniques can be used to support a Business System Option?

5. Develop some alternative Business System Options for the Car Allowance System.

6. Develop a set of Business System Options for the Telephone Directory System described in Chapter 5, section 2.

   Assume the following mandatory functional requirements:

   - All staff to have immediate access to a copy of the telephone directory.
   - A central computer-based version of the directory will be maintained by the switchboard operators.
   - The switchboard operators have on-line access to the directory when dealing with calls.
   - On-line access by name, job title, department or extension number.
   - Staff can be allocated more than one extension number. Each extension number may be in a different location.

   Assume the following non-mandatory functional requirements:

   - All directors and their secretaries to have on-line access to the telephone directory.
   - All staff to have on-line access to the telephone directory (no printed version).
   - Automatic dialling once a telephone directory number selected.
   - Printed version of directory (if any) should have alphabetical listing by name and also an alphabetical listing within department.

7. Prepare some Business System Options for the Student Administration System described in Appendix 2.

CHAPTER EIGHT

Function Definition

8.1 Introduction

Function definition is a procedure which starts with the identification of functions from existing SSADM products. It then references all the SSADM products that provide the detailed specification of the function components. A function is the user view of system processing. The grouping of processes which make up a function is carried out by the analyst and user working in close consultation.

There are two clear phases in Function Definition. The first phase occurs once the Required System Data Flow Model has been produced. Update and major enquiry functions can then be identified from the Data Flow Model. Enquiry functions can be identified from the Requirements Catalogue.

The second phase occurs after Entity Life History analysis has been carried out (see Chapter 11, Entity-event Modelling). Additional events will be identified and the previously identified functions may be modified or new functions created.

The activities in Function Definition can be repeated because of information coming to light later. The output from Function Definition is input to both the Logical System Specification and Physical Design Modules. Once functions have been identified they are documented on a Function Definition Form, see Figure 8.1. As Function Definition is an iterative technique, this form is completed over time as more information becomes available about the function.

Function Name:	Registration of car allowance claim	**Function ID:** 1
Function type:	Update On-line User	
User Roles:	Finance Clerk	

Function description

Error handling

DFD processes

Events	**Event Frequency**

I/O Description refs:

I/O Structure refs:

Requirements Catalogue ref:

Volumes:

Related functions:

Enquiries	**Enquiry frequency**

Common processing:

Dialogue names:

Service level requirement

Description	**Target value**	**Range**	**Comments**

Figure 8.1 Extract from a Function Definition Form for 'Registration of Car Allowance Claim' function.

In addition to the referencing information contained on the Function Definition Form the inputs and outputs of a function can be represented as Input/Output Structures. Input/Output Structuring represents the inputs and outputs of a function in a structured way, using Jackson-like notation.

8.2 Functions

8.2.1 What is a function

A function is a set of system processes which the user wishes to carry out at the same time. Functions are input to physical design and provide the basis for the creation of program specifications. Each function will become one or more programs.

8.2.2 Function types

Functions must be classified on the Function Definition Form according to each of the following three sets of criteria:

i) Enquiry or update.
An update function may include enquiries.

ii) On-line or off-line.
This refers to the database update or enquiry processing.

iii) User or system initiated.

The function type classification can be seen near the top of the Function Definition Form in Figure 8.1.

8.2.3 Function components

Functions can be broken down into data streams and processes. The data stream components are inputs, outputs and the flows between processes. Function Definition identifies functions and references the SSADM products which define the function components. The only function components defined during Function Definition are the function inputs and outputs. They are documented as Input/Output Structures.

8.2.3.1 Inputs

Input data is made up of groups of data items. There are three kinds of component: events, enquiry triggers and redundant data. An event is a something that triggers a process to update the database and is specified during Entity Life History analysis. An enquiry trigger is a group of data items which is the entry point to the Logical Data Model and is defined along with the Enquiry Access Paths during Logical Data Modelling. Events and enquiry triggers are listed on the Function Definition Form with a reference to their full specification. During Function Definition the analyst should check that the data items for the events and enquiry triggers are contained in the input structure of any function including that event or enquiry,

Some input data items are redundant since they are not needed by an update or enquiry process. They are present as control data items used to validate the input data before it is accepted by the system. Control data is not defined until Physical Design. Input/Output Structures, Dialogue Design and the Function Component Implementation Map define the input component of a function.

8.2.3.2 Outputs

Output data is determined by the needs of the business activity supported by the function. Error handling is not part of Function Definition. Output related to error handling is defined in Logical Process Design and Physical Design.

Input/Output Structures, Dialogue Design and the Function Component Implementation Map define the valid output from a function.

8.2.3.3 Processes

A function can consist of one or more processes. Update and enquiry processes are defined during Logical Database Process Design as Update Process Models and Enquiry Process Models. The output from Function Definition is used as a basis for the production of these models.

8.2.3.4 Flows between processes

The flows between data processes are groups of data items which can carry event and enquiry triggers. These are defined as explained in sections 8.2.3.1 and 8.2.3.2.

8.3 Developing functions

There are a number of activities involved in developing functions.

i) Identify update functions
ii) Identify enquiry functions
iii) Modify functions to reflect results of Entity-event Modelling
iv) Update functions to reflect the results of Specification Prototyping

Function Definition is an iterative process so these activities are not sequential.

8.3.1 Identify update functions.

8.3.1.1 Function initiation

An update function has the effect of changing the data in the database. Update functions may be either user or system initiated. The update functions are initially identified from the processes on the Required System Data Flow Diagrams.

8.3.1.2 User-initiated update functions

To identify user-initiated update functions start with the bottom level Required System Data Flow Diagrams. Look for input data flows from each external entity. For each input data flow, trace its path through the process or processes that handle the data on that flow, and identify all the updates required to data stores. The objective is to identify all the processes, output data flows and data store updates that take place before all the data on the original data store have been processed. Usually there will only be one process for each function, but where inter-process data flows have been used then further processes may be grouped in the same function.

8.3.1.3 System-initiated update functions

System-initiated update functions are time-based functions that the system invokes automatically. They appear as processes on the Required System Data Flow Diagrams but have no input from an external entity. System initiated functions are often associated with transient data stores.

Once the user-initiated functions have been identified look for outputs which have not yet been assigned to any function. Trace each output back to the process that produces them. Identify the updates to data stores carried out by these processes. The processes and the outputs will form a system-initiated function.

8.3.1.4 Checking functions

The user-initiated functions are identified first, followed by the system-initiated functions. Then a check is made of all the bottom level Required System Data Flow Diagrams to ensure that all processes with their inputs and outputs have been assigned to at least one function. If a function is to be implemented both on-line and off-line then a function must be created for each type.

The events within each function are the start-up events for Entity Life History analysis. They must be identified and listed on the Function Definition Form (see Chapter 11, Entity-event modelling).

8.3.1.5 User involvement in function identification

The composition of each function must be discussed in close consultation with users. The user can provide detailed information about job activities and interdependencies which helps the analyst to validate functions and identify additional functions.

Some functions may be split because a user needs to invoke part of a function independently. The functions must support the way in which the user works. An example from the Car Allowance System might be the creation of an Authorised Car User. The user may point out that the current function includes the creation of car-phone information but that this is not usually available at the time the authorization is recorded and is normally added later. A new function should be created to handle the addition of the car phone information.

Some functions may be merged because the user always invokes them in sequence. An example might be where two user-initiated functions have been identified in an order processing system. The first function creates one or more orders and the second function prints some order documentation. The two functions are always carried out in sequence and very close in time.

When changes are made to Function Definitions care must be taken to ensure that all the affected Function Definition Forms are updated. Particular attention should be paid to checking the cross-references to other related functions.

8.3.2 Identify enquiry functions

Some major enquiries may be identified from the Required System Data Flow Diagrams. The remaining enquiry functions are identified from the Requirements Catalogue, the Required System Data Flow Diagrams or directly from users. The detail of enquiry processing is found in the Enquiry Access Paths from the Logical Data Model.

8.3.3 Modify functions to reflect results of Entity-event Modelling

The second phase of Function Definition takes place after Entity-event Modelling has taken place in Step 360. A more detailed view of system update processing should now be available from the Effect Correspondence Diagrams, making it possible to develop a full set of functions. Each event must be allocated to at least one function. New functions may be created as a result. All additions and changes must be reflected on a Function Definition Form. The Required System Data Flow Model should be updated to show any new processing which has been identified. User consultation is still essential at this phase of Function Definition and may result in merging or splitting of functions.

Entity Life History analysis may find that some enquiries affect the life of an entity. For instance, an order entity may not be progressed until a supervisor has checked the order. The supervisor check updates the state indicator value for that entity, no further updates can be made to the entity until the state indicator value is updated. Such a function would be reclassified as an update function (see Chapter 11, Entity-event Modelling).

The grouping of events into functions can be checked once Entity-event modelling is complete. The input data can be viewed as a batch of events that may be grouped together in one function if they meet some of the following criteria:

- have the same, or related, external entity as their point of origin
- send outputs to the same, or related, external entities
- occur at the same time or very close together
- affect the same entities by having either the same or closely-related entry points to the database or the same access paths.

The more of the above criteria that apply, the stronger the case for grouping.

8.3.4 Update functions to reflect results of Specification Prototyping.

The prototyping procedure may lead the user to identify additional combinations of events which will be documented as additional functions. Amendments to existing functions may also be necessary.

8.4 Document the function

As each function is identified a Function Definition Form is created, see Figure 8.1 for a sample form.

The function name, function ID, type, user roles, function description, DFD processes, Requirements Catalogue reference, volumes, enquiry name and enquiry frequency can all be completed when a function is created.

Error handling information can be added as discussions with users proceed. Error handling is not considered formally but useful information is recorded. This information is referred to during the formal documentation of error handling, Entity-event modelling and Logical Database Process Design.

After Entity-event modelling the event reference and event frequency can be recorded on the form. By the end of Stage 5 the information from the Entity Life Histories and Effect Correspondence Diagrams has been converted into an Update Process Model identified by the event names. The Function Definition Form should be annotated with a reference to these Update Process Models.

As Input/Output Structures are developed the I/O description and I/O Structure references should be completed.

Service level requirements may be partially documented in the Requirements Catalogue but the formal documentation on the Function Description Form must be completed by the end of Step 370, Confirm System Objectives. The service level requirements are required for input to creation of Technical System Options (see Chapter 12). If more than one dialogue can initiate a function then there may be different service level requirements for each dialogue.

Bottom level processes from the Required System Data Flow Diagrams will be documented as Elementary Process Descriptions. This fairly informal definition of processing is mainly replaced by the formal definition of functions, events and enquiries.

Common processing and Dialogue name information is added as it is identified during Step 330, Derive System Functions. Common processes are processes which occur more than once on the Required System Data Flow Diagrams. A common process Elementary Process Description which is a function, event or enquiry is marked not to be carried forward in the documentation. It is replaced by the Function Description Form. Any remaining common process Elementary Process Descriptions are annotated with the function, event or enquiry names which use them. They are also referenced on the Function Definition Form.

8.5 Develop Input/Output Structures for each function

Input/Output Structures are developed to specify the user interface for each function.

Input/Output Descriptions are part of the Required System Data Flow Model. For each data flow they list the data items carried by the flow and document any supplementary information such as repeating groups, conditions and options. This information is one of the inputs to the creation of Input/Output Structures for update and major enquiry functions.

The majority of enquiry functions will be identified from the Requirements Catalogue. These enquiries will not have Input/Output Descriptions. The input and output data items must be identified for each enquiry. In practice this is done at the same time as the production of the Input/Output Structure for the enquiry.

A completed Input/Output Structure consists of an Input/Output Structure Diagram and an Input/Output Structure Description and must be produced for each function.

8.5.1 Input/Output Structure Diagrams

Input/Output Structure Diagrams provide a pictorial view of the data item on the Input/Output Descriptions. They do not include error handling responses. The Input/Output Structure Diagrams use Jackson-like notation to represent sequences, selections and iterations. The production of Input/Output Structures treats on-line inputs and outputs differently to off-line inputs and outputs.

The completion of all of the Input/Output Structures and their Descriptions provides a full specification of the input and output data items for a function.

8.5.1.1 Sequence

A sequence represents a group of data items entered in a definite order. Figure 8.2 shows a portion of a simple on-line dialogue in an order processing system.

The user enters an item code, the system responds with the item description and price details, finally the user enters the quantity required for an item.

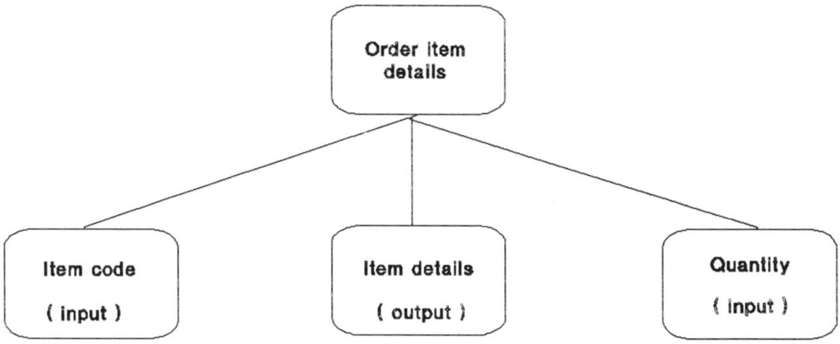

Figure 8.2 Input/Output Structure showing sequence

8.5.1.2 Iteration

An iteration is used to represent a repeating group of data items. For example, in an order processing system the user may be able to create a multi-item order. The item details are a repeating group. Figure 8.3 shows a portion of an on-line dialogue which allows zero, one or more items to be created. The repeating group is shown as an iteration and this is indicated by the "set of order items" box with an "order item" box below it marked with an asterisk (*).

8.5.1.3 Selection

A selection is used to represent optional groups of data items. For example, in an order processing system, the delivery address might not be entered if it was the same as the invoice address. Delivery address would be an optional group of data items. Figure 8.4 shows this, delivery address has become a

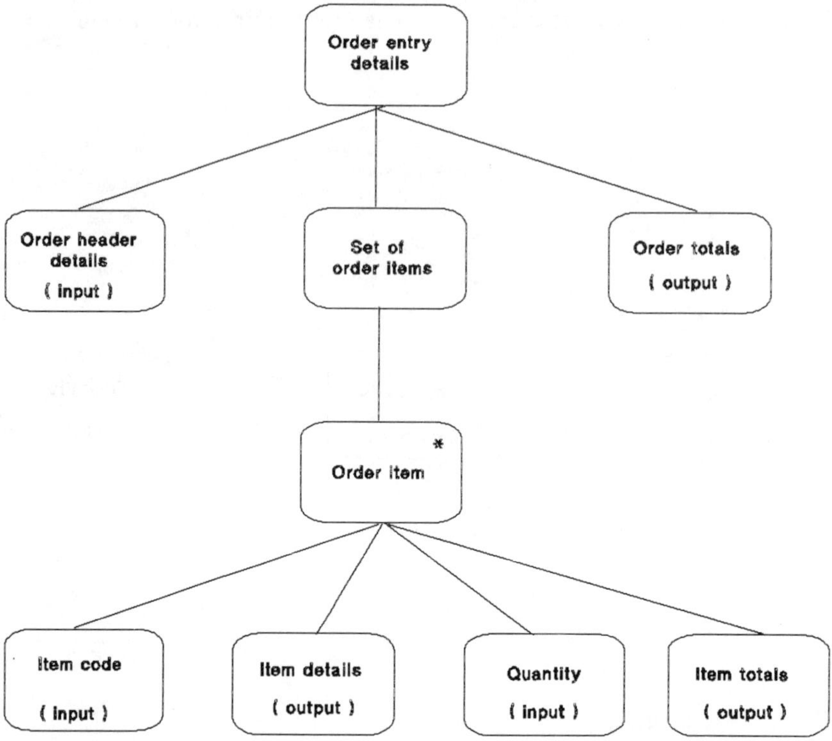

Figure 8.3 Input/Output Structure showing iteration.

separate box following order header details in sequence. The option is indicated by the sequence box "possible delivery address" with the two option boxes below, each option having a ^{O} symbol in the top right of the box. The option of no delivery address entered is shown by the blank box (dotted line).

A selection is also used to represent a mutually exclusive group of data items, in this case there could be no blank option box.

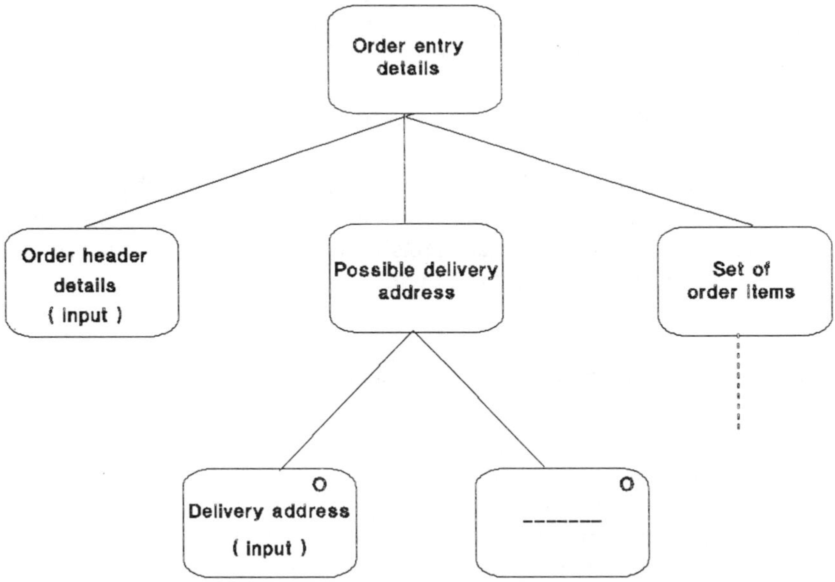

Figure 8.4 Input/Output Structure showing selection

8.5.2 On-line inputs and outputs.

The first task is to identify all of the input and output dataflows belonging to a particular function. These dataflows will be referenced on the Function Description Form as Input/Output Descriptions and represent the dialogue between the user and the system for that function.

Discussion with the user should identify groups of data items that the user will input to the system and the system responses to these inputs. Some system responses may be shown on the Required System Data Flow Diagrams and will have an Input/Output Description. Most system responses will not be documented in this way.

System responses will often be for validation items. For instance, in the Car Allowance System, when a claim form is processed the first data item entered is the Employee's payroll number, the system will return the claimant's name, job details, car allowance grade and car details to confirm that the correct claimant has been identified.

There is a set of rules to follow when grouping data items:

- input and output items should not be grouped together
- mandatory and optional items should not be grouped together
- repeating groups of data items should be separate from items which do not repeat with that group.

Keeping these rules in mind, use the following procedure

- group data items input by the user
- group data items which are the system responses
- identify the sequencing of the groups of inputs and outputs
- draw an Input/output Structure to represent the sequencing
- use iterations to show repeating groups
- use selection to show optional groups or mutually exclusive groups
- record each Input/output Structure element on an Input/Output Structure Description, including a list of the data items which make up that element

8.5.3 Example

The processing of a Claim Form in the Car Allowance system involves the user entering the employee payroll number. The system responds with the claimant's name, job details, car allowance grade and car details (up to two cars may be listed). Having visually checked this information the total mileage and the total amount claimed are entered. If these agree then, for 85% of claims, the claim details are accepted. The other 15% of claim forms will require a further check, the details of each journey making up the claim will require to be entered.

The following groups of data can be identified:

employee payroll number	user
employee car allowance details	system
car details	system
total claim details	user
journey details	user

There are two repeating groups of data items: car details and journey details.

Figure 8.5 shows an example of an Input/Output Structure for the Car Allowance System on-line update. Figure 8.6 shows an example of the information recorded on an Input/Output Structure Description.

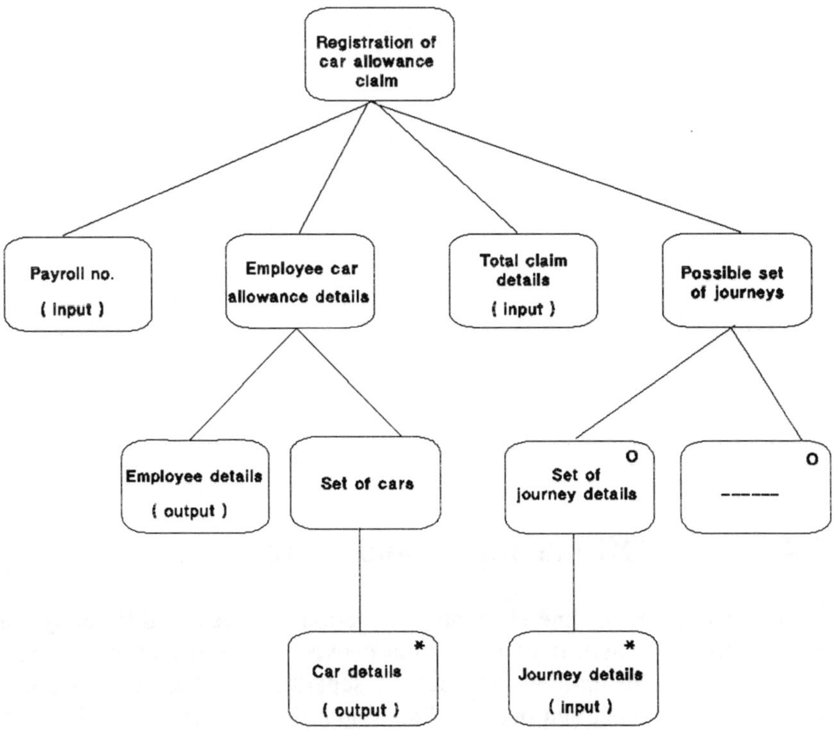

Figure 8.5 Input/Output Structure for an on-line update.

I/O Structure Element	Data Item	Comments
Employee payroll no.	Pay no.	
Employee details	Employee name Job title Job location Allowance grade	
Car detail	Car make Car model Engine cc Registration no.	
Total claim detail	Total mileage Total claim value	
Journey detail	Start odometer reading Finish odometer reading	15% claims only

Figure 8.6 Input/Output structure elements with data items for function 'Registration of car allowance claim'.

8.5.4 Off-line inputs and outputs

Off-line functions or off-line elements of functions are treated differently from on-line functions. There is no interaction between the user and the system as there would be in an on-line dialogue. A separate Input/Output Structure is produced for each input and output. Each Input/Output Structure will be only input or only output.

8.6 The Place of Function Definition in SSADM

8.6.1 Requirements Specification Module

8.6.1.1 Step 330 Derive System Functions

Update functions are identified from the processes on the Required System Data Flow Diagram. The events and enquiries contained within each update function must then be identified.

Enquiry functions are identified from the Requirements Catalogue, the Required System Data Flow Diagrams or directly from users.

Input/Output Structures are developed to specify the user interface for each function.

The required system dialogues are identified using the User Role/Function Matrix. Dialogues critical to the success of the required system should be noted.

The service level requirements are defined for each function.

8.6.1.2 Step 340 Enhance Required Data Model

Functions whose input/output specifications are to have relational data analysis applied are identified. The normalised relations for each function are converted into a Logical Data Model style submodel. Each submodel is compared against the Required System Logical Data Model and changes made as necessary.

8.6.1.3 Step 350 Develop Specification Prototypes

Input/Output Structures are an input, Function Definitions a reference during specification prototyping (see Chapter 10).

8.6.1.4 Step 360 Develop Processing Specification

Function definition identifies a start-up set of events for the creation of Entity Life Histories. Functions are defined or redefined in Step 330 for additional events specified.

8.6.1.5 Step 370 Confirm System Objectives

The Function Definitions are reviewed to ensure each function is fully defined including objective measures and service level requirements.

8.6.1.6 Step 380 Assemble Requirements Specification

A check for the completeness and consistency of the Requirements Specification Module includes a review of the Function Definitions, Input/Output Structures and the User Role/Function Matrix.

8.6.2 Logical System Specification Module

8.6.2.1 Step 510 Define User Dialogues

Function Definitions and Input/Output Structures are used as input to this Step (see Chapter 3, Dialogue Design).

8.6.2.2 Step 520 Define Update Processes

Function Definitions and Input/Output Structures are used as input to this Step (see Chapter 13, Logical Database Process Design).

8.6.2.3 Step 530 Define Enquiry Processes

Function Definitions and Input/Output Structures are used as input to this Step (see Chapter 13, Logical Database Process Design).

8.6.2.4 Step 540 Assemble Logical Design

The Function Definitions, Input/Output Structures and User Role/Function Matrix become part of the Logical Design after all the products of Stage 5 have been checked for completeness.

8.6.3 Physical Design Module

8.6.3.1 Step 620 Create Physical Data Design

The Function Definitions are required as one of the inputs when preparing the Physical Data Design (first cut) and the space estimation (see Chapter 14 Physical Data Design).

8.6.3.2 Step 630 Create Function Component Implementation Map

Specifies the syntax error handling, physical input/output formats and physical dialogues for each function. The Function Component Implementation Map is created and this identifies duplicate and common function components; the relationship between all the function components (see Chapter 15 Physical Process Specification).

8.6.3.3 Step 640 Optimise Physical Data Design

The Physical Data Design is validated against the performance information contained in the Function Definitions and the Requirements Catalogue.

8.6.3.4 Step 650 Complete Function Specification

Program specifications are produced for the function components requiring procedural code.

8.6.3.5 Step 660 Consolidate Process Data Interface

This Step identifies any mismatch between a function component to handle data access according to the Required System Logical Data Model and the Physical Data Design (optimised). Amendments to the Function Definitions may be required as a result of this series of activities (see Chapter 15, Physical Process Specification).

8.6.3.6 Step 670 Assemble Physical Design

The completed Function Definitions become part of the Physical Design Document.

8.7 Summary

Function Definition is a central technique in SSADM. A function is the user view of processing in the required system and the technique must be carried out in close consultation with users. Function Definition identifies the processing requirements of the required system and describes them in sufficient detail for Logical System Specification and Physical Design. The main concern is to annotate the Function Description Form with references to other SSADM products that provide the detailed specification of the function components.

The technique starts with the identification and documentation of updates and major enquiries from the Required System Data Flow Diagrams. Other enquiries are identified from the Requirements Catalogue. The output of Entity-event Modelling can cause changes and updates to the Function Descriptions. Function inputs and outputs are documented using Input/Output Structures.

8.8 Keywords

Function
Function type
Function component
Update process
Enquiry process
Input/Output Structures
Input/Output Structure Description
Function Description Form
Enquiry Access Path
Required Data Flow Model
Logical Data Model
Event
Event trigger
Enquiry trigger
Entity-event modelling
Requirements Catalogue
User-initiated function
System-initiated function
Sequence
Selection
Iteration

8.9 Exercises

1. Describe the activities involved in Function Definition.

2. Outline the links from Function Definition to other SSADM techniques.

3. Identify as many update and enquiry functions for the Car Allowance System as you can (see Chapters 3, 4, 5, 6 and 7 for further information).

4. Develop an Input/Output Structure for the function which registers new authorized users on the Car Allowance System.

5. Identify functions and prepare Function Definition Forms and Input/Output Structures for the Telephone Allowance System described in Chapter 5, section 2.

6. Identify functions and prepare Function Definition Forms for the Student Administration System described in Appendix 2.

CHAPTER NINE

Relational Data Analysis

9.1 Introduction

Relational Data Analysis is a technique used to assist in understanding the data of a system under investigation. By applying the technique to a large amount of seemingly unrelated data, a clear picture emerges of the essential form of the data. The end result of the technique is a set of tables of data in a form known as Third Normal Form. These tables form the basis of the logical data design of the system. It is from this logical design that the physical implementation of the data is derived. This may be in the form of conventional files or a more sophisticated database such as ORACLE, IDMS, or IMS. The need for a rigorous approach to data analysis is best illustrated with a simple example. Suppose we have a retail company which has a file of sales information. The company has several stores and the file has a record for every product line on sale at each store. The records look as in Figure 9.1.

	Store	Item-Code	Description	Annual-Sales To-Date
Record 1	10	AB13	Towel	1100.00
Record 2	10	CF99	Handkerchief	350.00
Record 3	10	HK76	Jeans	1700.00
Record 4	20	AB13	Towel	840.00

Figure 9.1 - Product lines.

Now imagine the sales manager asks that the system be amended to include price per item on the file. Obviously this will mean some kind of file manipulation to find every record with, say, Item-Code AB13. To make matters worse, the manager also wants to include future price changes with their Effective-Date. The data as the manager sees it is shown in Figure 9.2.

	Item-Code	Description	Price	Effective-Date
Record 1:	AB13	Towel	1.15	30/06/88
Record 2:	CF99	Handkerchief	0.38	30/06/88
Record 3:	CF99	Handkerchief	0.47	31/10/88
Record 4:	HK76	Jeans	26.99	30/06/88

Figure 9.2 - Product price changes.

When this data is merged with that in Figure 9.1, the result might look like Figure 9.3.

	Store	Item	Description Code	Annual-Sales to-Date	Price	Effective Date
Record 1	10	AB13	Towel	1100.00	1.15	30/06/88
Record 2	10	CF99	Handkerchief	350.00	0.38	30/06/88
Record 3	10	CF99	Handkerchief	*	0.47	31/10/88
Record 4	10	HK76	Jeans	1700.00	26.99	30/06/88
Record 5	20	AB13	Towel	840.00	*	*

Figure 9.3 - Product lines with price changes.

The entries marked * have values which have already been entered. Is it worth storing the Price and Effective-Date every time that item occurs in the file? It is quite possible that the item will be stocked by all the shops in the company! One needs no knowledge of computing to know that the file design is wrong. A lot of data is duplicated because of the way the file is organised. For instance if AB13 is a Towel, is it necessary to store the word "Towel" every time we store the Item-Code AB13?

Not only is this situation wasteful in terms of storage space, but it can also lead to inconsistencies in the data. If the manager subsequently decides to change one of the prices or its Effective- Date, every occurrence of this data will have to be changed. It would be quite possible to accidentally miss out some of the occurrences leading to the dangerous situation of two values for the same item.

The data would lack integrity. Files such as this have been created in real life, and Relational Data Analysis is a formal way of avoiding the trap. A little application of common-sense would have reorganised this one file into three separate files as shown in Figure 9.4:

File 1

	Item-Code	Description
Record 1:	AB13	Towel
Record 2:	CF99	Handkerchief
Record 3:	HK76	Jeans

File 2

	Store	Item-Code	Annual-Sales-To-Date
Record 1:	10	AB13	1100.00
Record 2:	10	CF99	350.00
Record 3:	10	HK76	1700.00
Record 4:	20	AB13	840.00

File 3

	Item-Code	Effective-Date	Price
Record 1:	AB13	30/06/88	1.15
Record 2:	CF99	30/06/88	0.38
Record 3:	CF99	31/10/88	0.47
Record 4:	HK76	30/06/88	26.99

Figure 9.4 - Product details in three files

All the unnecessary duplication of data is removed. In our example Item-Code appears in all three files but this duplication is necessary so that we can find information such as the price of towels in July 1988. The Item-Code is used to link the two separate files of data. The relationship of one data item to another is very important in relational data analysis. A careful study of the three files shows that in File 2 the value of Annual-Sales-To-Date is determined by (dependant on) the Item-Code and the Store, ie for a given value of Store and a given value of Item-Code only one value is possible for

Annual-Sales-To-Date. In File 1 Description is determined by Item-Code. In File 3 Price is determined by Item-Code AND Effective-Date. It is this idea of DETERMINACY that is the basis of Relational Data Analysis.

The above process was done by applying common-sense but, with more complicated examples, a more formal method is required. This is the technique of NORMALISATION which is is the subject of this chapter.

9.2 Exercises

1. Identify the duplicated data in the following table of Employee Details:

Employee No.	Employee Name	Job Code	Job-Title	Start Date	Finish Date
123	Smith	A1	Trainee Analyst	3/2/80	5/2/81
349	Cairns	P3	Senior Programmer	3/2/81	3/9/81
541	McPhee	P3	Senior Programmer	5/2/81	7/4/83
123	Smith	A2	Analyst	6/2/81	7/5/83
541	McPhee	P4	Chief Programmer	8/4/83	
123	Smith	A3	Senior Analyst	8/5/83	10/10/85
632	Keith	A2	Analyst	9/4/84	
123	Smith	M1	Project Manager	11/10/85	

2. If the Sales Manager wanted to add the following data to the files in Figure 9.4

   (a) Supplier name for each item
   (b) Name of store manager for each store
   (c) Maximum quantity of each item to be stored in each store

   Where would this data be stored ie. File 1, 2 or 3 or would any new files be required?

9.3 Relational Data Analysis and SSADM

Relational Data Analyis is used in SSADM in partnership with Logical Data Modelling. The Logical Data Model provides a top down view of data structures. Relational Data Analysis builds a bottom up view of the data structures which can be used to verify the Logical Data Model. Relational Data Analysis can be used when creating the Logical Data Model to check that the entities are in third normal form. An entity in the Logical Data Model corresponds to a relation in Relational Data Analysis.

The Input/Output Structures devloped during Function Definition are then taken as inputs to Relational Data Analysis. The Input/Output Structures and their Descriptions are selected for analysis if they are complex, high volume, of high frequency or of critical importance. Relational Data Analysis is applied separately to each structure. The resulting relations are checked for consistency with the Logical Data Model.

9.4 Relations

In relational data analysis it is convenient to think of data as a collection of tables. A table, also known as a RELATION, is equivalent to a file of data. A sample relation of data is given in Figure 9.5. It is part of a results table for students studying for a qualification in computing. The qualification is made up of a number of courses from which students take a selection. This table may already exist as a document in a student records system or may have been formed by merging a number of documents containing results for individual courses. This table is an UN-NORMALISED form and is the starting point for the process of normalisation.

Before analyzing this data formally, there are a few points worth mentioning.

(a) The table has only THREE rows! This may seem a surprising statement but the table is presented in the above form for convenience. The three rows contain data for the three courses SYA, COB and PAS. The rows are of unequal length as the student data is repeated several times in the same row and, since there is insufficient room to present these long rows on a page, the student details are shown one below the other.

Course Code	Course Title	Stud. Code	Student Name	Date-of Birth	Tutor Code	Tutor Name	Grade	Result
SYA	Systems Analysis	A2345	Smith	20.08.69	1746	Jones	A	Dist.
		A7423	Barker	03.04.59	1746	Jones	C	Pass
		B3716	Green	23.02.70	1330	Jarvis	D	Pass
		A3472	Harris	17.07.69	1746	Jones	F	Fail
		B9843	Green	10.11.68	1330	Jarvis	B	Merit
COB	Cobol	A7423	Barker	03.04.59	1520	Hooper	E	Fail
		A4217	Morris	17.01.68	1520	Hooper	B	Merit
		B8238	Carter	09.12.69	1520	Hooper	C	Pass
PAS	Pascal	A4217	Morris	17.01.68	1520	Hooper	A	Dist.
		B9843	Green	10.11.68	1283	Trotter	B	Merit
		A3393	Davies	30.09.69	1283	Trotter	E	Fail
		A4247	Cross	25.12.69	1520	Hooper	C	Pass

Figure 9.5 - Student results by course

(b) As already mentioned, the table can be compared to a file. Taking the comparison further, each column in the relation is equivalent to a field and each row equivalent to a record (in this case a variable length record).

(c) The table shows two different students with the same name - a not uncommon occurrence. A name is therefore a very bad choice for an identifier for a person, a unique code for each person is nearly always used. In the example the two students are differentiated by codes B3716 and B9843.

(d) It is extremely important to really understand the data, and the more data available to the analyst the better. For example, if the only data analyzed were for the COBOL course, the analyst may well be left with the impression that each course has only one tutor. Examination of the other courses shows this to be false. A misinterpretation such as this could eventually lead to incorrect file design and in the worst case a working computer system which only allowed one tutor per course!

(e) Other important points to come out of close examination of the table are:
- a student can take more than one course (e.g. Barker)
- a tutor can tutor on more than one course (e.g. Hooper)
- a student can have the same tutor on more than one course (e.g. Morris)

9.5 Exercises

1. Given the following table are the following statements true or false?
   (a) A customer can have more than one salesman.
   (b) A salesman can have more than one customer.
   (c) A discount code is associated with only one discount percentage.
   (d) The total sales to date is determined solely by customer number.

Salesman Number	Salesman Name	Cust. Number	Cust. Name	Cust. Disc-Code	Cust. Disc-%	Total-Sales To-Date
002	Kellerman	257	Jones	A	10	2272
		286	Brown	B	15	189
		295	Foster	B	15	23652
014	Adams	317	Green	C	20	24272
		352	Tate	A	10	5734
027	Jennings	463	Young	O	0	5734
		494	Peacock	C	20	4153
		295	Foster	B	15	2253

9.6 Identifying Key Fields

Every relation must have a key field or fields. The value in the key field(s) must provide a unique reference to each row in the relation of data. Since a key should be as short as possible the key should be numeric or a code in preference to a text field, where a choice exists. In the Student results example in Figure 9.5 the best choice of key field for the relation is Course-Code. Course-Title is a possible key but it is possible that another course could be added to the relation, which would have a different Course-Code but the same Course-Title.

9.7 Exercises

1. Choose a key field for the Salesman table in Exercise 9.5.1

2. Choose a key field for the Employee Details table in Exercise 9.2.1

9.8 Normalisation

9.8.1 First Normal Form (FNF)

DEFINITION:

Any relation is in First Normal Form when it contains no repeating groups.

A repeating group is a field or set of fields which occur more than once for a single value of the key. If you look at the Student Results table in Figure 9.5 you can see that for each course there is a repeating group of data about students. A row in our table can be considered to be the course identification fields plus the repeating group of fields about students. To produce relations in First Normal Form, the original un-normalised relation is split into two. The fields that do not repeat are removed into one relation as shown in Figure 9.6.

Course Code	Course Title
SYA	Systems Analysis
COB	COBOL
PAS	Pascal

Figure 9.6 Course details.

and the repeating data produces another relation that has appended to it the original key - Course Code, as shown in Figure 9.7.

We must now identify keys for the two relations in Figures 9.6 and 9.7. A given value of Course-Code uniquely identifies one row in the Course details relation in Figure 9.6, so Course-Code is a suitable key for this relation.

Course-Code does not uniquely identify a row in the Course student details relation so we require a COMPOUND KEY. A compound key is made up of two or more fields which together uniquely identify a row.

Course Code	Student Code	Student Name	Date of Birth	Tutor Code	Tutor Name	Grade	Result
SYA	A2345	Smith	20.08.69	1746	Jones	A	Dist.
SYA	A7423	Barker	03.04.59	1746	Jones	C	Pass
SYA	B3716	Green	23.02.70	1330	Jarvis	D	Pass
SYA	A3472	Harris	17.07.69	1746	Jones	F	Fail
SYA	B9843	Green	10.11.68	1330	Jarvis	B	Merit
COB	A7423	Barker	03.04.59	1520	Hooper	E	Fail
COB	A4217	Morris	17.01.68	1520	Hooper	B	Merit
COB	B8238	Carter	09.12.69	1520	Hooper	C	Pass
PAS	A4217	Morris	17.01.68	1520	Hooper	A	Dist.
PAS	B9843	Green	10.11.68	1283	Trotter	B	Merit
PAS	A3393	Davies	30.09.69	1283	Trotter	E	Fail
PAS	A4247	Cross	25.12.69	1520	Hooper	C	Pass

Figure 9.7 Course student details.

If Student-Code alone was the key to Course student details then we would not be able to find out the title of a course which a student is taking. By identifying a compound key we can maintain the link between the two relations. Course-Code and Student-Code provide a suitable compound key for this relation, as Student-Code provides a unique identifier for each occurrence of the repeating group.

The relations in Figures 9.6 and 9.7 are now in First Normal Form as they do not contain any repeating groups. Writing out relations in the form of data tables can be very time- consuming and, once the data has been thoroughly digested and understood, it is normal practice to show the normalisation process in terms of field names as in Figure 9.8.

9.8.2 Exercises

1. Remove the repeating groups from the Salesman Table in Exercise 9.5.1 to produce First Normal Form Tables. Show this process in terms of field names (as in Figure 9.8).

2. Remove the repeating groups from the Employees Table in Exercise 9.2.1 to produce First Normal Form Tables. Show this process in terms of field names.

UNF	FNF	SNF	TNF
Course-Code	Course-Code		
Course-Title	Course-Title		
Student-Code			
Student-Name	Course-Code		
Date-of-Birth	Student-Code		
Tutor-Code	Student-Name		
Tutor-Name	Date-of-Birth		
Grade	Tutor-Code		
Result	Tutor-Name		
	Grade		
	Result		

UNF - Un-normalised Form **FNF - First Normal Form**
SNF - Second Normal Form **TNF - Third Normal Form**

The key fields are underlined.

Figure 9.8 Student results by course in first normal form.

9.8.3 Second Normal Form (SNF)

DEFINITION:

Any relation already in First Normal Form is also in Second Normal Form if either the key is a single item or the non-key items are fully dependent on the WHOLE key.

First Normal Form (FNF) analysis has yielded the relations shown in Figures 9.6 and 9.7 - the Course relation and the Course-Student relation respectively.

In Second Normal Form (SNF) analysis, each non-key field is examined to see whether it is dependent on the whole key or on only part of the key. The first relation has a single data item as its key - Course-Code (this is termed a SIMPLE key) and so SNF analysis cannot simplify the relation. The relation is said to already be in SNF. However, the second relation has a COMPOUND key made up of two fields Course-Code and Student-Code. Each non-key field in this relation is now examined.

Student-Name and Date-of-Birth are determined by Student-Code alone i.e. given a value of Student-Code the values of Student-Name and Date-of-Birth can be determined exactly.

Tutor-Code, Tutor-Name, Grade and Result are whole key dependent - they are determined by Course-Code AND Student-Code. Neither of these is alone sufficient to determine the four non-key fields.

As Student-Name and Date-of-Birth are dependent only upon Student- Code they are removed from the Course-Student relation to give another relation shown in Figure 9.9.

It should be noted that in this Student relation each Student-Code only occurs once, in contrast to the Course-Student relation (Figure 9.3) where a Student-Code can appear in more than one row (for example A7423). This is one of the aims of normalisation - to eliminate data redundancy. There is no point in storing Student-Name every time the Student-Code is stored - it wastes space and can lead to inconsistencies. However some duplication of keys is essential to maintain the link between relations.

Having removed Student-Name and Date-of-Birth the Course-Student relation now looks like Figure 9.10.

Student Code	Student Name	Date-of Birth
A2345	Smith	20.08.69
A7423	Barker	03.04.59
B3716	Green	23.02.70
A3472	Harris	17.07.69
B9843	Green	10.11.68
A4217	Morris	17.01.68
B8238	Carter	09.12.69
A3393	Davies	30.09.6
A4247	Cross	25.12.69

Figure 9.9 Student relation.

Course Code	Student Code	Tutor Code	Tutor Name	Grade	Result
SYA	A2345	1746	Jones	A	Dist.
SYA	A7423	1746	Jones	C	Pass
SYA	B3716	1330	Jarvis	D	Pass
SYA	A3472	1746	Jones	F	Fail
SYA	B9843	1330	Jarvis	B	Merit
COB	A7423	1520	Hooper	E	Fail
COB	A4217	1520	Hooper	B	Merit
COB	B8238	1520	Hooper	C	Pass
PAS	A4217	1520	Hooper	A	Dist.
PAS	B9843	1283	Trotter	B	Merit
PAS	A3393	1283	Trotter	E	Fail
PAS	A4247	1520	Hooper	C	Pass

Figure 9.10 Course-Student relation.

This process is often termed removal of part-key dependencies. Writing out the whole process in terms of field names, as done with First Normal Form, gives the table in Figure 9.11.

UNF	FNF	SNF	TNF
<u>Course-Code</u>	<u>Course-Code</u>	<u>Course-Code</u>	
Course-Title	Course-Title	Course-Title	
Student-Code			
Student-Name	<u>Course-Code</u>	<u>Course-Code</u>	
Date-of-Birth	<u>Student-Code</u>	<u>Student-Code</u>	
Tutor-Code	Student-Name	Tutor-Code	
Tutor-Name	Date-of-Birth	Tutor-Name	
Grade	Tutor-Code	Grade	
Result	Tutor-Name	Result	
	Grade		
	Result	<u>Student-Code</u>	
		Student-Name	
		Date-of-Birth	

Figure 9.11 Normalisation table to second normal form for Student Results example.

9.8.4 Exercises

1. Perform second normal form analysis on the salesman table in exercise 9.5.1. Present the results in terms of field names.

2. Perform second normal form analysis on the employees table in exercise 8.2.1.

9.8.5 Third Normal Form (TNF)

DEFINITION:

> Any relation already in Second Normal Form is also in Third Normal Form if all non-key fields are independent of all other non-key fields and all key fields are independent of all other key fields.

So far in our example, we have three relations in SNF: the Course relation (Figure 9.6), the Course-Student relation (Figure 9.10) and the Student relation (Figure 9.9). The first step is to look at all the non-key fields in each relation and see whether any of them are dependent upon any other. The Course relation has only one non-key field Course-Title and so this is not investigated further.

The Course-Student relation, however, has some interesting properties. Firstly, Tutor-Name is determined by Tutor-Code i.e. given a value for Tutor-Code there is only one possible value for Tutor Name. Secondly, examination of the data shows that Result is determined by Grade i.e. given a value for Grade there is only one possible Result. The reverse is not true - a value of Result does NOT give only one possible Grade. For example, a Result of 'Pass' is associated with a Grade of C OR D.

The Student relation does not have any non-key interdependencies. Both non-key fields Student-Name and Date-of-Birth are determined by the key field Student-Code.

The second step, which is often overlooked, applies to relations with a COMPOUND key. It is similar to the previous step except that now inter-key dependencies are examined. This is only relevant to the Course-Student relation. The questions to ask are:

(a) "Given a value of Course-Code is there only one possible value for Student-Code?" - Answer NO

(b) "Given a value for Student-Code is there only one possible value for Course-Code?" - Answer NO

Hence there are no inter-key dependencies. The non-key dependencies are now moved from the Course-Student relation to give two new relations - Tutor (Figure 9.12) and Grade (Figure 9.13). No data has been lost by splitting this relation, we can still find the name of student A2345's tutor and that Grade A means a Distinction.

Tutor Code	Tutor Name
1746	Jones
1330	Jarvis
1520	Hooper
1283	Trotter

Figure 9.12 Tutor relation.

Grade	Result
A	Dist.
B	Merit
C	Pass
D	Pass
E	Fail
F	Fail

Figure 9.13 Grade relation.

The new Course-Student relation is now shown in Figure 9.14. Note that the keys of the new relations Tutor-Code and Grade are retained in the Course-Student relation to maintain the links between relations.

The field name table for the complete normalisation process can now be drawn and is shown in Figure 9.15.

Course Code	Student Code	Tutor Code	Grade
SYA	A2345	1746	A
SYA	A7423	1746	C
SYA	B3716	1330	D
SYA	A3472	1746	F
SYA	B9843	1330	B
COB	A7423	1520	E
COB	A4217	1520	B
COB	B8238	1520	C
PAS	A4217	1520	A
PAS	B9843	1283	B
PAS	A3393	1283	E
PAS	A4247	1520	C

Figure 9.14 Course-Student relation.

UNF	FNF	SNF	TNF
Course-Code	Course-Code	Course-Code	Course-Code
Course-Title	Course-Title	Course-Title	Course-Title
Student-Code			
Student-Name	Course-Code	Course-Code	Course-Code
Date-of-Birth	Student-Code	Student-Code	Student-Code
Tutor-Code	Student-Name	Tutor-Code	Tutor-Code
Tutor-Name	Date-of-Birth	Tutor-Name	Grade
Grade	Tutor-Code	Grade	
Result	Tutor-Name	Result	Student-Code
	Grade		Student-name
	Result	Student-Code	Date-of-Birth
		Student-Name	
		Date-of-Birth	Tutor-Code
			Tutor-Name
			Grade
			Result

Figure 9.15 Complete normalisation table for Student Results example.

The original relation (Figure 9.5) has produced five relations which are fully normalised and shown as a summary in Figure 9.16.

Course Relation

Course Code	Course-Title
COB	COBOL
PAS	Pascal
SYA	Systems Analysis

Course-Student Relation

Course Code	Student Code	Tutor Code	Grade
SYA	A2345	1746	A
SYA	A7423	1746	C
SYA	B3716	1330	D
SYA	A3472	1746	F
SYA	B9843	1330	B
COB	A7423	1520	E
COB	A4217	1520	B
COB	B8238	1520	C
PAS	A4217	1520	A
PAS	B9843	1283	B
PAS	A3393	1283	E
PAS	A4247	1520	C

Tutor Relation

Tutor Code	Tutor Name
1330	Jarvis
1520	Hooper
1283	Trotter
1746	Jones

Student Relation

Student Code	Student Name	Date-of Birth
A2345	Smith	20.08.69
A7423	Barker	03.04.59
B3716	Green	23.02.70
A3472	Harris	17.07.69
B9843	Green	10.11.68
A4217	Morris	17.01.68
B8238	Carter	09.12.69
A3393	Davies	30.09.69
A4247	Cross	25.12.69

Grade Relation

Grade Code	Result
A	Dist.
B	Merit
C	Pass
D	Pass
E	Fail
F	Fail

Figure 9.16 The five normalised relations for the Student Results example

A convenient notation for recording TNF relations is shown in Figure 9.17. The asterisks are placed against FOREIGN keys. A foreign key is a non-key field in one relation which is a key, or part of a key, in another relation.

Course	**Student**	**Course -Student**	**Tutor**	**GRADE**
Course-Code	**Student-Code**	**Course-Code**	**Tutor-Code**	**Grade**
Course Title	**Student Name**	**Student-Code**	**Tutor Name**	**Result**
		Date of Birth	***Tutor Code**	
			***Grade**	

Figure 9.17 TNF relations for Student Results Example.

9.8.6 Exercises

1. Perform third normal form analysis on the salesman example in Exercise 9.5.1.

2. Perform third normal form analysis on the employees example in Exercise 9.2.1.

9.9 Overview

The three stages of normalisation are summarised below:

1. First Normal Form - remove repeating groups

2. Second Normal Form - remove part-key dependencies

3. Third Normal Form - remove non-key interdependencies and inter-key dependencies.

9.10 Another example

The example used to demonstrate the normalisation process - the Student Results relation - is in the form of a report. Reports of one kind or another occur in all systems and will need to be normalised if the system is to be properly analy. However, they are not the only documents of interest. There are also transactional documents such as orders, invoices, credit notes etc. which trigger some action such as production of goods, payment of bills, purchase of materials etc. The example chosen is an invoice, a sample of which is shown in Figure 9.18.

The choice of key for this document is not difficult, Invoice-Number uniquely identifies an invoice. There is also a repeating group corresponding to a line of the invoice i.e. product details. We shall have to assume however that a given product will only ever appear ONCE on an invoice, so that a line on an invoice can be identified by the Invoice-Number and Product-Code alone. The normalisation process is shown in Figure 9.19. The relations produced are shown in Figure 9.20.

The process illustrated in Figure 9.19 obviously needs some explanation. Producing FNF is straightforward enough - the repeating group corresponding to a line on the invoice is removed. SNF is also reasonably easy as Description, Unit of Sale and Price are determined by Product Code alone and so can be removed. In TNF, the Customer data is removed form the Invoice relation as Customer Name and Customer Addr. are determined by Customer Number but also four fields Total (ex. VAT), VAT, Total Payable and Amount have disappeared! The reason for this is that they are all DERIVABLE fields. Their values can be obtained from other fields by calculation. Amount is obtained by multiplying Price by Quantity, Total (ex. VAT) is obtained by summing all the Amount fields for a particular invoice, VAT is obtained by multiplying Total (ex. VAT) by 0.15, and Total Payable is obtained by adding Total (ex. VAT) and VAT.

These derivable fields are therefore determined by other fields and are hence removed in Third Normal Form but they are not quite the same as the Grade/Result fields in the Student records example. These latter fields are related by a "look-up" table which is removed as a separate relation (see Grade relation in Figure 17). Derivable fields are related by a mathematical or logical expression. There is no logical reason why these fields should not be calculated every time they are required - they are logically redundant.

However, when the relations are implemented physically and form the basis of a database or set of files, it may be decided that some or all of these derivable values should be stored to avoid recalculating them every time they are required. If they are, it will be essential to maintain consistency between the derivable fields and the rest of the data.

GUY, LEJK AND MELDRUM LTD
INVOICE

Invoice Number **346782** **Date 9/7/88**

Customer Number **2657**

Name & Address **F. D. Jones & Son**
Preference House
Market Rd.
Manchester
M20 7MY

Product Code	Description	Unit of Sale	Price	Quantity	Amount
BC100	Blue paper towel	3600	9.25	100	925.00
GR100	Green roll towel	18	23.25	10	232.50
MS123	P.V.C. waste sack	25	20.80	30	624.00
WP250	Clear polythene bags	1000	3.50	10	35.00

Total (exclusive of VAT)	1816.50	
VAT @15%	272.47	
Total payable		2088.97

Figure 9.18 Sample invoice to be normalised.

UNF	FNF	SNF	TNF
Invoice-Number	Invoice-Number	Invoice-Number	Invoice-Number
Invoice Date	Invoice Date	Invoice Date	Invoice Date
Cust. Number	Cust. Number	Cust. Number	Cust. Number
Customer Name	Customer Name	Customer Name	
Customer Addr.	Customer Addr.	Customer Addr.	Customer-Number
Total (ex. VAT)	Total (ex. VAT)	Total (ex. VAT)	Customer Name
VAT	VAT	VAT	Customer Addr.
Total Payable	Total Payable	Total Payable	
Product Code			Invoice-Number
Description	Invoice-Number	Invoice-Number	Product-Code
Unit of Sale	Product-Code	Product-Code	Quantity
Price	Description	Quantity	
Quantity	Unit of Sale	Amount	Product-Code
Amount	Price		Description
	Quantity	Product-Code	Unit of Sale
	Amount	Description	Price
		Unit of Sale	
		Price	

Figure 9.19 Complete normalisation table for Invoice example.

Invoice	Invoice -Product	Product	Customer
Invoice-Number	Invoice-Number	Product-Code	Cust.-Number
Invoice Date	Product-Code	Description	Customer Name
*Customer Number	Quantity	Unit of Sale	Customer Addr.
		Price	

Figure 9.20 The four normalised relations for the Invoice example.

9.11 Exercise

9.11.1 Normalise the data on the following car insurance certificate.

Certificate Number **253/390610/86/2**

Description of Vehicle **ANY PRIVATE MOTOR CAR THE PROPERTY OF THE POLICYHOLDER OR HIRED TO THE POLICYHOLDER UNDER A HIRE PURCHASE AGREEMENT.**

Name of Policyholder **MRS M JONES**

Date of commencement **Date of expiry**
17TH. JUNE 1988 **16TH. JUNE 1989**

PERSONS OR CLASSES OF PERSONS ENTITLED TO DRIVE AS DEFINED IN BCF BELOW

A) **The Policyholder**
B) **The Policyholder, who may also drive a private type motor car not belonging to him/her and not hired to him/her under a hire purchase agreement.**
C) **The Policyholder's spouse.**
D) **Any person who is driving on the order of or with the permission of the Policyholder**
E) **Any person other than the person or persons specified at (G) below**
F) **Names persons as specified at (G) below.**
G) **MS. E. JONES, MR. J. JONES**

LIMITATIONS AS TO USE AS DEFINED IN PARAGRAPHS MN BELOW BUT SUBJECT TO THE EXCLUSIONS U BELOW

M) **Use for social domestic and pleasure purposes including use for journeys between residence and permanent place of business**
N) **Use by the Policyholder in person in connection with his/her business**
P) **Use for the business of the Policyholder and/or the Policyholder's employer or partner**

EXCLUSIONS

T) **Use in connection with any trade, business or profession**
U) **Use for commercial travelling**
V) **Use for any purpose in connection with the motor trade**

9.12 Sensible choice of keys

Returning to the first example - Student Results - the choice of key for the un-normalised form of Figure 9.5 was, to a large extent, influenced by the way the data was presented. The table was in order of Course-Code and so Course-Code was a sensible choice of key. However, the examinations officer may well have wanted the results presented by grade as shown in Figure 9.21.

Grade	Result	Student Code	Student Name	Date of Birth	Course Code	Course Title	Tutor Code	Tutor Name
A	Dist.	A2345	Smith	20.08.69	SYA	Sys Anal	1746	Jones
		A4217	Morris	17.01.68	PAS	Pascal	1520	Hooper
B	Merit	A4217	Morris	17.01.68	COB	COBOL	1520	Hooper
		B9843	Green	10.11.68	SYA	Sys Anal	1330	Jarvis
		B9843	Green	10.11.68	PAS	Pascal	1283	Trotter
C	Pass	A4247	Cross	25.12.69	PAS	Pascal	1520	Hooper
		A7423	Barker	03.04.59	SYA	Sys Anal	1746	Jones
		B8238	Carter	09.12.69	COB	COBOL	1520	Hooper
D	Pass	B3716	Green	23.02.70	SYA	Sys Anal	1330	Jarvis
E	Fail	A7423	Barker	03.04.59	COB	COBOL	1520	Hooper
		A3393	Davies	30.09.69	PAS	Pascal	1283	Trotter
F	Fail	A3472	Harris	17.07.69	SYA	Sys Anal	1746	Jones

Figure 9.21 Student Results By Grade

On the face of it, we should be able to adopt the same approach as when the data was presented in Course Code sequence. We now have six rows with repeating student data and a key of Grade would seem to be sensible. Normalisation would then proceed as in Figure 9.22.

This looks rather complicated and "messy". Comparing this table with Figure 9.16 shows that the normalisation process gives some different relations in FNF, SNF and finally TNF. The relation produced in FNF by removing the repeating group has a compound key made up of three part keys i.e. Grade, Student Code and Course Code. As no fields depend upon ALL three of these together, the three keys end up as a KEY-ONLY relation in SNF. Examination of inter-key dependencies shows that Grade is determined by Student Code and Course Code, so the key-only relation is modified in TNF to one with Student Code and Course Code as a compound key and Grade as a non-key field. In TNF there are therefore two relations with the same key as shown in Figure 9.23.

UNF	FNF	SNF	TNF
Grade	Grade	Grade	Grade
Result	Result	Result	Result
Student Code			
Student-Name	Grade	Grade	Student-Code
Date-of-Birth	Student-Code	Student-Code	Course-Code
Course-Code	Course-Code	Course-Code	Grade
Course Title	Student Name		
Tutor Code	Date of Birth	Student-Code	Student-Code
Tutor Name	Course Title	Course-Code	Course-Code
	Tutor Code	Tutor Code	Tutor Code
	Tutor Name	Tutor Name	
			Tutor-Code
		Student-Code	Tutor Name
		Student Name	
		Date of Birth	Student-Code
			Student Name
		Course-Code	Date of Birth
		Course Title	
			Course-Code
			Course Title

Figure 9.22 Normalisation table for Student Results By Grade example

Student-Code	Student-Code
Course-Code	Course-Code
*Grade	*Tutor Code

Figure 9.23 Two TNF relations with the same key in Student Results By Grade example.

A process called optimisation (see Section 9 in this chapter) allows these relations to be merged to form one as shown in Figure 9.24:

<u>Student-Code</u>
<u>Course-Code</u>
***Grade**
***Tutor Code**

Figure 9.24 Optimised TNF Relations.

So, the net result is the same. Normalisation is based on sound mathematical principles and, in theory, the choice of key for the un- normalised relation is immaterial - the answer will be the same whatever key is chosen. In practice, however, an uneducated choice of key can lead to a complicated normalisation process as the above example illustrates. It would be easy to make a mistake.

The basic problem in the example is that Grade is itself determined by Student Code and Course Code and is hence a bad choice of key. A good rule of thumb is to pick a key for the un-normalised relation which is NOT determined by any other field or combination of fields and which still uniquely identifies a row. There may not be one single field for which this is true and a compound key may have to be chosen for the un-normalised relation. For the student results example there are only two CANDIDATE keys - Student Code and Course Code. One could argue that Student Code is determined by all the other fields associated with it but it is theoretically possible for two students to have the same name, be born on the same day, study the same courses with the same tutor and achieve the same results. They will however have different Student Codes. It is therefore necessary to be cautious about choice of key and it is sometimes wise to rewrite the data in a different form to arrive at a sensible choice.

9.13 Exercise

1. Rewrite the salesman table in Exercise 9.5.1 in Customer-Number sequence and make the salesman a repeating group within customer. Normalise this table.

9.14 Optimisation

In practice, the fields which a relation contains will be obtained from several sources. It is extremely unlikely that all the data associated with an entity will appear in only one document. If several documents are normalised it is likely that some of the resulting relations will have the same key. Optimisation is the process of merging relations with identical keys.

Returning to the Student Results example, another document dealing with student records has been normalised and produced the relation shown in Figure 9.25.

<u>Student-Code</u>
Student Name
Student Home Address
Student Home Tel No
Student Term Address
Student Term Tel No

Figure 9.25 Additional relation for Student Results example.

We already have a Student relation from the first document and it is shown again in Figure 9.26.

<u>Student-Code</u>
Student Name
Date of Birth

Figure 9.26 Student relation.

The two relations are identified by the same key and they are separate relations simply because the different details associated with a student are held in different places in the student records system. They can be merged to produce one Student relation as in Figure 9.27.

<u>Student-Code</u>
Student Name
Date of Birth
Student Home Address
Student Home Tel.No.
Student Term Address
Student Term Tel No

Figure 9.27 Merged Student Relations.

Any other student details obtained from other sources could then be merged with this relation so that all the fields determined by Student Number are held in the same place.

Although this appears a simple, mechanical process, great care must be taken not to lose some hidden meaning or real world significance by merging relations with the same key. For example, the student records office keep the details of students who have withdrawn from a course separate to students who are still studying. They also append the withdrawal date to the student record and delete their term time details so that two relations could arise as shown in Figure 9.28.

Current Student	**Withdrawn Student**
<u>Student-Code</u>	**<u>Student-Code</u>**
Student Name	**Student Name**
Date of Birth	**Date of Birth**
Student Home Address	**Student Home Address**
Student Home Tel.No.	**Student Home Tel.No.**
Student Term Address	**Withdrawal Date**
Student Term Tel No	

Figure 9.28 Relations for Current Student and Withdrawn Student.

If these relations are merged because they have the same key, we could lose a useful way of distinguishing between current and withdrawn students. As a result, the relations can be left separate or a status indicator added to the Student relation (a simple flag would suffice with 'C' for current and 'W' for withdrawn).

9.15 Composite Keys

One of the difficulties students of data analysis tend to experience is the ability to distinguish between COMPOUND and COMPOSITE keys. They are different and they both occur widely in practice. The problem is that they appear very similar and the difference between them is rather subtle. The difference is best illustrated with an example. The table in Figure 9.29 shows the breakdown of student marks on different courses by assignment number.

Course Code	Course Title	Student Code	Student Name	Ass. No.	Ass. Subject	Ass. Mark
SYA	Systems Analysis	A2345	Smith	1	Data Flow Diagrams	72
				2	Normalisation	67
				3	Dialogue Design	83
		A7423	Barker	1	Data Flow Diagrams	59
				2	Normalisation	47
				3	Dialogue Design	62
		B3716	Green	1	Data Flow Diagrams	45
				2	Normalisation	42
				3	Dialogue Design	51
COB	COBOL	A7423	Barker	1	Sequential Files	37
				2	Relative Files	31
		A4217	Morris	1	Sequential Files	69
				2	Relative Files	62

Figure 9.29 Student Assignment Marks

In this example, we have a repeating group within a repeating group. This is termed a NESTED repeating group. For each course there is repeating student data and for each student there is repeating assignment data. How this is dealt with in the first stage of normalisation is quite logical and is shown later in Figure 9.32.

During normalisation, one of the problems will be uniquely identifying a particular assignment. Course-Code is not sufficient as a there is more than one assignment per course. The key will have to be a combination of Course-Code and Ass.-Number which appears to be a COMPOUND key containing two SIMPLE keys. However, this is an example of a COMPOSITE key not a COMPOUND key and it is written as in Figure 9.30 with brackets surrounding the constituent parts.

(Course-Code)
(Ass.-Number)

Figure 9.30 Composite key

The Ass. Number has to be qualified by a higher level simple key. Ass. Number is not a unique key because it does not uniquely identify anything. An Ass. Number of 1 could refer to a number of assignments for different courses. In contrast the key in Figure 9.31

Course-Code
Student-Code

Figure 9.31 Compound key

is a COMPOUND key as both Course Code and Student Code are unique keys - a given Course Code uniquely identifies a particular course and a given Student Code uniquely identifies a particular student. The nature of the data determined by this compound key is the reason for these two unique keys having to be combined. When Converting FNF to SNF, a composite key should be treated as a special case of a simple key. It is not possible to have part-key dependency on the lower non-unique part of the key but it is possible on the higher unique part. The normalisation is now shown in Figure 9.32.

The TNF relations are shown in Figure 9.33.

The nested repeating groups are dealt with by applying the rules for FNF twice: once to remove the student data and then again to remove the assignment data.

The key of the MARK relation is a COMPOUND key made up of a SIMPLE key, Student Code, and a COMPOSITE key, Course Code and Ass. Number.

UNF	FNF	SNF	TNF
Course-Code	Course-Code	Course-Code	Course-Code
Course Title	Course Title	Course Title	Course Title
Student Code			
Student Name	Course-Code	Course-Code	Course-Code
Ass. Number	Student-Code	Student-Code	Student-Code
Ass. Subject	Student Name		
Ass. Mark			
	Student-Code	Student-Code	Student-Code
	Student Name	Student Name	(Course-Code)
			(Ass.-Number)
	Student-Code	Student-Code	
	Ass. Subject	(Course-Code)	(Course-Code)
	Ass. Mark	(Ass.-Number)	(Ass.-Number)
			Ass. MarkAss. Mark
		(Course-Code)	(Course-Code)
		(Ass.-Number)	(Ass.-Number)
		Ass. Subject	Ass. Subject

Figure 9.32 Normalisation table for Student Assignment Marks example.

COURSE	COURSE -STUDENT	STUDENT	MARK	ASS/MENT
Course-Code	Course-Code	Stud.-Code	Stud.-Code	(Course-Code)
Course-Title	Stud.-Code	Stud.-Name	(Course-Code)	(Ass.-Number)
			(Ass.-Number)	Ass.-Subject
			Ass. Mark	

Figure 9.33 TNF relations for Student Assignment Marks example.

9.16 Exercise

9.16.1 Normalise the following statement from a mail-order catalogue.

Period covered by this statement
24TH. MAR TO 21ST. APR

MRS. M. JONES
32 EASTCLIFFE RISE
WHITLEY BAY
TYNE & WEAR
NE23 4RT

Agents's Number	Statement Number	Page Number
9680805-5	21	1

Ref No	Date	Description	Quantity	Value
		BALANCE BROUGHT FORWARD		57.54
0157	18 APR	PAYMENT - THANK YOU		20.25-
		<u>RETURNS</u>		
0159	19 APR	FG086 TROUSERS CORAL 134	1	18.99-
0165	20 APR	FX469 KNITTED SHIRT PEACH 134/14	1	5.99-
		<u>ORDERS</u>		
T0149	7 APR	FG086 TROUSERS CORAL 134	1	8.99
T0155	7 APR	JG201 SHOES WHITE 2	1	13.99
		<u>OTHER ITEMS</u>		
0144	25 MAR	INSUFFICIENT COMMISSION CHARGE		33.58
		<u>ITEMS NOT CHARGED</u>		
T0130	25 MAR	FG138 SHIRT MINT 122/12	1	
T0140	25 MAR	FX469 KNITTED SHIRT PINK 122/12	1	
		BALANCE OUTSTANDING AT 21.4.88		78.87

9.17 Generated Keys

Suppose the invoice shown in Figure 9.18 were modified to allow the situation shown in Figure 9.34 where a product could appear on more than one line of an invoice.

Invoice Number **346782** **Date 9/7/88**

Customer Number **2657**

Name & Address **F. D. Jones & Son**
Preference House
Market Rd.
Manchester
M20 7MY

Product Code	Description	Unit of Sale	Price	Quantity	Amount
BC100	Blue paper towel	3600	9.25	100	925.00
GR100	Green roll towel	18	23.25	10	232.50
MS123	P.V.C. waste sack	250	20.80	30	624.00
WP250	Clear polythene bags	1000	3.50	10	35.00
GR100	Green roll towel	18	23.25	20	465.00
		Total (exclusive of VAT)			2281.50
		VAT @ 15%			342.23
		Total payable			2623.73

Figure 9.34 Modified Invoice example.

In this case, a compound key of Invoice-Number and Product-Code is NOT sufficient to uniquely identify a line and a GENERATED key will have to be invoked. This could be Invoice-Line-No. and would be introduced in FNF as in Figure 9.35.

UNF	FNF	SNF	TNF
Invoice-Number	Invoice-Number	Invoice-Number	Invoice-Number
Invoice Date	Invoice Date	Invoice Date	Invoice Date
Customer No.	Customer No.	Customer No.	Customer No.
Customer Name	Customer Name	Customer Name	
Customer Addr.	Customer Addr.	Customer Addr.	Customer-No.
Total (ex. VAT)	Total (ex. VAT)	Total (ex. VAT)	Customer Name
VAT	VAT	VAT	Customer Addr.
Total Payable	Total Payable	Total Payable	
Product Code			(Invoice-No.)
Description	(Invoice-No)	(Invoice-No.)	(Line-No.)
Unit of Sale	(Line-No.)	(Line-No.)	Product Code
Product-Code	Product Code	Product Code	Quantity
Price	Description	Description	
Quantity	Unit of Sale	Unit of Sale	Product-Code
Amount	Price	Price	Description
	Quantity	Quantity	Unit of Sale
	Amount	Amount	Price

Figure 9.35 Normalisation table for Modified Invoice example.

Note that the Invoice-Line-No. does not exist in the real system but is simply generated for convenience. It also forms part of a composite key and this is almost always the case with generated keys.

9.18 TNF Tests, Transitive Dependence and Implied Keys

In order to check that a TNF relation is really in Third Normal Form, there are two tests which can be applied:

(1) For a given value of the key, is there just one possible value for each of the non-key fields? If the answer is 'No', the relation is not in TNF.

(2) Are all of the non-key fields DIRECTLY dependent upon the key? Again, an answer of 'No' implies that the relation is not a true TNF relation.

The first test is relatively easy to apply. The second test is catered for in the transition from SNF to TNF but it is possible for relations to 'slip through the net' as the following example illustrates. A company offers discount at various rates to customers and a sample of this data is shown in Figure 9.36.

Customer Code	**Discount Rate (%)**
A1745	10
A5123	0
C7923	5
F3326	15
D4988	10
B5419	20
G4429	5

Figure 9.36 Customer Discount Codes

This yields the TNF relation in Figure 9.37.

Customer-Code
Discount Rate

Figure 9.37 TNF relation for Customer Discount Codes example

Applying the first TNF test to this relation gives an answer of 'Yes'. A given value of Customer-Code gives one and only one Discount-Rate. However, careful investigation of the company shows that each customer has a Discount-Code and it is this that determines the Discount-Rate according to the table in Figure 9.38.

Discount Code	Discount Rate (%)
A	0
B	5
C	10
D	15
E	20

Figure 9.38 Discount Code relation.

So the original relation is split in two, one of them having an IMPLIED key of Discount Code as shown in Figure 9.39.

Customer Code	Discount Code	Discount Code	Discount Rate (%)
A1745	C	A	0
A5123	A	B	5
C7923	B	C	10
F3326	D	D	15
D4988	C	E	20
B5419	E		
G4429	B		

Customer-Code	Discount-Code
*Discount Code	Discount Rate

Figure 9.39 Normalisation table and TNF relations for Customer Discount Codes example.

Splitting the table like this makes sense from a practical point of view. If the company were to change all or some of the discount rates, they would only have to change the second 'look-up' table, which can be done quickly as there are only five rows in it. The alternative would be changing the discount rate of all or a good proportion of the customers which could be very time-consuming.

The above is an example of transitive dependence in which a field which does have a unique value for a given key is not directly dependent on that key but on another key, part or all of which is dependent on the first key.

9.19 Key-only Relations

Sometimes a TNF relation is obtained after normalisation which consists entirely of keys. There is no data associated with the key. An example is the Course-Student relation shown in Figure 9.33 and shown again in Figure 9.40.

Course-Student

<u>Course-Code</u>
<u>Student-Code</u>

Figure 9.40 Relation consisting entirely of keys.

However, there is another relation with the same key which does contain some data in Figure 9.17 and this is shown again in Figure 9.41.

Course-Student

<u>Course-Code</u>
<u>Student-Code</u>
***Tutor Code**
***Grade**

Figure 9.41 Second Course Student Relation

These two relations can obviously be merged (optimised) to give the one in Figure 9.41 and so the key-only relation disappears.
There are occasions, however, where key-only relations remain after optimisation and the analyst/designer MAY be able to remove them from the final set of optimised TNF relations.

For example, consider the situation where, in a factory, the start and stop time of a machine is recorded for the various jobs it undertakes. A job will use several different machines and the normalisation process may appear as in Figure 9.42.

UNF	FNF	SNF	TNF
Machine-No.	Machine-No.	Machine-No.	Machine-No.
Job No.			
Job Start Time	Machine-No.	Machine-No.	Machine-No.
Job Finish Time	Job-No.	Job-No.	Job-No.
	Job Start Time	Job Start Time	Job Start Time
	Job Finish Time	Job Finish Time	Job Finish Time

Figure 9.42 Normalisation table for Machine Job Times example

The key-only relation Machine-No. has no data and serves no useful purpose, and during optimisation this type of relation can be dropped.

In contrast, consider the situation where a member of staff can be working on a number of projects at the same time and this situation leads the normalisation process in Figure 9.43.

The key-only data structure obtained is a valid TNF relation and it CANNOT be discarded if it persists after optimisation. Its removal would remove the link between a staff member and a project and hence its retention is vital.

Great care must be taken not to delete key-only relations which do serve some purpose. If the relation has any practical value or provides the only occurrence of a required link between the elements of the relation, then it should be retained.

UNF	FNF	SNF	TNF
<u>Personnel-No.</u>	**<u>Personnel-No.</u>**	**<u>Personnel-No.</u>**	**<u>Personnel-No.</u>**
Name	**Name**	**Name**	**Name**
Department	**Department**	**Department**	**Department**
Project-No.			
Project Name	**<u>Personnel-No.</u>**	**<u>Personnel-No.</u>**	**<u>Personnel-No.</u>**
Project Leader	**<u>Project-No.</u>**	**<u>Project-No.</u>**	**<u>Project-No.</u>**
	Project Name	**Project Leader**	
		<u>Project-No.</u>	**<u>Project-No.</u>**
		Project Name	**Project Name**
		Project Leader	**Project Leader**

Figure 9.43 Normalisation table for Staff Project Details example.

9.20 Worked Example

One of the outputs of Function Definition is the Input/Output Structures and Descriptions. The data items on important Input/Output Structures can be normalised and the resulting relations drawn as a Logical Data Structure. This Logical Data Structure can be compared with the Logical Data Model to ensure that the data structure can support the processing requirements. During analysis of the Car Allowance System the Logical Data Model was informally normalised as part of the process of producing the Required System Logical Data Model.

Once Function Definition has taken place the important Input/Output Structures can be normalised. As an example we will use the Input/Output Structure shown in Figures 8.5 and 8.6, 'Registration of car claim'. Figure 9.44 shows the normalisation process.

The four Third Normal Form relations are shown in Figure 9.45. Note that Total-claim-value can be calculated if the Allowance-grade and Total-mileage are known, so it has been omitted from the TNF relations. Compare these relations with the Logical Data Structure in Figure 6.27. The relations Employee, Car and Claim all correspond to the Logical Data Model, the additional data items may be needed to support other functions. The relation Employee/Car is not shown. There is not an M:N relationship between Employee and Car. The link between the two can be handled adequately by adding the Pay-no to the Car entity data items.

UNF	FNF	SNF	TNF
Pay-no	Pay-no	Pay-no	Pay-no
employee-name	employee-name	employee-name	employee-name
job-title	job-title	job-title	job-title
salary grade	salary grade	salary grade	salary grade
job-location	job-location	job-location	job-location
allowance grade	allowance-grade	allowance-grade	allowance-grade
car-make	total-mileage	total-mileage	total-mileage
car-model	total-claim-value	total-claim-value	
engine-cc			
registration-no	Pay-no	Pay-no	Pay-no
total-mileage	Registration-no	Registration-no	Registration-no
total-claim-value	car-make		
start-odometer	car-model	Registration-no	Registration-no
finish-odometer	engine-cc	car-make	car-make
		car-model	car-model
	Pay-no	engine-cc	engine-cc
	start-odometer		
	finish odometer	Pay-no	Pay-no
		Start-odometer	Start-odometer
		Finish-odometer	Finish-odometer

Figure 9.44 Normalised Input/Output Structure

EMPLOYEE	EMPLOYEE/CAR	CAR	CLAIM
Pay-no	Pay-no	Registration-no	Pay-no
employee-name	Registration-no	car-make	Start-odometer
job-title		car-model	Finish-odometer
job-location		engine-cc	
allowance grade			
total-mileage			

Figure 9.45 TNF relations for Input/Output Structure

9.21 Place of Relational Data Analysis in SSADM

9.21.1 Feasibility Study

Relational Data Analysis may be used to assist in the development of the Logical Data Model during the Feasibility Module.

9.21.2 Requirements Analysis

9.21.2.1 Step 140 Investigate Current Data

Relational Data Analysis can be used to help in the preparation of the Logical Data Model during this Step.

9.21.3 Requirements Specification

9.21.3.1 Step 320 Develop Required Data Model

Normalisation can be used an aid when building the Required Logical Data Model.

9.21.3.2 Step 340 Enhance Required Data Model

Relational Data Analysis is used during this Step to improve the quality of the Logical Data Model. A selection of inputs and outputs are normalised and the normalised relations can be built into individual data submodels for comparison with the Logical Data Model.

9.22 Summary

Relational Data Analysis is used to assist in understanding the data of a system under investigation. In SSADM the technique is applied to the documents and files in the system. The output from the process becomes the basis of file or database design. The process involves normalising data to third normal form. Data in first normal form has no repeating groups. Data in second normal form has no non-key data items which are dependant on only part of the key. Data in third normal form has no dependencies between key data items and no dependencies between non-key data items.

9.23 Keywords

Keyfields
Dependency
Determinacy
Unnormalised data
Compound key
Foreign key
Simple key
Repeating group
Relation
Logical Data Model
Input/Output Structures
First Normal Form
Second Normal Form
Third Normal Form
Repeating group
Composite key
Generated key
Optimisation
Nested repeating group
Entity
Function Definition
Key only relations

9.24 Exercises

1. Describe the process of normalising data to First Normal Form.

2. Describe the process of normalising data to Second Normal Form.

3. Describe the process of normalising data to Third Normal Form.

4. Develop a data submodel for the TNF relations in Figure 9.45.

5. Apply relational data analysis to any other Input/Output Structures which you have prepared for the Car Allowance System. Prepare a data submodel and compare this with the Logical Data Model in Figure 6.27.

CHAPTER TEN

Prototyping

10.1 Introduction

One of the main objectives of a system development project is to produce a system which meets the business and user needs. The production of a Requirements Specification states what the analyst thinks the business and the user need but it can be a very large volume of paperwork to digest. Although the users have been involved throughout the process of producing the Requirements Specification it is difficult to relate all the paper-based information to the software which they will eventually use. It would be helpful if the users could see a mock-up of at least part of the required system, some sort of software model of the system. The equivalent in manufacturing would be producing a scale model of a new car, rather than just presenting a drawing of the car.

Specification Prototyping in SSADM involves the production of such a software model. Selected parts of the user-interface with the system, dialogues and reports, are presented as a prototype. The prototype is a piece of software which contains menus and dialogues and can produce printed reports. The users view and use the prototype in a structured way and the outcome of each prototyping session is documented. Analysts are looking to users to identify areas such as missing functionality, confirmation of data formats and changes to dialogue to reflect the user method of working. The resultant changes are then made to the specification. For instance, the addition of new data items or processes would require additional documentation, minor changes to dialogues would cause modifications to existing documents.

The prototype allows users to gain a better idea of the end-product which they will be using but there are dangers. Users are presented with something which looks like a working system and wonder why it will take so long to implement. Users need to be given a clear vision of the scope and purpose of Specification Prototyping. The prototype demonstrations may raise the users' awareness of the capabilities of computer systems resulting in requests for all sorts of extra functionality. It is very important to avoid uncontrolled changes to the boundaries of the required system.

SSADM does not rule out the wider use of prototyping but Specification Prototyping has been built in to ensure the best possible Requirements Specification is produced.

10.2 Prototyping tools

Specification Prototyping requires a software tool which provides facilities for screen, menu and report painting. There should also be a data dictionary and a facility for on-line navigation. If a CASE tool is being used to develop the system then this should interface with the prototyping software, some CASE tools provide the facilities necessary for Specification Prototyping. A variety of specialist tools are available but some general purpose software, such as a 4GL, may also be used if it provides the necessary facilities.

The software product used for prototyping need not be the same product as is used to implement the full system since the prototype is usually discarded. Sometimes elements of the prototype are kept in the final system, for example report layouts and screen displays. In such circumstances compatibility between the software used for prototyping and full implementation would be required.

10.3 Specification Prototyping

10.3.1 Identify scope

The starting point for Specification Prototyping is a scoping document which defines the boundaries and the objectives of the exercise. This will have been provided by management. Using this document as a basis, the prototyping team require to select the aspects of the Requirements Specification which are to be prototyped.

Critical dialogues can be identified from the User Role/Function Matrix and these would normally be prototyped. In addition the users may request the inclusion of some other dialogues.

It is also useful to prototype output reports, particularly those which are constrained by factors external to the system. This might include outputs to other systems; outputs covered by legal constraints; documents required by external organisations such as the Inland Revenue.

10.3.2 Prototype Menu and Command Structures

The prototyping is based on the Menu and Command Structures produced by Dialogue Design (see Chapter 3). The prototypes should conform to the Installation Style Guide as far as possible. The menu prototypes are demonstrated to the users belonging to the appropriate user roles. Changes requested and agreed are implemented and the prototypes re-demonstrated. The changes are documented as described in section 10.3.6. SSADM products such as the Requirements Catalogue, Menu Structures etc. must be amended to incorporate the outcome of prototyping.

10.3.3 Prototype interaction of menus, screens and reports

Each dialogue or report to be prototyped is defined as a Prototype Pathway. This shows the route of the dialogue or report through the pathway for each User Role. The pathway shows the linking together of all the user interface requirements for the dialogue or the report, from the initiation point such as a main menu, through to the conclusion of the dialogue or report.

There are three types of component in a pathway: menus, screens and reports. Menus are identified from the Menu Structure for a User Role, these are a product of Dialogue Design (see Chapter 3). Screens are defined by identifying the Logical Groupings of Dialogue Elements for each of the Input/Output Structures required for prototyping (see Chapter 3). Reports are identified from the Input/Output Structures, the Input/Output Structure Description giving a list of the data items.

The pathway components can be combined in a diagram to create a Prototype Pathway. Each occurrence of a component type is represented by a square-cornered box. The components are linked by vertical lines. The diagram shows the progression through a dialogue from menu option to completion. Figure 10.1 shows a Prototype Pathway based on the Car Allowance System Case Study. It shows the menu and screen components of the "Register car claims" function and would be demonstrated to users representing the Accounts Officer User Role. The Input/Output Structure for this example is shown in Figure 3.9, the Menu Structure in Figure 3.10. Once a Prototype Pathway has been completed it can be implemented on the prototyping tool linking in to the existing menu prototypes.

10.3.4 Demonstrate and review prototypes

A Prototype Demonstration Objective Document is prepared for each Prototype Pathway (see section 10.6). This sets out an agenda for the demonstration. The prototype is demonstrated using appropriate demonstration data. The queries raised in the Prototype Demonstration Objective Document are examined in turn and the results of these deliberations are recorded in a Prototype Result Log with one of seven grades recorded for each potential change (see section 10.6).

10.3.5 Update the prototypes

The Team Leader must decide what action should be taken for each potential change. Some changes will require further demonstrations of a Prototype Pathway, particularly if major changes have been necessary. Care has to be taken to control the number of iterations of prototyping to ensure that the process is still adding value to Requirements Specification. Changes must be carefully considered and approved before being incorporated in the Requirements Specification. Any SSADM products affected by such changes must be updated to reflect the amended Requirements Specification. Any additional requirements identified must be recorded in the Requirements Catalogue.

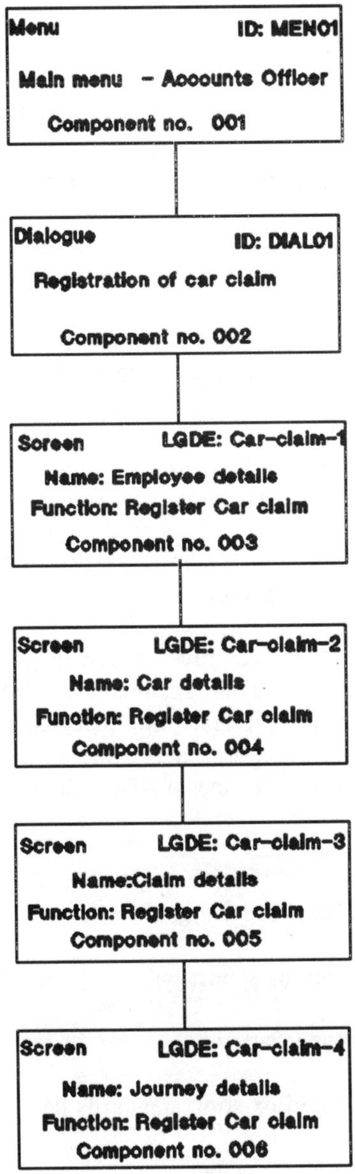

Figure 10.1 Prototype Pathway

10.3.6 Documentation

10.3.6.1 Prototype Pathways

The Prototype Pathway Document records one version of a Prototype Pathway, giving the function name, User Role, pathway no and a pathway diagram. Each version of a pathway is given a separate pathway no.

10.3.6.2 Prototype Demonstration Objective Documents

This document is prepared for every demonstration of a Prototype Pathway. It lists an agenda for the demonstration which can include administrative details such as " Explain the procedure of prototyping". It then lists a number of pathway components and identifies for each a particular query which the demonstration should resolve. For instance a report might be examined to ensure that the format of some specified data items is correct.

10.3.6.3 Prototype Result Logs

The Prototype Demonstration Objective Document lists a number of queries about pathway components. This document records the outcome of the deliberations for each of the queries. For instance it might record that the format of the data items on a report needs to be amended to a stated format. Each potential change is awarded one of seven change codes:

N No change required

C Cosmetic, affects presentation only

D Affects dialogue or report only

P affects Prototype Pathway

S Standards, should existing standards be changed to permit this?

A Analysis may be incorrect

G Global, this change has effects beyond the system boundary

10.3.6.4 Prototyping Report

Once all the changes to the documentation have been completed the Prototyping Report requires to be written. This discusses whether the prototyping process achieved the following:

i) matched the original prototyping scope

ii) met the objectives set

iii) changed the Requirements Specification

iv) added value to the project (if any)

10.4 Place of Specification Prototyping in SSADM

10.4.1 Requirements Specification

10.4.1.1 Step 320 Develop required data model

The Required Logical Data Model and the Data Catalogue are inputs to Specification Prototyping. The results of prototyping may be fed back into this Step if changes have been identified such as the addition of entities or of extra data items.

10.4.1.2 Step 330 Derive System Functions

The User Role/Function Matrix and the Input/Output Structures produced in this Step are inputs to Specification Prototyping. Function Definitions and User Roles are used as a reference.

Any changes to system processing identified by prototyping are fed back to this step so that the SSADM products concerned can be suitably modified.

10.4.1.3 Step 350 Develop Specification Prototypes

A set of Specification Prototypes is developed for critical dialogues and for any additional dialogues and reports selected by the analysts and users. The prototypes are demonstrated to the users, any changes required are documented and a final report is prepared. Other SSADM products may require to be updated as a result of Specification Prototyping. This step runs more or less in parallel with Step 330.

10.4.1.4 Step 360 Develop Processing Specification

Specification prototyping may identify new events. This will result in changes to the Entity-event Model which, in turn, will result in changes to the documentation produced in Step 330.

10.4.2 Logical System Specification

10.4.2.1 Step 510 Define User Dialogues

Dialogues at this point are defined as Logical Groupings of Data Elements. The Command Structures, Menu Structures and Prototyping Report produced during Step 350 are used as a reference during the process of Dialogue Design.

10.5 Summary

Specification Prototyping provides an opportunity for users to see a 'working model' of the user interface of the required system. The technique is used to identify gaps and errors in the Requirements Specification and to clarify issues such as presentation of data and users' preferred methods of working. The whole process must be carefully controlled and documented to ensure that it is adding value to the project. Any accepted changes affecting SSADM products must be implemented.

10.6 Keywords

Specification prototyping
Dialogues
Reports
Logical Data Model
Function Definition
Input/Output Structures
Menu Structures
Command Structures
Installation Style Guide
Prototype Demo. Objective Document
Prototype Pathway
Requirements Catalogue
Entity-event Modelling
Prototyping scope
Data Catalogue
User Role/Function Matrix
Prototyping Report
Screen formats
Prototype Result Logs

10.7 Exercises

1. Prototype selected dialogues and reports for the Car Allowance system.

2. Prototype selected dialogues and reports for the Telephone Allowance System.

3. Prototype selected dialogues and reports for the Student Administration System.

CHAPTER ELEVEN
Entity-event Modelling

11.1 Introduction

Entity-event Modelling is the SSADM technique which shows the sequence of events that affect groups of data held within a system. For every entity about which we want to hold data, an Entity Life History diagram depicts the events that can happen to that entity, and the time relationships between the events. Events affect an occurrence of an entity in a number of ways. For instance, in the Car Allowance System, an effect of the 'Register car claim' event is to create an occurrence of the Car Claim entity. Effect-Correspondence Diagrams show the relationship between effects for each event.

Just like Relational Data Analysis, an Entity Life History can be drawn purely from the viewpoint of a single system, and later, when that system's requirements have been defined, it can be fused with other Entity Life Histories of the same entity, which may occur in other systems. That, of course, assumes that the organization has some central controlling function to coordinate data processing development.

Entity Life Histories are mainly used in three ways in the creation of a new system. Firstly they are an aid to the analyst in gaining an understanding of the system he is investigating. Secondly, they are used to check the accuracy and completeness of prior work. Finally, they define the circumstances under which data can be inserted, modified and deleted in systems files.

Initially the analyst simply collects the events which affect the system, and notes them down for future reference. As he becomes more familiar with the system, the sequence of events can be deduced, and a diagram can be drawn for each of the entities in the system.

In fact, it would be more accurate to say that a number of versions of the set of diagrams can be drawn, because the thought required to document the life cycle of an entity usually uncovers incomplete prior analysis work. Moreover, because an Entity Life History describes the changes in state of an entity, it is a complex task to draw it. A moving target it harder to hit than a sitting one.

The checking of an Entity Life History by a user requires him to imagine every possible state which an entity can assume, and then to predict the conditions which cause the entity to change state. As many of these conditions will be exceptions, they will not spring readily to mind, and a number of iterations can be expected.

Once the system has been documented, the Entity-event Model shows the combinations of events with which the system must cope. In a computer-based system each event will lead to some update of the system's files. Therefore for each event there will be a program, or a program function. The analyst will need to define these functions, and then package them into programs, depending upon the limitations of the hardware and software to be employed.

A further use of the Entity Life Model is in peer group reviews of the analyst's work product. The diagrams are said to be easy to understand, and the group should be able to detect if anything is missing, or not completely understood. One of the worst mistakes that can be made in the design of a new system is the overlooking of some function which updates the system database. Entity-event Modelling is one way of avoiding such mistakes.

11.2 Definitions.

11.2.1 Entity

An entity is something about which we wish to collect data. It can be something real, such as an employee, a customer, or a machine; or it can be purely conceptual, such as the popularity rating of a political party at a given time.

11.2.2 Entity Occurrence

An entity occurrence is a particular instance of an entity. For example, in a Payroll system there would probably be an entity called Employee. If there are two hundred employees on the payroll, there will be two hundred entity occurrences. Each occurrence will have its own individual life history; but every such life history should conform to the same potential pattern.

NB: students who are familiar with programming, may find it helpful to think of an entity as a computer file, and an entity occurrence as a computer record. The analogy can be discarded later, once the concepts are understood properly.

11.2.3 Event

An event is a happening which is reported to the system and to which the system must respond, e.g. a customer walks into a shop, the whistle blows for the end of the day's work, a machine tool breaks down on the factory shop floor, or, as Sherlock Holmes pointed out, a dog does not bark in the night. It is something that triggers a process which changes the status of the data within the system.

11.2.4 Effect

This is the result of the process triggered by an event. In a computer-based system, it means the change in status that will occur to the database or system files. An effect will affect an occurrence of an entity in one of the following ways:

- create an entity occurrence
- amend an entity occurrence
- delete an entity occurrence
- alter the state indicator value (see section 11.4.6).

When looking at systems, it is easy to confuse events and effects. If you check with a dictionary, you will find that many of the words used to describe an effect are also used to describe an event. The word 'event' is also used to describe things which in SSADM terms are a process (e.g. a church fete). In computer terms, an effect is a change to a record in a file, and an event is the cause of that change.

11.3 Entity Life History Diagram Conventions.

11.3.1 Starting The Diagram

An Entity Life History is started with an oblong box at the top of the diagram containing the name of the entity. As an example, consider a system for a registry of births, marriages, and deaths. Such a system would probably deal with an entity called 'Man', a title which would include woman. Thus the Entity Life History appears as in Figure 11.1.

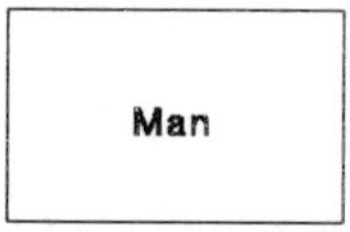

Figure 11.1 Subject entity of Entity Life History

11.3.2 Sequence

Two events which affect the entity 'Man' are his birth and death. For the purposes of this system assume that each event will only occur once for each occurrence of the entity, and the two events can only happen in one defined sequence. There is a convention for drawing such a combination of events. Each event is shown as a box with the name of the event within. As we will see later, there is the possibility of 'null' events being included. The 'Man' Entity Life History might appear as in Figure 11.2.

Such a pattern is called a Sequence. Every event in a Sequence must occur, and it must occur in the sequence defined by the positions of the event boxes from left to right.

11.3.3 Iteration

In the registry system, we also want to record marriages. A person can be married once, more than once, or not at all. This is known as an Iteration of

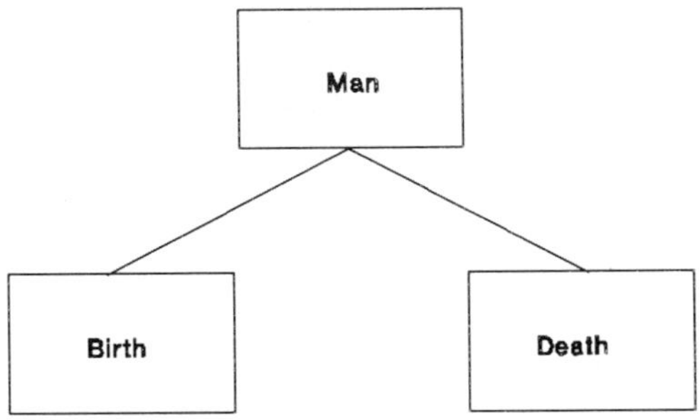

Figure 11.2 Entity Life History showing sequence.

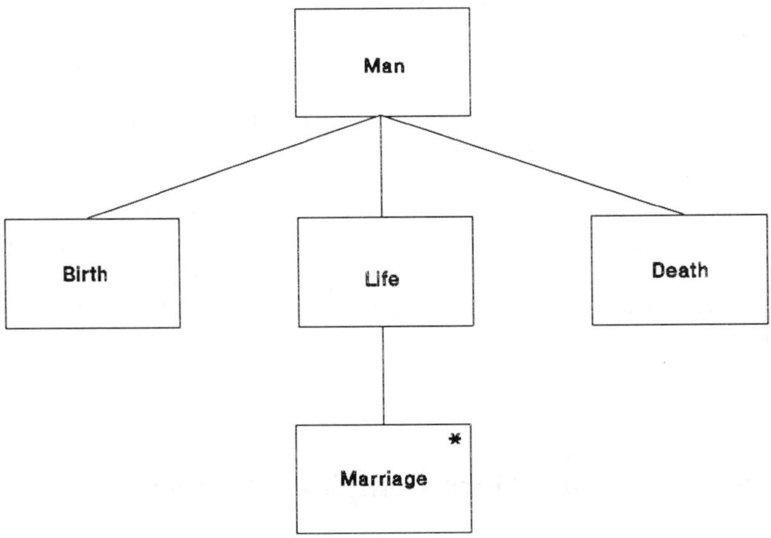

Figure 11.3 Entity Life History showing iteration.

events. Clearly, the iteration occurs in the middle of the Birth-Death sequence. However, in the interests of clarity, there is a convention in drawing Entity Life Histories that you cannot mix different types of event structures at the same level in the diagram. So a 'structure box' is included in the sequence in order to maintain the convention. The structure box need not be labelled, but if a meaningful description can be found, so much the better. In this case we can infer that there is something called Life intervening between Birth and Death as shown in Figure 11.3. The asterisk in the top right hand corner of the event box 'Marriage' denotes an Iteration construct.

11.3.4 Selection

However, the situation is a little more complex than it is represented. One talks of marriage as taking place, but it is also a state of life. As such, it has a beginning and an end. It starts with an event known as a wedding, and it may be concluded by one of a number of different events, of which the type is not known in advance.

In particular, a marriage can be ended by divorce, or by the spouse's death, or by the entity occurrence itself dying. To cater for this sort of situation there is a convention, called a Selection construct. It means that one only of the events shown can happen. There is also a null event to show that none of the events shown need occur. An example is shown in Figure 11.4. Note the null event. We could perhaps have called it 'Dissolution' or some such, but that would have added very little to the readability of the diagram. The small circle in the top right hand corner in the bottom row of events indicates the Selection construct.

11.3.5 Some More Complex Situations.

No doubt, a real life registry system would need to deal with more events than have been depicted above. Let us take another example: the life history of a spare part, stocked in a warehouse for sale. For the purposes of the system to be installed, the following events affect the entity 'Part':-

(1) Someone makes a business decision that the part should be stocked.

(2) A supplier delivers stock against a Purchase order.

(3) A customer places an order to buy the part.

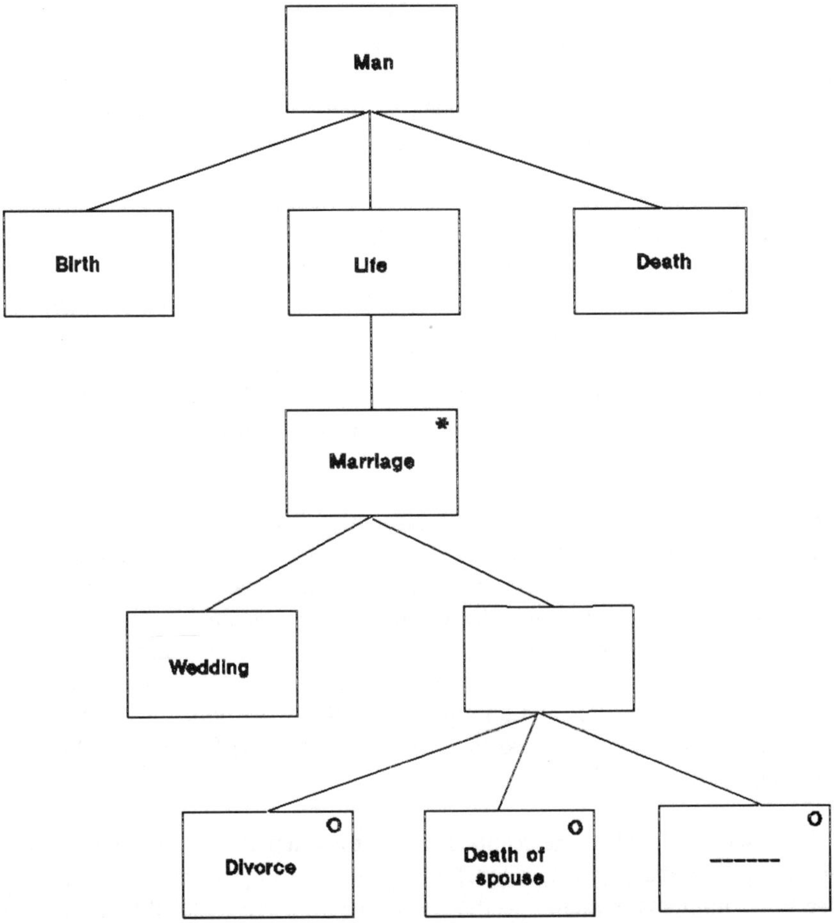

Figure 11.4 Entity Life History showing selection

(4) Someone decides that the part should be superseded by another part.

(5) Someone decides to discontinue stocking the part.

Note that the three 'someones' can be three different people acting independently, the supplier is not under company control, and the customer makes his decisions without reference to the company running the warehouse.

However there are some time dependencies. Events (2), (3), and (5) presumably cannot happen until event (1) has happened. Event (4) is a little different. A warehouse can stock parts, which have been superseded; indeed specialist firms dealing with old motor cars may stock only superseded parts. But just for the time being, let us imagine that event (1) will always precede event (4). Let's not look too closely at event (3) either, just for the moment.

It is easy to see that there will be a sequence of Stocking and Discontinuance with something in between to cater for Delivery, Sale and Supersession. It can't be a Sequence, because that would imply a known order to the events, and the order of events is, in fact, unpredictable. It can't be an Iteration, because that implies a repetition of only one event type. It can't be a Selection, because a Selection means that only one of the events can happen, whereas these events can happen simultaneously. There is therefore a Parallel structure, denoted by two parallel lines with event boxes suspended below them.

Supersessions present a further problem. They can occur for many reasons, such as product improvement, ease of assembly or a new type of raw material. Some of those reasons will have no effect on whether the existing part should be stocked or not. On the other hand, sometimes parts are superseded for safety reasons, and must be withdrawn from sale immediately. In that case the normal life history of the entity is interrupted; to cover this situation a Quit and Resume construct is provided. The event which changes the order of events is marked with the letter 'Q' and a number, and the event which takes place next is marked with the letter 'R' and the same number. The Entity Life History of a part might look like Figure 11.5.

Here the second level of the Entity Life History depicts a Sequence, the third level a Parallel, and the bottom level a Selection. If the supersession is normal, there is no immediate change to the life of a part. No doubt the supersession will be recorded on the database for further action, and in due course the discontinuance will be decided by management. On the other hand, a supersession for safety reasons will immediately cause a discontinuance to be activated, so that Delivery and Sale can no longer take place.

Note that there is a difficulty with regard to the delivery. Presumably, the company cannot prevent the supplier filling the order, and are bound to accept the delivery. The event will have an effect on a Purchase Order entity, but as the goods are not taken into stock, it does not affect the Part entity.

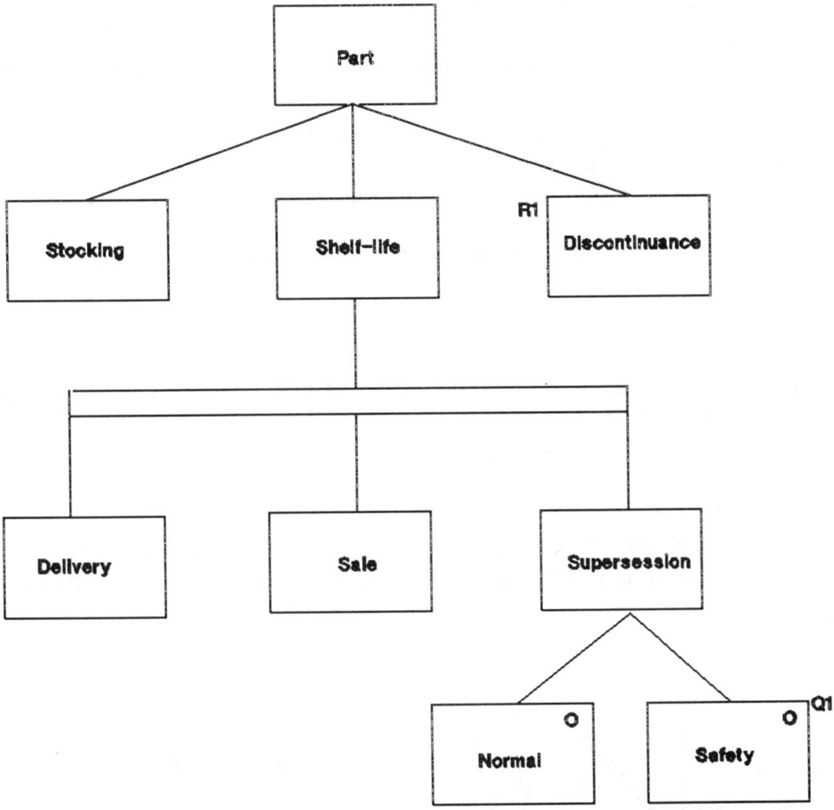

Figure 11.5 Quit and resume construct

11.4 Steps in Entity-event Modelling

There are six steps in Entity-event Modelling:

i) Create Entity/Event Matrix
ii) Draw draft Entity Life Histories
iii) Review Entity Life Histories
iv) Add operations
v) Create Effect Correspondence Diagrams
vi) Add State Indicators

11.4.1 Create an Event/Entity Matrix

The starting point for drawing an Entity Life History is the Logical Data Model of the system in which we are interested. For every entity shown on the Logical Data Model we should be able to draw an Entity Life History. If there are no events which affect the entity, there is not much point in collecting data about it. So the first step is to list the entities along the top of the matrix.

The events identified through Function Definition should be entered down the side of the matrix.

The body of the matrix contains an entry for every occasion on which an event has an effect upon one of the entities in the system. The entry in the matrix will be 'C', 'M', or 'D', depending whether the event creates a new occurrence of the entity, modifies it, or deletes it from the database.

Using the Car Allowance System as an example, the entities have been taken from the Logical Data Model in Figure 6.27. Some events identified during Function Definition have been included. The resulting matrix might look as in Figure 11.6.

Entity / Eventy	Employee	Appl. History	Car	Claim	Journey	Grade
Register authorized user	C		C			
Register change of job	M	C				
Register change of car		C	C/M			
Register claim				C		
Check journey details					C/D	

Figure 11.6 Entity/Event Matrix

The entity 'Grade' is never created, modified or deleted. This entity contains the information about car allowance grade values. The Data Flow Model and Function Definition have not identified the event which creates this entity. After further analysis, the analyst establishes that Grade is created by an event 'Create grade' which allows new grades to be added. The rates payable are modified annually by an event 'Record new grade values'. Other events exist, for example to allow grade boundaries to be altered.

The Function Definitions and Required System Data Flow Diagram should be updated to include any missing events.

Note that a modification to the database may not always be obvious. Sometimes an entity may change its status, simply because a process has taken place. For example, one goes on holiday by air, and before returning, one confirms one's flight. The only thing (if any) that happens, is that a flag is set on your record on the database, and that may affect the calculations of the airline's overbooking rate. It is possible that for a particular entity, all that needs to be done is to record that the event has occurred; the accompanying details may be recorded in some other Entity's data.

11.4.2 Draw Draft Entity Life Histories

Once the matrix has settled into a semi-permanent state, it is possible to look at each entity individually to build the Entity Life History diagrams. The Logical Data Model should have been drawn in such a way that there is a hierarchy of entities, i.e. one or more master entities at the top and various levels of detail entities below. Entity Life History diagrams should be drawn starting from the lowest level entities first. The reason is that the insertion or deletion of such an entity occurrence will not affect the existence of its masters. The converse is not true.

The attributes of the entities 'Employee' and 'Car', from the Car Allowance System are listed, followed by the steps in drawing up the Entity Life History.

EMPLOYEE	**CAR**
Pay-no	**Pay-no**
Name	**Make**
Address	**Model**
Job-title	**Year**
Job-location	**Engine-cc**
Salary-grade	**Reg-no**
Current-allowance-grade	**Check-date**
Date-authorised-driver	**Check-details**
Driver-test-details	

i) Identify the birth event, ie the event which creates the primary key. The primary key of 'Employee' is 'Pay-no', this is created when an employee is first awarded a car allowance by the event 'Register authorised user'.

ii) Identify events which change the mid-life of the entity. One of the main events affecting 'Employee' is 'Register change of job' since this requires re-authorisation and a possible change of grade.. Another important event is 'Register change of car' which can also alter the grade of allowance authorised.

iii) Identify the death events, ie the event which would result in the removal of an occurrence of the entity. Employee details are retained in the 'Employee' entity until either the driver leaves the company, or, the driver dies. Both circumstances require the occurrence of the 'Employee' entity to be deleted and relevant details to be archived. The event 'Leave company' handles both circumstances.

iv) Check the Entity/Event Matrix to ensure that all the events affecting the entity have been included. Then, the next step is to examine the attributes of the entity and determine the following:

- are all the attributes born when the entity is born? With the current list of entities for 'Employee' the answer is 'yes'. If some attributes can be added later then an additional event is necessary to do this.

Consider what could happen if the 'Car' entity had to retain the phone number of a car-phone which the company installed in an employee's car. This phone may not be installed when the other car details are created. A separate event would be necessary to allow the car-phone information to be created at a later time.

- look at each attribute and determine how it can be altered through the entity lifespan. In 'Employee' the following additional events could happen: change of name due to marriage; change of employee address; change of job location (still same job). An event 'Change employee details' could handle changes like this which do not require authorization and/or a change of grade. Also check whether all the attributes die with the entity. This might not always be the case. For instance the car-phone information for 'Car' could die before the remaining car details. The employee may change jobs within the company and still use the same car but no longer have a car-phone.

The important point at this stage is to consider the events that are likely to happen. Unlikely events can be considered later.

It might appear to be reasonable to assume that events which create an entity occurrence will precede events which modify the entity.
Initially the diagram should be drawn in this way, as if parallelism and interrupts to the normal life do not exist. In many cases parallel constructs can be represented as Selections for clarity.

Having determined sequence, or lack of it for parallel events, one is in position to draft the diagram. The term 'draft' is used advisedly, because the next step is to take it back to the users for verification.

A first attempt at an Entity Life History for the Employee entity from the Car Allowance System is shown in Figure 11.7.

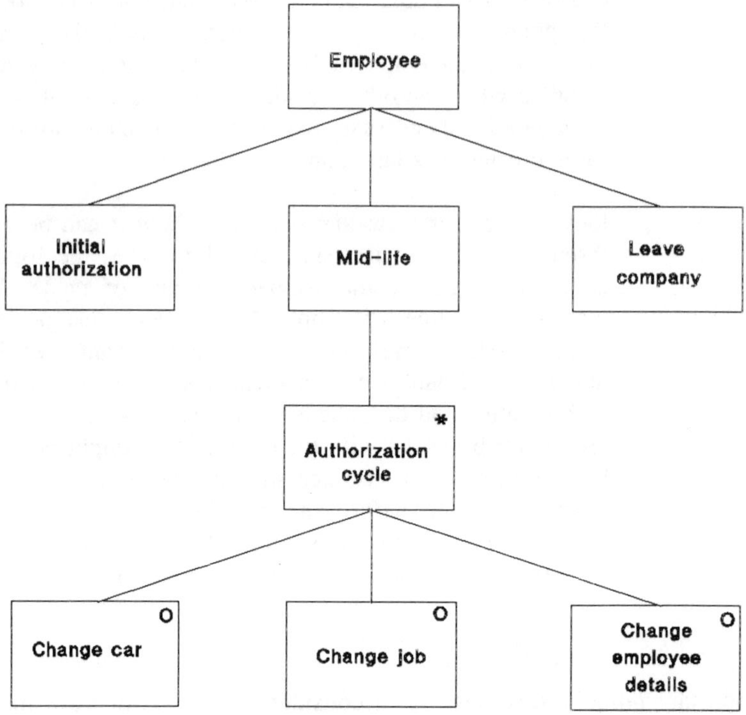

Figure 11.7 Draft Entity Life History

11.4.3 Review Entity Life Histories

11.4.3.1 Check for parallelism

So far we have tried to assume that an event is created before it can be modified. However, some modifications will logically affect an entity before it is created. In the example given in section 11.3.5, if a part was superseded before it was stocked, the entity occurrence may not physically have existed on the database, but its status has changed from current to superseded. A similar position could arise in an Insurance system. The first notification that a policy exists might be a claim. This is a result of the peculiar nature of the insurance business, and may account for the wealth of judicial law that it has produced.

The analyst is well advised to check all Selection and Sequence constructs to ensure that they are not potential Parallel events. The system may need to be altered so that the Parallels can be implemented as Selections, but it must be known in advance. A Sequence may need to be implemented as a Parallel, simply as a result of the sequence of events as notified to the database. In the case mentioned above where the first event which occurs to a Policy is a claim, one might quite reasonably say the system should reject the event as an error. The general principle in data processing is to keep errors out of your data at all costs.

But nowadays one tends to deal with systems which interact with the public; the clerk at the claims desk can't just tell the claimant to go away. In reality, there may be several possibilities. The claimant may be talking to the wrong Insurance Company, and an error has indeed occurred. The policy may have been issued, but somehow not arrived on the database. Or a Cover Note may have been issued by an Agent, in which case the Policy may or may not be issued in due course.

Another example is a typical Job Costing/Time Recording system. A Job consists of a Sequence: Sale, Life and Billing. During its Life time may be booked to the Job. Such a system would be implemented by the Sale event adding a record to the Jobs database, and the Billing event removing it. Many such systems have been installed, usually with less than satisfactory acceptance. One problem was what to do with records that didn't match the database. You could add dummy records with default values to the database, and risk putting up errors caused by transposition errors; or you could reject the unmatched records, and risk having your error report being ignored.

Also such systems suffered other inflexibilities. Take the case of a customer who is billed for a job, and subsequently complains about the work. Let us assume it is cheaper to spend some time on rework, than it is to argue; so extra work is carried out. Also a sale with a short deadline is likely to be made, so the Production Manager tells the Tool Room Foreman to get on with making the required jigs and dies 'just in case'. The computer system cannot deal with either case, but the overall system will find a way almost inevitably. The work will be booked down to some other job, and the job cost records will be wrong.

By systematically looking at all Sequences and Selections it is hoped to avoid such inflexibilities. In practice there will be political problems, because managers are not likely to take kindly to the fact that a system may allow for unauthorized departures from company policy.

11.4.3.2 Check with Logical Data Model.

The next step is to check each Entity Life History starting from the top level of the Logical Data Model. Each event in the master entity should be considered with relation to each of detail entities. Does a change in status of the master (especially its deletion) depend upon the status of the details?

One can imagine that an airline system will hold data on the entity 'Flight', which is a master of the entity 'Passenger'. If a flight is cancelled, the 'Flight' entity needs to be deleted, but it is unlikely that the airline would want to lose its passengers as well. Checking the Entity Life History suggests that something is amiss with the Logical Data Model. Perhaps there is some other entity required, such as 'Reservation'. This is shown in Figure 11.8.

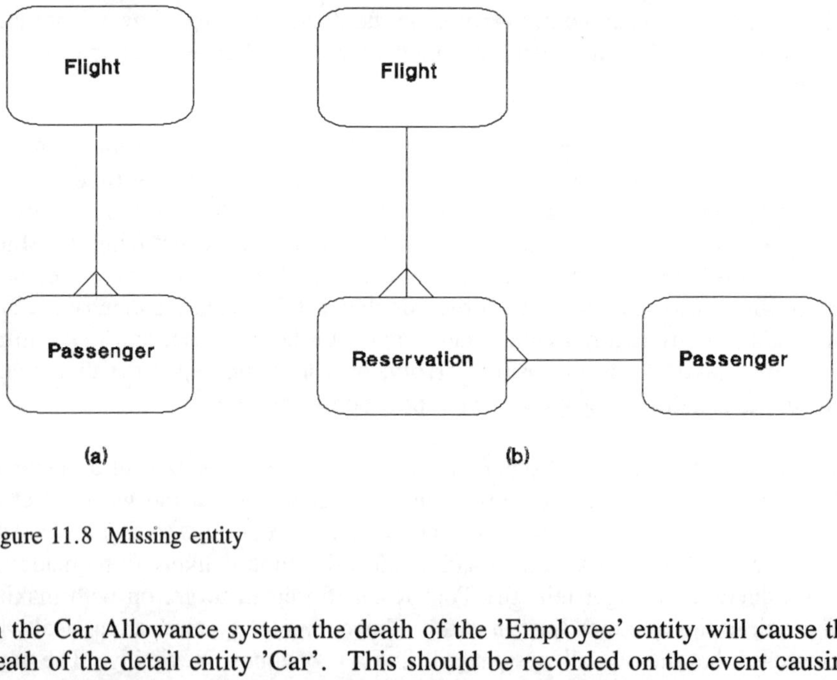

Figure 11.8 Missing entity

In the Car Allowance system the death of the 'Employee' entity will cause the death of the detail entity 'Car'. This should be recorded on the event causing the death of the master as a death effect on the life of the detail.

In some circumstances a master may only die once all its details have died. In the Car Allowance System this could happen if employees could only be removed from the system if they have no claims during the current financial year. The Entity Life History for the 'Claim' entity must show the event causing the death of the master after the death of the detail.

If a detail can exist without a master, the deaths of the master and detail should be shown as options using the Selection structure.

Random events which can be identified can be handled using the Quit and Resume structure.

11.4.4 Add operations

Having documented effects on the Entity Life History, one must then document the individual operations relating to each effect. The effects are shown as the bottom boxes in the Entity Life History structure. An operation is a discrete unit of logical processing which contributes to part, or all, of an event's effect.

Draw up a list of the major operations relating to the effects on the Entity Life History. The following operations are used:

i)	**Store keys**	**user enters a primary key value, birth event only**
ii)	**Store <attribute>**	**user sets the value of an attribute which is not a primary key, birth event only**
iii)	**Store remaining birth attributes**	**user sets values of attributes not set by i) and ii), event only.**
iv)	**Store <value> using <expression>**	**user sets value of attribute to result of expression, birth event only**
v)	**Replace <attribute>**	**user modifies attribute value**
vi)	**Replace <attribute> using <expression>**	**user alters value to result of expression**
vii)	**Tie to <entity>**	**links this entity with a master entity**
viii)	**Cut from <entity>**	**removes link from this entity to a master entity**
ix)	**Gain <entity>**	**link this entity to a detail entity**
x)	**Lose <entity>**	**remove link between this entity and a detail entity**

The Entity Life History for 'Employee' is shown in Figure 11.9 with the operations for each effect.

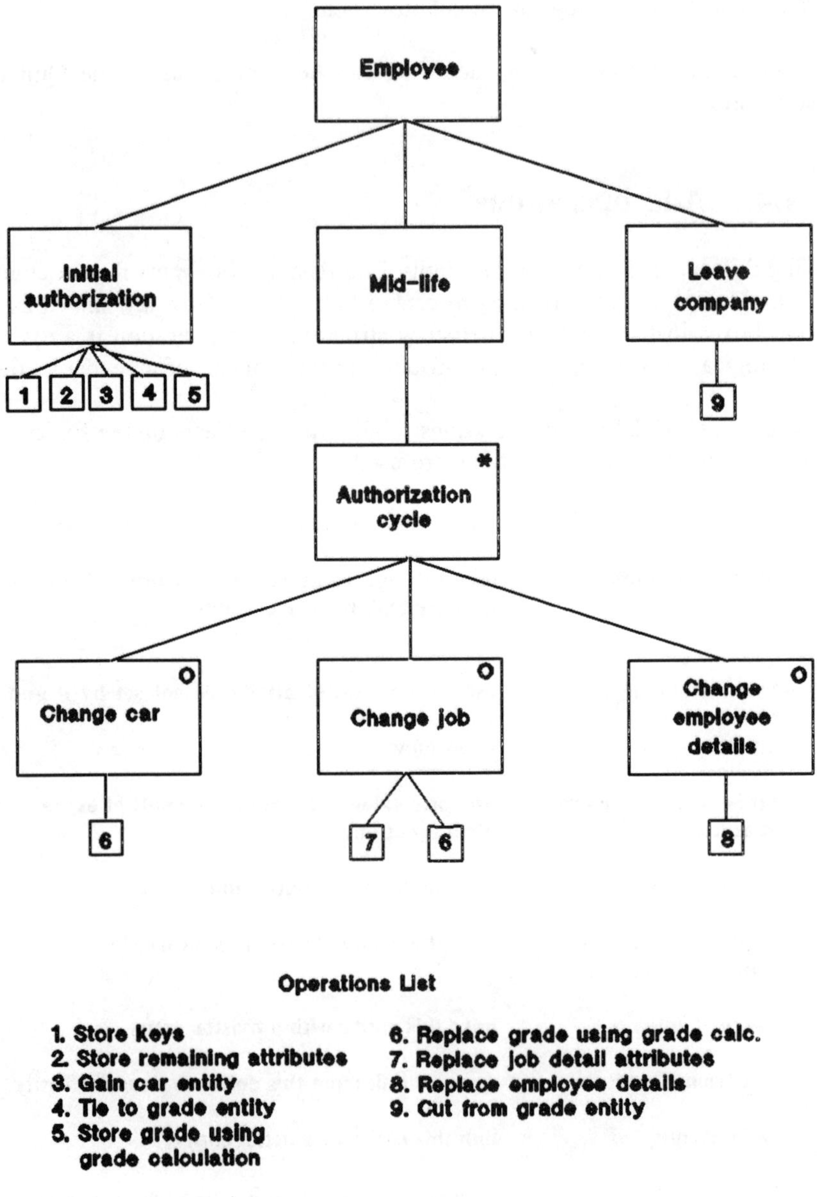

Figure 11.9 Entity Life History with operations

11.4.5 Create Effect Correspondence Diagram

The creation of Effect Correspondence Diagrams is important in validating the Entity Life History analysis. An Effect Correspondence Diagram must be drawn for each event identified. An event can affect data in more than one entity, the Effect Correspondence Diagram shows all the effects which an event has on system data. The attributes of the event which are input to an update process require to be specified. The set of Effect Correspondence Diagrams provides the update access paths used in logical design and provide the basis for the development of Update Process Structures.
A simple illustration is provided for the event 'Register authorised user' from the Car Allowance System. The resulting diagram is shown in Figure 11.10.

The entities affected by the event 'Register authorised user' are 'Employee', 'Car' and 'Grade'. The operations on the Entity Life History help to identify links to other entities. These links are shown by correspondence arrows.

The event creating 'Employee' also creates 'Car'. A correspondence arrow shows this link. An occurrence of the event can cause the creation of more than one set of car details, so 'Car' is shown as an iteration.

The creation of 'Employee' requires an access to the 'Grade' entity, this link is shown by a correspondence arrow.

The attributes which are to be input to the update process are now entered. The input attribute for the example event is 'Pay-no' and this is shown on the diagram.

11.4.6 Add State Indicators.

When the combination and sequence of events which can affect an entity are complex, it is valuable to know precisely which events have occurred at a particular moment. The combination of prior events can affect the validity of a further attempt to update that entity's data. It ought to be possible to discover the state of the entity by the state of its accompanying data, but the logic to unscramble the facts may be unreasonably complex. Hence the need for an Entity State Indicator.

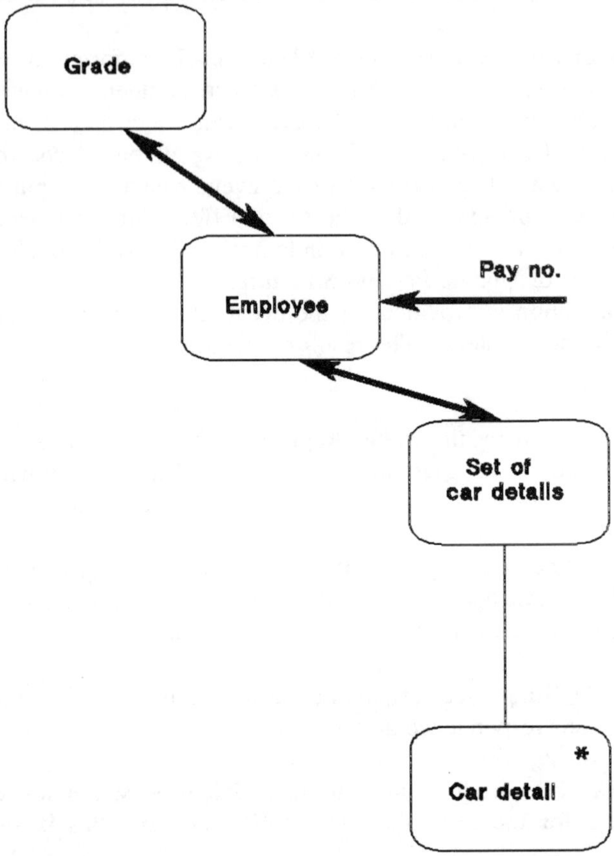

Figure 11.10 Effect Correspondence Diagram for the event 'Register authorized user'.

As far as the Entity Life History diagram is concerned, the State Indicator is just a number to show what the state of the entity is, after the effects of an event have occurred, and the allowable states before the event can be accepted as valid by the system. More than one State Indicator may be needed to cater for parallel events.

The convention is that the State Indicators will be shown under the lowest levels of the Entity Life History in the form k,l,m/p or k-n/p, where k,l,m,n are permissable states before the event, and p is the resultant state after the event. The symbol '-' indicates the null state, before any events occur.

In setting State Indicators all the arguments with regard to whether a Sequence should be a Parallelism, need to be considered and settled. If an event can convert the state of an entity from its previous state to one (and only one) new state, then it is in sequence with the prior event.

Every rule with regard to allowability of events will reduce the flexibility of the system, whilst making it easier to implement. It is another example of the problem of whether to reject invalid data ruthlessly, or to accept it, and then devise methods of controlling the erroneous data. The Car Allowance System Entity Life History for the entity 'Employee' might look like Figure 11.11.

11.5 Place of Entity-event Modelling in SSADM

11.5.1 Requirements Specification

11.5.1.1 Step 310 Define Required System Processing

The Required System Data Flow Model may require to be updated as a result of Entity-event Modelling identifying additional processes..

11.5.1.2 Step 320 Develop Required Data Model

The Required System Logical Data Model may require to be updated as a result of Entity-event Modelling identifying additional entities, or attributes of entities.

11.5.1.3 Step 330 Derive System Functions

Function Definitions are not complete until the end of Step 360 when the Entity-event Modelling concluded. Additional events may be identified for a function or the creation of new functions may be necessary.

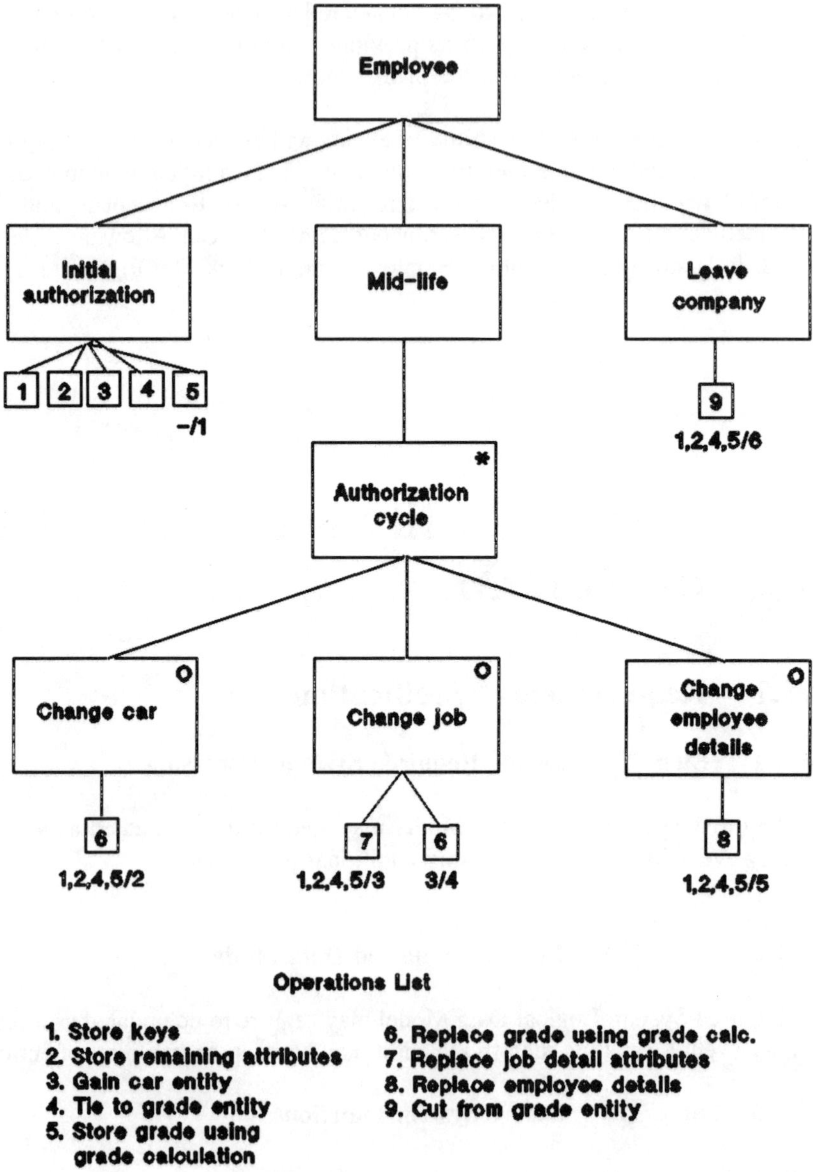

Figure 11.11 Entity Life History with State Indicators

11.5.1.4 Step 360 Develop Processing Specification

Entity Life Histories are created for each entity in the Logical Data Model, working from the bottom of the structure to the top. An Effect Correspondence Diagram is then created for each event. The Requirements Catalogue, Logical Data Model, Data Flow Model and Function Definitions may all require revision as a result of this process.

The Logical Data Model can now have Enquiry Access Paths added for each enquiry function and can be annotated with entity and relationship volumes.

11.5.1.5 Step 380 Assemble Requirements Specification

The Entity-event Model becomes part of the Requirements Specification.

11.5.2 Logical System Specification

11.5.2.1 Step 520 Define Update Processes

The state indicator values are added to Entity Life Histories, the meanings of each value are documented in the Entity Description.

The Effect Correspondence Diagrams are converted into a processing structure.

The operations for each event are identified from the Entity Life Histories and then allocated to the processing structure.

11.5.2.2 Step 530 Define Enquiry Processes

Entity Life Histories are input to the definition of Enquiry Processes.

11.5.2.3 Step 540 Assemble Logical Design

The Entity-event Model becomes part of the Logical Design document which provides the basis for Physical Design.

11.5.3 Physical Design

11.5.3.1 Step 620 Create Physical Data Design

The Effect Correspondence Diagrams are used in the creation of the Physical Data Design.

11.5.3.2 Step 640 Optimise Physical Design

The Effect Correspondence Diagrams are used to help validate the Physical Data Design so that it meets the performance requirements.

11.6 Summary

The Entity-event Model consists of two sets of components. Each entity in the system is documented on an Entity Life History. Each effect in the system is documented by an Effect Correspondence Diagram.

The Entity Life History shows the sequence of events which affect groups of data held within a system. These events indicate processes which change one or more of the attributes of an entity. Events must be identified which create, amend or delete an occurrence of the entity The Entity Life History also identifies the time relationships between events. It allows the analyst to check that there is an event which creates an occurrence of the entity before it can be amended or deleted. Mid-life events may occur in a certain order and/or be repeated during the life of the entity occurrence. There may be more than one event which can delete an occurrence of the entity.

The Effect Correspondence Diagram records how an effect relates to the entities in the system. An event may cause changes to data in several entities and access to data in other entities. The Effect Correspondence Diagrams become the basis for Update Process Structures.

The Entity-event Model draws on information derived from Function Definition and the Logical Data Model. The process of preparing the Entity Life History Diagrams and the Effect Correspondence Diagrams may identify events which have been missed during Function Definition or may show up errors in the Logical Data Model.

11.7 Keywords

Entity
Sequence
Selection
Parallelism
Entity-event Model
Effect Correspondence Diagram
Logical Data Model
State indicator
Iteration
Quit and Resume
Event/Entity Matrix
Operation
Function Definition

11.8 Exercises

1. In the aircraft industry it is a normal procedure for purchasers of aircraft to buy an option to order, so as to book a space on the production schedule of the aircraft. In due course the purchaser can take up the option by placing a firm order, or he can let the option lapse if his planned requirement for the aircraft has not eventuated. Draw an Entity Life History of a purchase option.

2. Draw an Entity Life History for a life assurance policy.

3. Imagine you are working on a real-time system, which monitors the status of pedestrian crossing traffic lights. Draw an Entity Life History (complete with state indicators) of the signal which controls motor traffic on a straight section of road,

(a) assuming the signal works continuously, and

(b) allowing for interruption for routine and breakdown maintenance.

5. Imagine you are working for a car hire firm. One of the entities, about which the firm wants to keep data is 'Car'. Events which affect this entity are its Purchase and Sale (or Write-off) and its Hiring and Return (or Non-return). Draw an Entity Life History with state indicators for 'Car'.

6. Add operations and state indicators to the Entity Life History in Figure 11.9.

7. Develop Entity Life Histories and Effect Correspondence Diagrams for as much of the Car Allowance System as possible.

8. Develop an Entity-event model for the Telephone Directory System described in section 5.2.

9. Develop an Entity-event Model for the Student Administration System described in Appendix 2.

CHAPTER TWELVE

Technical System Options

12.1 Introduction

Technical System Options are created as part of the Logical System Specification Module. They allow analysts and users to make detailed decisions about the implementation of the Selected Business System Option.

A number of areas require to be considered:

- specification of hardware requirements eg number and capability of terminals.
- software environments, eg development options might be: to use a 3GL, use a 4GL, or to buy a package.
- the impact of the options on the organisation and the users
- implications for system development of the remainder of the project
- costs

At this stage it is not necessary to specify particular makes and models of machines or to nominate particular suppliers. The concern is with identifying the facilities and performance required to achieve the system objectives.

12.2 Technical System Option Development

The development of Technical System Options can be divided into six stages:

i) Identify constraints
ii) Create outline Technical System Options
iii) Reduce the number of Technical System Options
iv) Develop the remaining Technical System Options
v) Select a Technical System Option
vi) Update the Technical Environment Description

12.2.1 Identify constraints

Before considering any Technical System Options it is sensible to determine any internal or external constraints which might restrict the potential choices available to the analyst.

The main external constraints should be documented in the Selected Business System Option. Typical constraints will be implementation date; budget; cost savings required; capital availability; hardware available; software available.

For instance, in the Car Allowance System, existing hardware and software has to be used. This means using either the existing mainframe system or using personal computers on a Local Area Network. There is a limited budget for buying terminals and peripherals. The software used must also be one of the software packages already in use in the company. The system has to be implemented by the start of the following financial year since it is collecting summary financial information.

Internal constraints are set for the project by the user requirements. They include factors such as data storage needs; service levels; security; system workload.

For instance the users have specified that the Car Allowance System must be on-line during normal working hours. The file sizes are determined by the Required System Logical Data Model and the number of authorised users. System workload peaks with the processing of claims in the first week of a month since the majority of users fill in claim forms for a calendar month. Security is handled with printouts such as a log of all new authorized car users. User numbers and passwords must also be used.

12.2.2 Create outline Technical System Options

The external and internal constraints provide the framework within which outline Technical System Options are prepared. Creative thinking is essential here and techniques such as 'brainstorming' can be of great use. The team preparing the options should come up with three to six outline Technical System Options. If the system is replacing an existing computer system then one of the options should normally be to maintain the status quo and stop the development project. Similarly, if the project is to replace an existing manual system, then one of the options could be the retention of the manual system.

12.2.3 Reduce the number of outline Technical System Options

At this stage the team should try to reduce the number of outline Technical System Options to about three before trying to research and document them in detail. This could be achieved by carrying out an informal impact analysis for each option in conjunction with the users. Features may be added to, or removed from, options during this process. The end result should be about three outline options which seem to be reasonably feasible.

12.2.4 Develop the remaining Technical System Options

The remaining Technical System Options now require to be specified in more detail to allow an informed choice to be made. The options should be documented to a standard which allows them to be referred to during the decision-making process. The following areas should be included in the specification of each option:

i) Outline Technical Environment Description
ii) System Description
iii) Impact Analysis
iv) Outline Development Plan
v) Cost/Benefit Analysis

12.2.4.1 Outline Technical Environment Description

An Outline Technical Environment Description must be prepared for each option. This will later be expanded to become an SSADM product for the Selected Technical System Option.

The outline must give the user enough information to understand how the system will work and to allow the selection of one option. Care must be taken not to provide too much detail. Significant aspects of design should be explained and detailed costings provided. It should cover factors such as hardware, software, data storage requirements, security and processing workload.

12.2.4.2 System Description

This describes how the option matches the Requirements Specification. Many of the major decisions will have been made when choosing the Selected Business System Option but sometimes choices may be required about trading off facilities against performance.

12.2.4.3 Impact Analysis

This explains how the option will impact on the system environment. It will include factors such as effect on the organisation structure, effect on jobs, training requirements, implementation issues. Any impact on the Requirements Catalogue should also be discussed.

12.2.4.4 Outline Development Plan

Estimates are required for future development costs. These include timescales and resource requirements. Costs may vary widely if development varies from implementing an off the shelf package to full scale in-house development.

12.2.4.5 Cost/Benefit Analysis

Carrying out a formal Cost/Benefit Analysis provides an objective way of comparing one option with another. Most of the information required should already be available to the analyst. Trying to quantify intangible benefits forces the analyst to consider how real these benefits might be.

12.2.5 Select a Technical System Option

A presentation should be made which outlines every option and explains the major implications of each. After considerable discussion with the users an option should be selected. This option will probably be a variation of the options discussed. The deliberations should be documented so that there is a clear record of the choices made.

The Selected Technical System Option should be formally reviewed to ensure that it will meet the service level requirements.

The process of considering the Technical System Options can bring forward problems which require analysis at an earlier Stage of SSADM. Such changes must be carefully controlled and all the relevant documents updated before development progresses.

12.2.6 Update the Technical Environment Description

The Technical Environment Description is the document which is carried forward to Physical Design. The remaining documents from the Selected Technical System Option are used for project management. The changes made during the selection procedure must be incorporated in the final version of the Technical Environment Description. The contents should include relevant information about the selected option. The following gives some idea of factors to include:

Hardware	eg. standards, communications needs, installation requirements, operational requirements, upgrades, maintenance, availability, etc.

Software	eg. system utilities, application packages, operating system facilities, development method, development environment, etc.
System Sizing	eg. data storage capacity, processing requirements
Other factors	eg. security, contingency plans, system access, maintenance, etc.

In addition the System Description and Impact Analysis should be updated and carried forward to Physical Design with the Technical Environment Description.

12.3 Place of Technical System Options in SSADM

12.3.1 Logical System Specification

12.3.1.1 Step 410 Define Technical System Options

This Step identifies and defines possible ways of physically implementing the Requirements Specification. The outputs of this Step are Technical System Options and the Capacity Planning Input.

12.3.1.2 Step 420 Select Technical System Option

During this Step the Technical System Options are presented to the project board and one option is selected to go forward to Physical Design.

12.3.2 Physical Design

The Selected Technical System Option will drive Stage 6, Physical Design.

12.4 Summary

Taking the Selected Business System Option as a basis, the Technical System Options technique provides a detailed implementation plan. A number of possible physical solutions are considered covering factors such as the technical environment; system functions; the impact of the new system on the organisation and the users; requirements for further development of the system. One solution must be selected and documented. The Selected Technical System Option drives the Physical Design Stage of the system.

12.5 Keywords

Outline Technical System Option
Selected Technical System Option
Selected Business System Option
Technical Environment Description
Outline Technical Environment Description
Impact Analysis
Outline Development Plan
Cost/Benefit Analysis
Installation Style Guide
Application Style Guide

12.6 Exercises

1. Outline the process of developing Technical System Options.

2. Describe the contents of an outline Technical System Option.

3. Describe the contents of the selected Technical System Option.

4. Consider possible Technical System Options for the Telephone Allowance System described in section 5.2.

5. Consider possible Technical System Options for the Student Administration System described in Appendix 2.

CHAPTER THIRTEEN

Logical Database Process Design

13.1 Introduction

Logical Database Process Design is concerned with specifying the processing for data that is input to, or output from, the logical database. The logical database is described in the Required System Logical Data Model. Data that is input to the database may create an entity, create attributes of an entity, or modify attributes of an entity. Data is output from the database as the result of an enquiry. An update may include an enquiry. Data and entities can also be deleted from the database. This technique looks at each entity and each data element and defines the processes which create, modify or delete them. The results are expressed in process models, each having its own operations list.

Enquiry Process Models are derived partly from Enquiry Access Paths created for the Logical Data Model (see Chapter 6). The other basis for building the model is the Input/Output Structures produced during Function Definition.

Update Process Models take Entity Life Histories and Effect Correspondence Diagrams as the starting point for creation of a model of each event.

The process models are logical descriptions of the requirements for processing the logical database. Processes are divided into sub-processes and combined in a structure diagram showing sequence, selection and iteration of these sub-processes. The structure diagram is then annotated with the operations required to access and update the data.

13.2 Modelling logical database processes

13.2.1 Description of technique

The technique uses the structure diagram principles already described for Entity Life Histories and Input/Output Structures. The following steps are followed:

i) Define input and output data structures showing sequence, selection and iteration of data groups.

ii) Identify correspondences between data items in the input and output data structures

iii) Merge the input and output data structures to form a process structure

iv) Assign operations and conditions to the process structure.

Update and Enquiry Process Models look very similar, but they are constructed from different bases. The development of an Enquiry Process Model is described in section 13.3. The development of an Update Process Model is described in section 13.4.

13.2.2 Operations

Operations were discussed in Chapter 11, section 11.4.4. In addition to the operations listed there the following operations are added to process models (square brackets denote optional clauses):

i)	**Read <entity-type> by key**	**read by key from the database using input key value**
ii)	**Define set of <entity-type>**	**members of set match the criteria in the input data**

iii)	**Read next <entity-type> in set**	**read next from currently defined set. Set must previously have been defined.**
iv)	**Read next <detail> of <master> [via <relationship>]**	**read next occurrence of detail linked to current occurrence of master. Give the relationship if more than one link between master and detail.**
v)	**Read <master> of <detail> [via <relationship>]**	**read master related to current occurrence of detail**
vi)	**Invoke <common process>**	**invoke a process defined elsewhere**
vii)	**Fail if state indicator of <entity> outside <value-range>**	**raise an error if state indicator is outside the valid range after reading an entity.**

Operation numbers are allocated to the diagram. They can be hung from iterated or optional components, but not from the component immediately above them. The operations should be itemised on a numbered list attached to the diagram.

13.2.3 Conditions

Conditions are annotated to the structure diagram above each option of a selection, and above each iterated component. Selection conditions often test the value of the entity's state indicator. Iteration conditions are often a test for the 'end of set'.

13.2.4 Logical Success Units

A logical success unit is a group of sub-processes which must succeed or fail as a group. If the group succeeds then the processing is a success and can be committed (written to the database). If the group fails then the system is restored to its position before the success unit began. All the data accessed by a success unit is locked until the unit fails or succeeds. Each update process should be considered a logical success unit. Enquiry processes should normally be a logical success unit to ensure data consistency. A long enquiry process can be divided into several small units, each being a logical success unit. This gives the user the option of abandoning the query.

13.2.5 Structure clashes

The merger of the input and output data structures can result in structure clashes. The handling of structure clashes in detail is beyond the scope of this book, but some brief examples are given of ordering clashes and boundary clashes.

An ordering clash arises when the sequence of data items in one data structure is different from that in another data structure. This typically arises when the sequence required for an output is different from the sequence of data in the logical database. This can be resolved by modifying the Logical Data Model or by defining additional sort/format processes.

Boundary clashes arise when data elements are grouped in different ways in different data structures. Again the problem usually arises when the grouping of data on an output differs from the grouping of data in the logical database. This can be resolved by using an application or report generator. An alternative is to define two processes which handle the different groupings and communicate with each other.

13.3 Worked example of Enquiry Process Model

An Enquiry Process Model is prepared for each enquiry which has been specified in detail as an enquiry function. Ad-hoc enquiries are not documented in this way and are not documented as a process model.

The enquiry input data structure is found from the Enquiry Access Path defined with the Logical Data Model. The output data structure is developed from the Input/Output Structure prepared during Function Definition. The input and output data structures are merged to produce the process structure. The addition of operations and conditions provides an Enquiry Process Model.

The following enquiry from the Car Allowance System will be modelled:

> **For a given Grade, list the name and salary grade of all employees on that Grade. For each Employee, list the engine capacity of the car(s) for which they can claim**

13.3.1 Identify required view of Logical Data Model

The first step is to look at the Logical Data Model and identify the required view of the data model. Figure 13.1 shows this for our example.

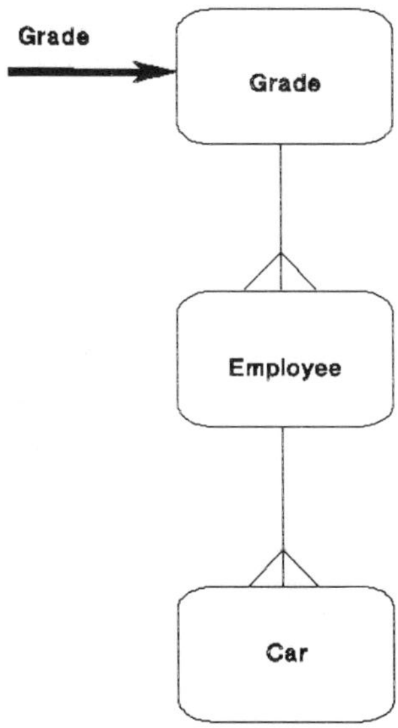

Figure 13.1 Required view of the Data Model.

13.3.2 Specify enquiry Name

Each enquiry should be given a unique name, as used in Function Definitions and Physical Process Specification. The enquiry in our example has the name 'Grade query'.

13.3.3 Specify enquiry trigger

The enquiry trigger is the data items input to the enquiry and is normally the key of the entry point entity on the Logical Data Model. The enquiry trigger is normally seen as a list of data items on the Enquiry Access Path. The enquiry trigger for our example is 'Grade', that is the reference letter used to identify the different levels of car allowance payable.

13.3.4 Specify Enquiry Access Path

The Enquiry Access Path for our example is shown in Figure 13.2.

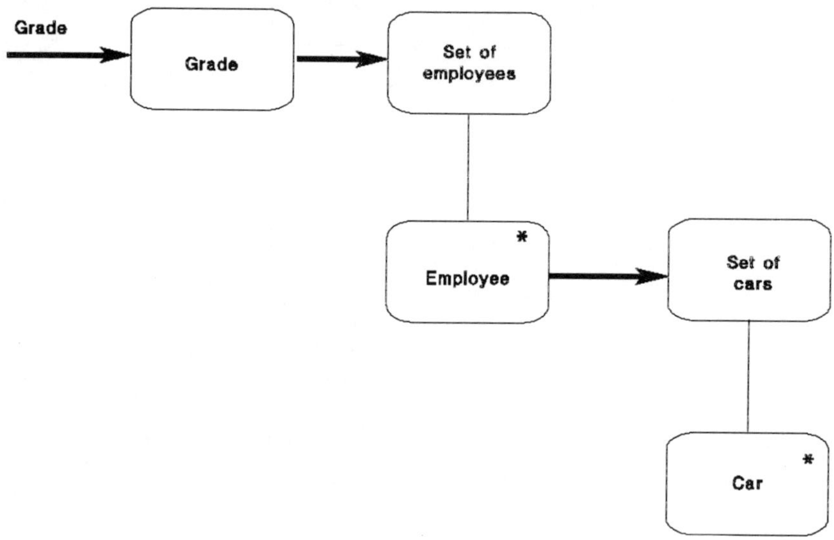

Figure 13.2 Enquiry Access Path

13.3.5 Prepare enquiry output data structure

The enquiry output consists of data items output from the enquiry. It can be derived from the Input/Output Structures from those functions which use the enquiry. This is simply done by taking the Input/Output Structure and removing all the input elements. Figure 13.3 shows the Input/Output Structure for our example. The Enquiry output data structure is shown in Figure 13.4.

Note that the structure box 'Set of allowance details' is no longer required when the input data element has been removed. The box changes shape from hard-cornered boxes in the Input/Output Structure to round-cornered boxes in the Enquiry output data structure.

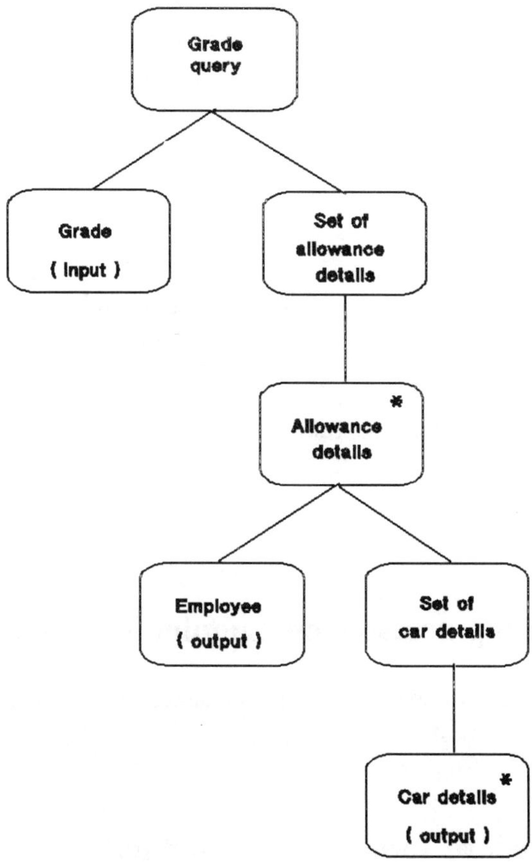

Figure 13.3 Input/Output Structure.

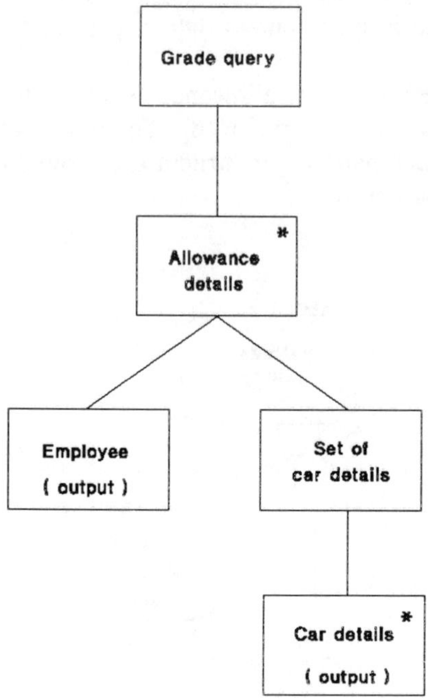

Figure 13.4 Enquiry output data structure.

13.3.6 Group accesses on Enquiry Access Path

Group the accesses in one-to-one correspondence on the Enquiry Access Path as shown in Figure 13.5.

13.3.7 Prepare Input Data Structure

The Enquiry Access Path with grouped accesses is then converted to a structure diagram. The grouped accesses become one box on the structure diagram. Extra structure boxes may be required to avoid mixing different structure types. Figure 13.6 shows the Input data structure for our example.

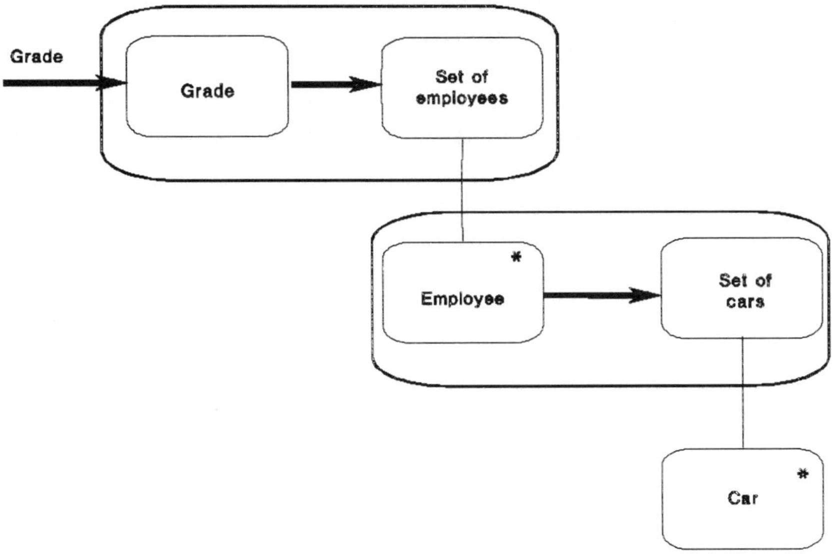

Figure 13.5 Enquiry Access Path with grouped accesses.

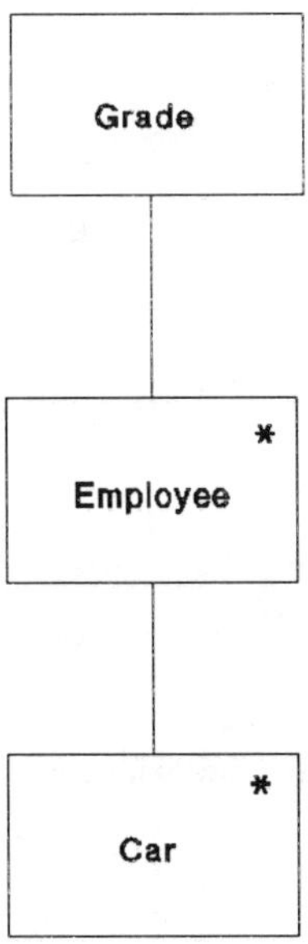

Figure 13.6 Enquiry input data structure.

13.3.8 Identify correspondences between input and output data structures

The correspondences between the input and output data structures must now be identified. This is shown in Figure 13.7. Structure clashes will become apparent at this stage.

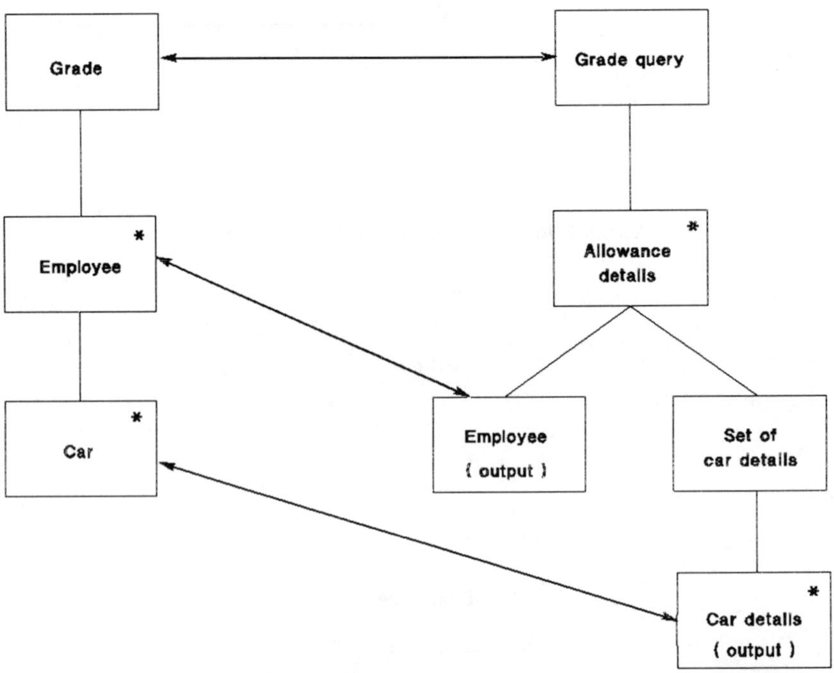

Figure 13.7 Input and output data structure with correspondences.

13.3.9 Merge input and output data structures

The next step is to merge the input and output data structures to form a process structure, as shown in Figure 13.8.

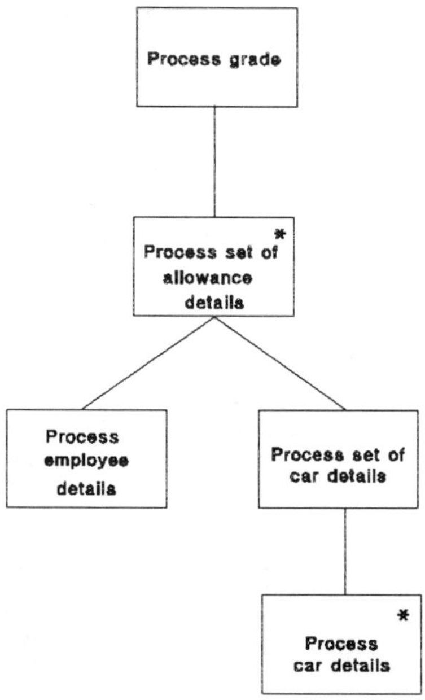

Figure 13.8 Process structure diagram.

13.3.10 Allocate operations and conditions to structure

The operations are then listed and allocated to the structure, as shown in Figure 13.9. The conditions are then recorded on the structure to give a completed Process Structure Model as seen in Figure 13.10.

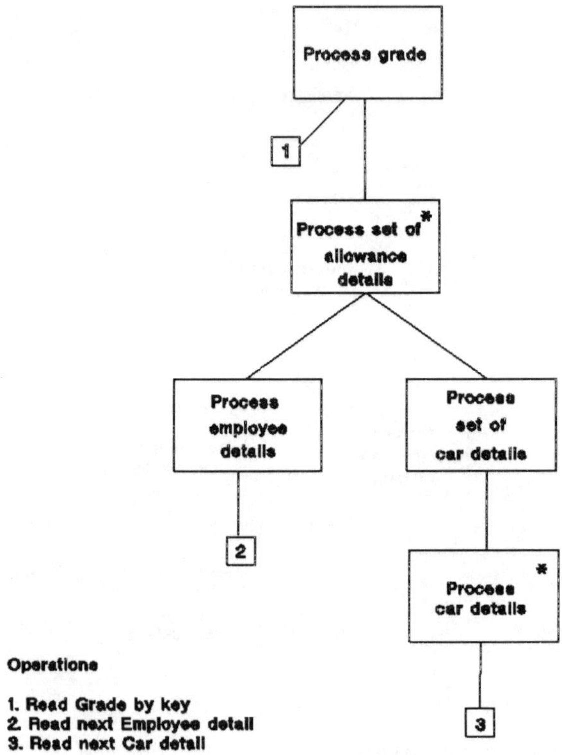

Figure 13.9 Process structure diagram with operations added.

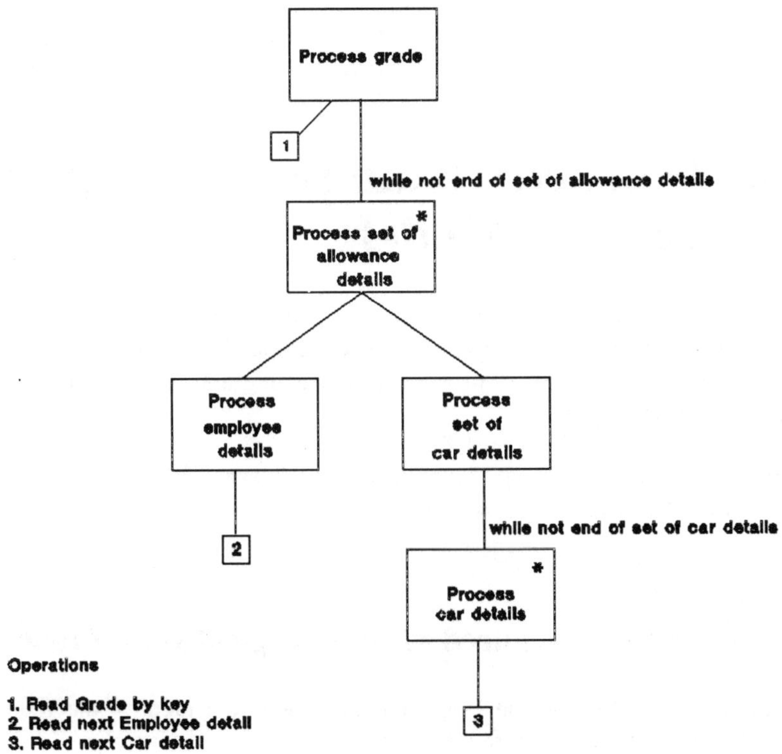

Figure 13.10 Process Structure Diagram with conditions added.

13.3.11 Identify integrity error conditions

Integrity error conditions are checked and documented as described in section 13.4.4. It is useful to have a 'structured walk through' of the Enquiry Process Model.

13.4 Worked Example of Update Process Model

An Update Process Model is prepared for each event within each update function. The process model for an event is developed by converting the Effect Correspondence Diagram into a process structure diagram. Operations are then added to the structure.

An Update Process Model will be created for the event 'Register authorized user' from the Car Allowance system.

13.4.1 Identify required view of Logical Data Model

The first step is to look at the Logical Data Model and identify the required view of the data model. Figure 13.11 shows this for our example.

13.4.2 Specify event name

The event is specified by the same unique name as used in Function Definitions, Entity Life Histories, Effect Correspondence Diagrams and Physical Process Specification. The event in our example has the name 'Register authorized user'.

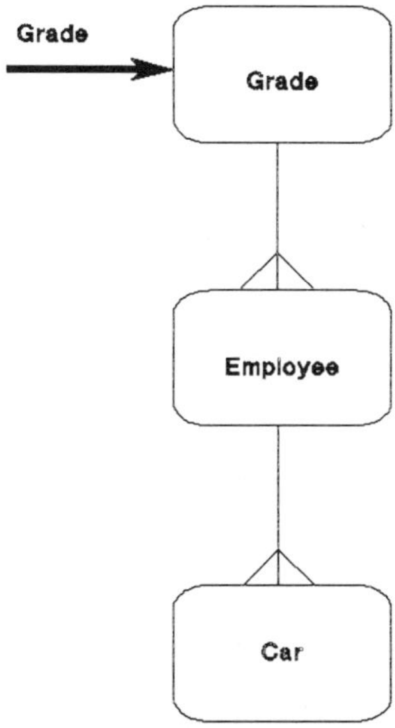

Figure 13.11 Required view of data model.

13.4.3 Specify event data

The event data consists of the data input to the event. This is usually the key of the entity which is the entry point to the Logical Data Model, plus some updating information.

An event may appear in more than one function, so the designer must check that the data items for the event appear in the function input structure, oı can be generated by it. Our example event appears in two Entity Life Histories, one for Employee and the second for Car. The Entity Life Histories are shown in Figures 13.12 and 13.13.

13.4.4 Specify Effect Correspondence Diagram 00

The Effect Correspondence Diagram for the event is completed during Entity-event modelling in Stage 3. The diagram for our example event is shown in Figure 13.14.

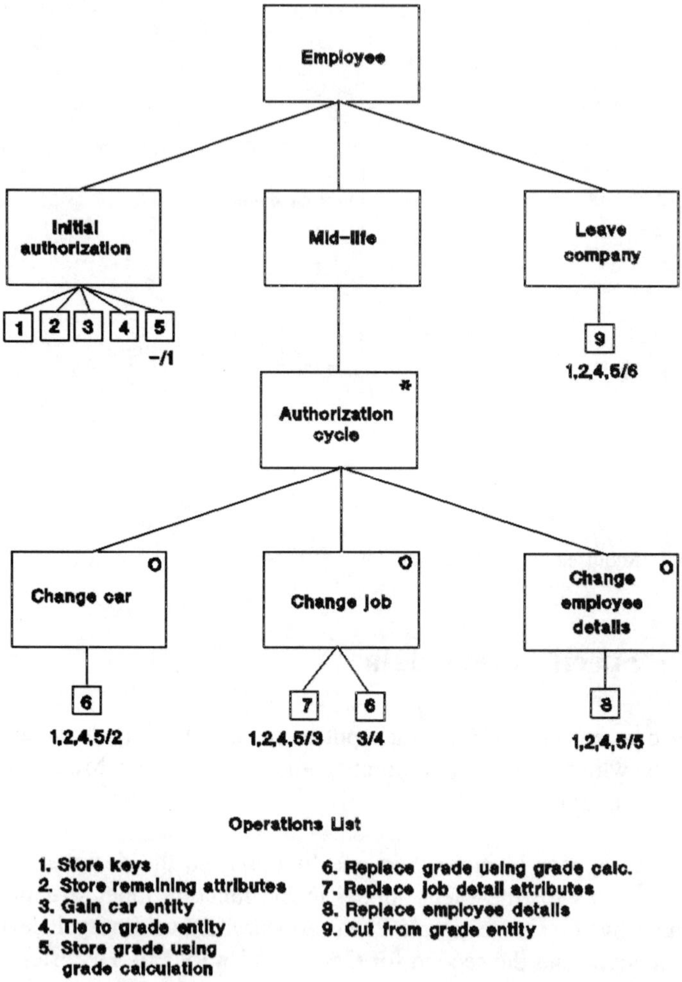

Figure 13.12 Entity Life History for 'Employee'.

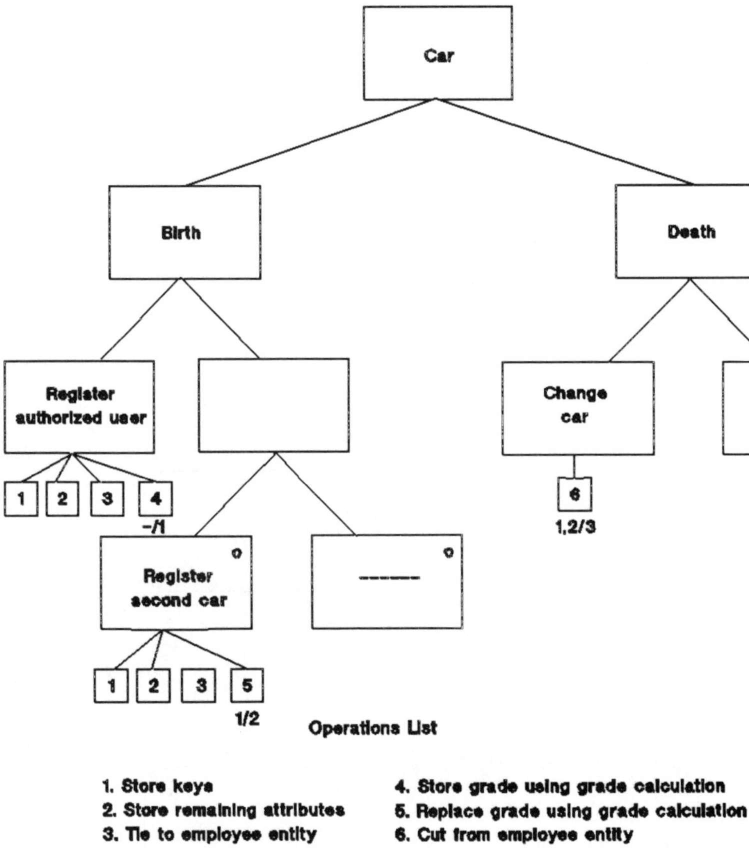

Figure 13.13 Entity Life History for 'Car@.

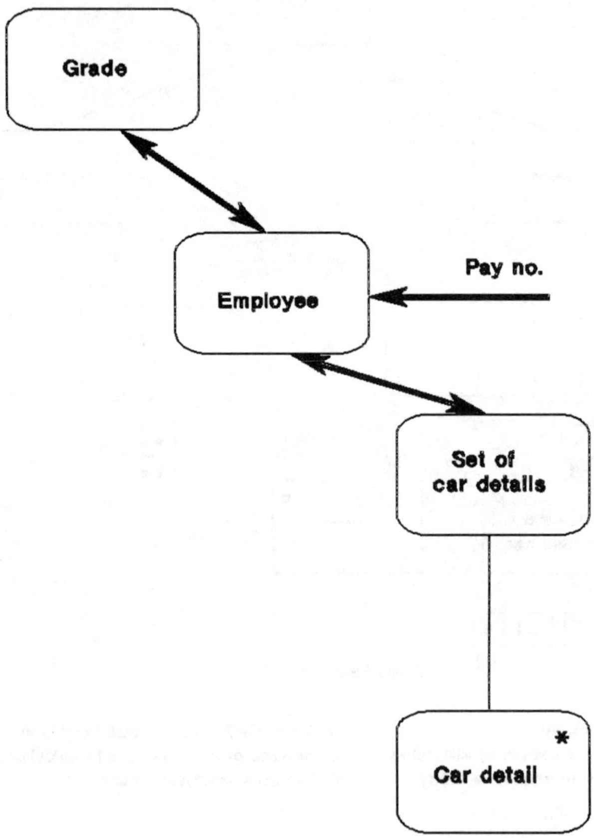

Figure 13.14 Effect Correspondence Diagram.

13.4.5 Specify event output

The event output should be specified. This may just be a message saying 'Record created'. If there is more substantial output then this should be defined in the same way as the enquiry output. Our example just requires a confirmation that a record has been created.

13.4.6 Extend Effect Correspondence Diagram

If an event has substantial output, then it may be necessary to extend an update process with enquiry-only entities. The Effect Correspondence Diagram is extended to these enquiry-only entities using the enquiry process modelling technique.

13.4.7 Group effects on Effect Correspondence Diagram

The effects in one-to-one correspondence on the Effect Correspondence Diagram are grouped. The grouped effects and any left-over elementary effects are named as processes. This is shown in Figure 13.15.

The example identifies two processes. 'New car user' creates an occurrence of the Employee entity, 'Car detail' creates an occurrence of the Car entity.

13.4.8 List operations

The operations are then listed by entity as shown in Figure 13.16. This makes it easier to check for omissions. Blank operations are used to divide the groupings by entity.

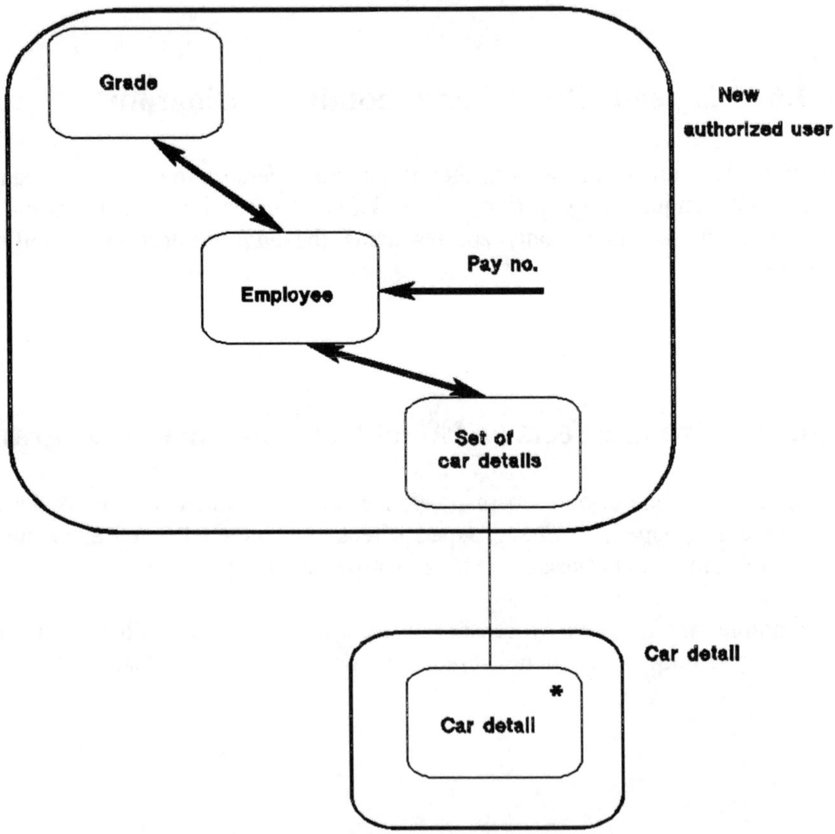

Figure 13.15 Effect Correspondence Diagram with grouped effects and named processes.

1. Read Employee by key
2. Fail if SI of Employee < > NULL
3. Create Employee
4. Store keys of Employee
5. Store remaining attributes of Employee
6. Store Grade using grade calculation
7. Set SI of Employee to 1
8. Write Employee
9.
10. Read Car by key
11. Fail if SI of Car < > NULL
12. Create Car
13. Store keys of Car
14. Store remaining attributes of Car
15. Set SI of Car to 1
16. Tie Car to Employee
17. Write Car

Figure 13.16 Operations List

The following changes are made to the operations used in Entity Life Histories (see section 11.4.4):

	ENTITY LIFE HISTORY	UPDATE PROCESS MODEL
i)	Gain <entity>	not used
ii)	Lose <entity>	not used
iii)	Store keys	Store keys of <entity>
iv)	Store remaining attributes	Store remaining attributes of <entity>
v)	Replace <attribute> [using <expression>]	Replace <attribute> of <entity> [using <expression>]
vi)	Tie to <entity>	Tie <entity> to <master-entity> [using <relationship>]
vii)	Cut from <entity>	Cut <entity> from <master-entity> [using <relationship>]

The following additional operations are used with update structures only:

i)	**Create <entity>**	**create without writing to database**
ii)	**Set state indicator of <entity> to <value>**	**set the entity's state indicator values before writing**
iii)	**Write <entity>**	**write entity to database**

13.4.9 Convert to structure diagram

The Effect Correspondence Diagram with grouped effects is now converted into a Process Structure Diagram as shown in Figure 13.17.

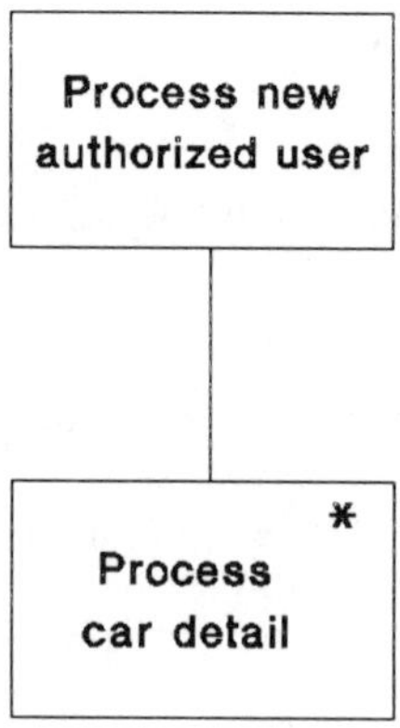

Figure 13.17 Process Structure Diagram

13.4.10 Allocate operations to structure

The operations are now allocated to the process box which represent the effect to which the operations apply. The operations should be allocated in the following sequence:

i) read the entity
ii) raise invalid SI (state indicator) value after read
iii) create
iv) (enhanced) operations from effects on the ELH for that entity
v) set the SI of the entity
vi) write entity

Figure 13.18 shows the Process Structure Diagram with operations added.

13.4.11 Allocate conditions to structure

Conditions should now be added above each option of a selection, and above each iterated component. This is shown in Figure 13.19.

13.4.12 Specify integrity error conditions

Operations must be added for any integrity error conditions which have been omitted.

The data in a database must be consistent, that is, it must retain its 'referential integrity'. Care must be taken when adding and deleting entity occurrences. For instance, in the Car Allowance Case Study, if a master entity occurrence of Employee was deleted and the occurrences of the detail entity Car belonging to that Employee were not deleted, we would have an integrity error. Car has the attribute 'Pay-no' which links a car to an Employee. If the Employee is deleted, then all Cars belonging to that Employee also require to be deleted.

Similarly we could not create a Car entity without first creating an Employee who owns that car.

In addition there may be some business rules which apply to the system. For instance in an Order Processing System, a company may have a rule that a Customer should not have a 'Total-balance-due' which exceeded the 'Credit-limit' for that customer.

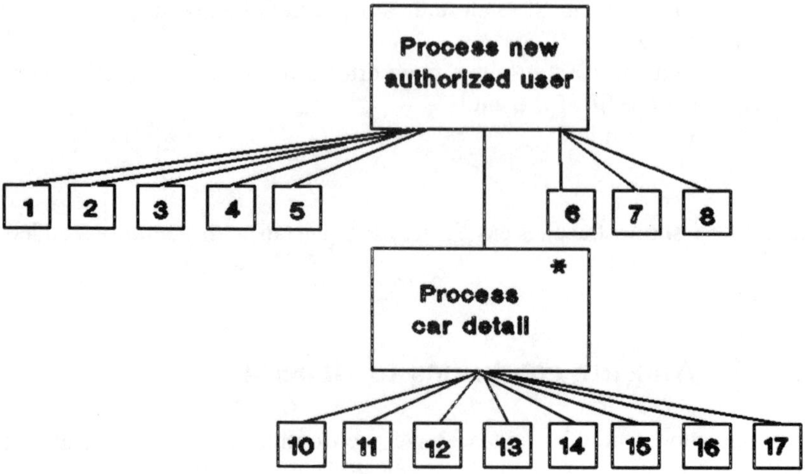

Operations List

1. Read employee by key
2. Fail if SI of employee <> NULL
3. Create employee
4. Store keys of employee
5. Store remaining attributes of employee
6. Store grade using grade calculation
7. Set SI of employee to 1
8. Write employee
9.
10. Read car by key
11. Fail if SI of car <> NULL
12. Create car
13. Store keys of car
14. Store remaining attributes of car
15. Set SI of car to 1
16. Tie car to employee
17. Write car

Figure 13.18 Process Structure Diagram with operations

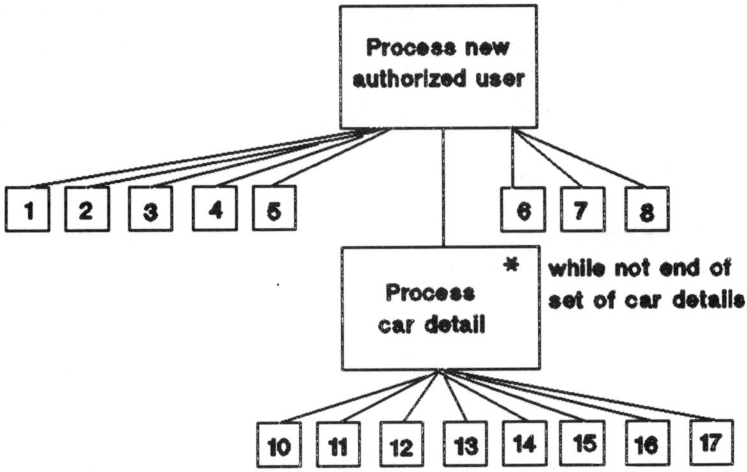

Operations List

1. Read employee by key
2. Fail if SI of employee <> NULL
3. Create employee
4. Store keys of employee
5. Store remaining attributes of employee
6. Store grade using grade calculation
7. Set SI of employee to 1
8. Write employee
9.
10. Read car by key
11. Fail if SI of car <> NULL
12. Create car
13. Store keys of car
14. Store remaining attributes of car
15. Set SI of car to 1
16. Tie car to employee
17. Write car

Figure 13.19 Process Structure Diagram with conditions.

In specifying the Update Process Model, care should be taken to specify all integrity error conditions as operations. Entity Life History analysis should have covered many of these integrity error conditions by specifying tests for valid states of state indicators or attributes. An example might be 'Fail if Total-balance-due > Credit-limit'.

Suitable error messages must be defined for every integrity error identified.

It is useful to have a 'structured walk through' of the Update Process Model' to ensure that the sequence makes sense.

13.5 Place of Logical Database Process Design in SSADM

13.5.1 Requirements Specification

The following outputs of Stage 3, Definition of Requirements Structure, are input to Logical Database Process Design: Required System Logical Data Model, Function Definitions, I/O Structures, Effect Correspondence Diagrams and Entity Life Histories.

13.5.2 Logical System Specification

13.5.2.1 Step 520 Define Update Processes

The logical specification of update functions is completed during this Step. State indicator values are added to Entity Life Histories. The Effect Correspondence Diagram for each event is turned into a processing structure. The operations for each event are identified, with the help of Entity Life Histories, and allocated to the processing structure. Error outputs are specified.

13.5.2.2 Step 530 Define Enquiry Processes

The Enquiry Access Path for the enquiry is converted into an input data structure. The output data structure is derived from the Input/Output Structure. The input and output data structures are then merged to form a single processing structure. Operations and conditions are added to the processing structure. Error outputs are specified.

13.5.2.3 Step 540 Assemble Logical Design

The Enquiry and Update Process Models become part of the Logical Design document.

13.5.3 Physical Design

13.5.3.1 Step 640 Optimise Physical Data Design

The Enquiry and Update Process Models are input to the process of optimising the Physical Data Design.

13.6 Summary

The Logical Database Process Design technique defines the processing for data input to, and output from, the logical database. An Enquiry Process Model is created for every enquiry function. An Update Process Model is created for every event included in the Update Functions. A process model consists of an Enquiry or Update Process Structure Diagram and an operations list.

13.7 Keywords

Logical Database Process Design
Enquiry Process
Update Process
Input/Output Structure
Enquiry Access Path
Logical success unit
Logical Data Model
Input/Output Structure
Structure clash
Enquiry Process Model
Update Process Model
Enquiry trigger
Enquiry output data structure
Enquiry input data structure
Enquiry process structure
Operation
Condition
Integrity error

13.8 Exercises

1. Prepare an Enquiry Process Models for the following enquiry from the Car Allowance System (see Logical Data Model in Figure 6.27):

   List the employee-name and total-claim-value for all employees for the financial year to date.

2. Prepare an Enquiry Process Model for the process which records a change of car for an employee.

CHAPTER 14

Physical Data Design

14.1 Introduction

Stages 1 to 5 of SSADM produce a Logical Design of the required system. Physical Design (Stage 6) deals with the implementation of the Logical Design in the selected physical environment. The physical data, processes, inputs and outputs must be specified using the features and language of the selected physical environment.

There are two main components of Physical Design. The first is a database design. The second is a set of process specifications. The database design is specified using the Physical Database Design technique described in this Chapter. The process specifications are specified using the Physical Process Specification technique described in Chapter 15.

Physical Data Design examines the physical groupings of data and the impact this has on access to data. The aim is to produce a Physical Data Design which implements the system data requirements, supports the processing requirements and meets the space and timing targets, as specified in the Logical Design.

The Physical Data Design technique provides some general principles which must be supplemented by detailed knowledge of the selected implementation environment. This Chapter discusses the general principles which should be applied in Physical Data Design.

14.2 Physical Data Design framework

Physical Data Design offers a framework which can be followed by designers. The Required System Logical Data Model is converted, through a series of steps, to a Physical Data Design. The Physical Design is expressed in terms of the physical storage and access facilities provided in the selected implementation environment. The SSADM framework for Physical Design requires the following design stages:

i) achieve an understanding of the selected implementation environment

ii) identify the facilities provided by, and constraints within, the selected implementation environment which will influence the physical design specification.

iii) define the Physical Data Design strategy

iv) produce a first-cut Physical Data Design

v) optimise and test the design

The first attempt at producing a physical data design is called the first-cut data design. The first-cut design is a physical schema which is the starting point for developing a tuned design. The final tuned design must be developed by somebody with an intimate knowledge of the selected physical environment and, because this process is so specific to a particular product and installation, this aspect is beyond the scope of this book. The remainder of this chapter will describe the production of the first-cut Physical Data Design and briefly describe some aspects of tuning the design.

14.3 Physical Data Design activities

The following activities are followed to produce a Physical Data Design:

i) produce an initial physical data model

ii) identify required entry points

iii) identify the roots of physical groups

iv) identify the allowable physical groups

v) apply least dependent occurrence rule

vi) determine block size

vii) split the groups to fit the block size

viii) apply the product specific rules

The first seven tasks produce the Physical Data Model and can be performed by an analyst, as they do not require product specific knowledge. The final task turns the model into a first-cut, product specific data design. The Physical Data Design produced by this process may require to be optimised.

The production of a first-cut Physical Data Design will be discussed using the Car Allowance Case Study as an example. A simple version of the Logical Data Model will be used as the basis for the design, see Figure 14.1.

14.3.1 Produce an initial physical data model

Some of the information on the Required System Logical Data Model is not required for Physical Design. One way of documenting the information needed for Physical Design is to convert the Required Logical Data Model into a Physical Data Model. This is done by making the following changes to the Required Logical Data Model, as seen in Figure 14.2:

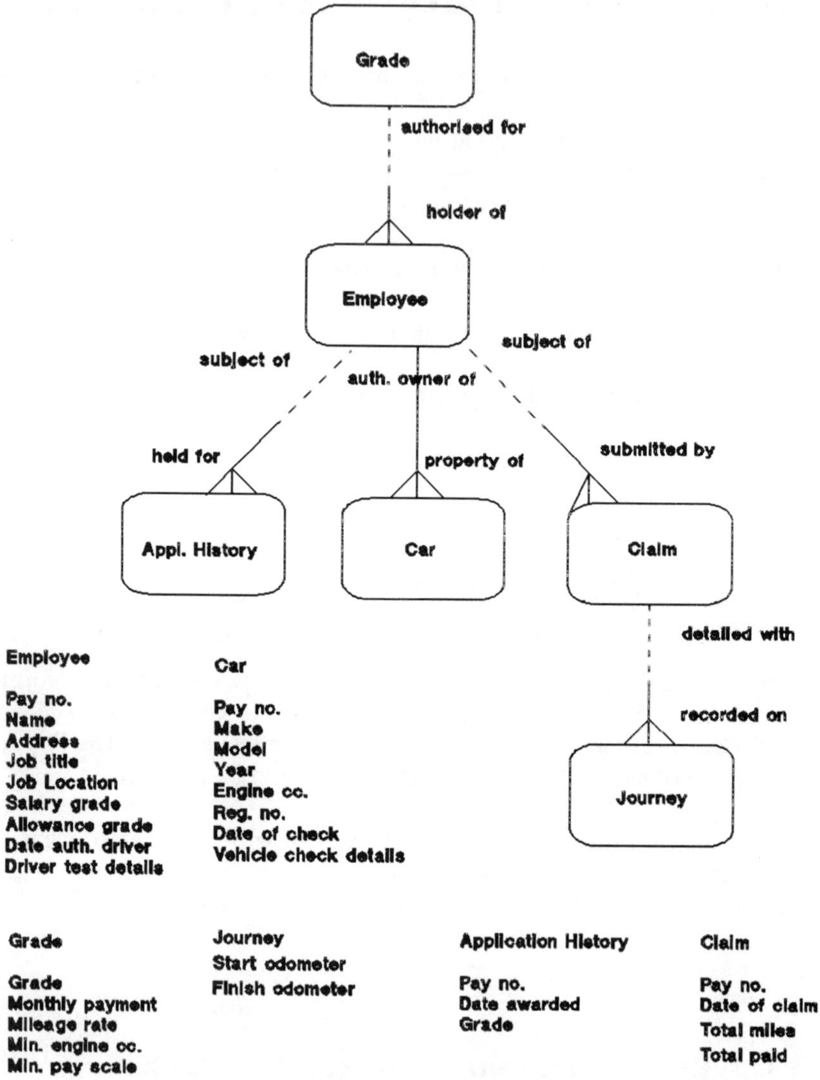

Figure 14.1 Logical Data Model

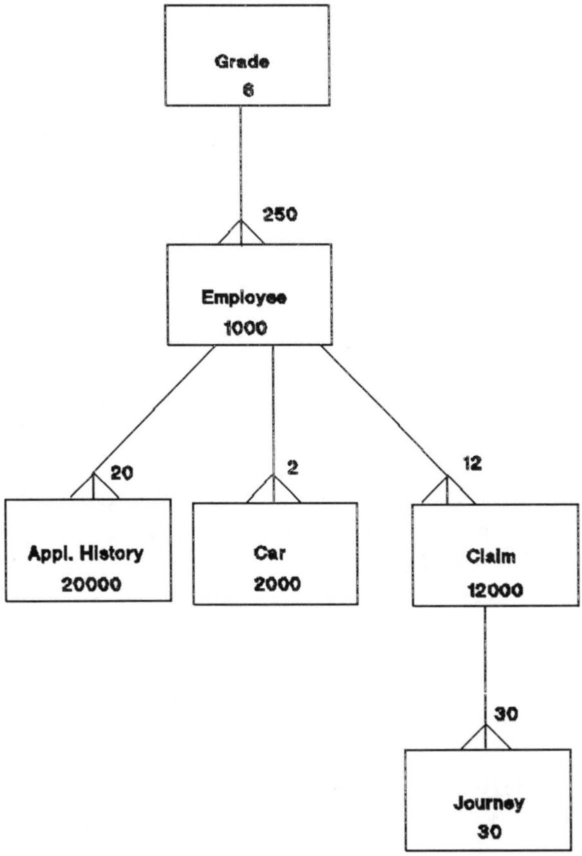

Figure 14.2 Physical Data Model

i) use hard-cornered boxes

ii) remove relationship names

iii) remove any reference to relationship optionality except that denoting whether a master must exist for a detail.
Where a relationship line is solid at the detail end and dashed at the master, replace this with a solid line.

Where a relationship line is dashed at the detail end (denotes master might not exist for detail), replace with a solid line with the 'O' symbol on it to denote optionality.

iv) Remove, or amend, exclusion arcs.

An exclusion arc between a master and two or more details is removed (shows detail of only one type must exist for an occurrence of master).

An exclusion arc between a detail and two or more of its masters is replaced by an 'O' denoting optionality (shows only one type of master will occur for each occurrence of detail).

v) carry over design volumes from the Required Logical Data Model. The number of occurrences for each entity is shown in the entity box. The numbers on the crow's feet show how many details there are for each occurrence of the master.

14.3.2 Identify required entry points

The next step is to define the required access entry points and distinguish those that are non-key. The access entry points, and the data items on which access is made, are derived from the Effect Correspondence Diagrams and Enquiry Access Paths.

Some access points may use data items which are not part of the entity key. Non-key access entry points represent secondary index requirements. Non-key entry points are represented by a sausage-shaped box linked to the entity it is indexing by a relationship line. Figure 14.3 shows two non-key access points on the Employee entity.

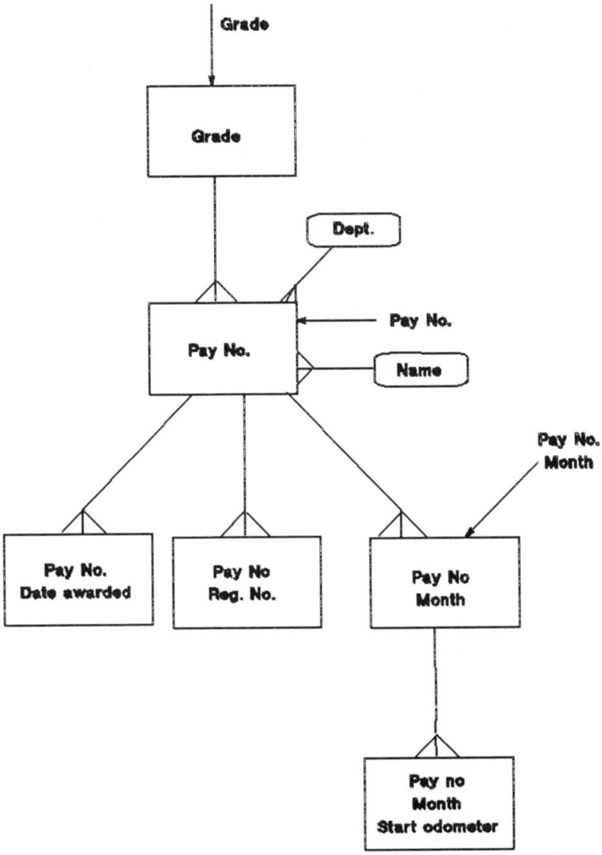

Figure 14.3 Identifying the entry points.

14.3.3 Identify the roots of the physical groups

Root entities are the entities without a master in the data model. They will normally appear at the top of the model. 'Grade' is an example of such a root entity. A root entity can also be an entity used as a direct access point, unless its key includes the key of one of its master entities and that master entity is already the top of a group. The master does not have to be the direct master of the detail. 'Employee' is an example of this type of root entity. 'Claim' is a direct access point, but it is not included as a root entity since its key includes 'Pay-no', the key of Employee which is already a root entity.

The resulting model is shown in Figure 14.4. A root entity is indicated by a stripe in the top of the entity box.

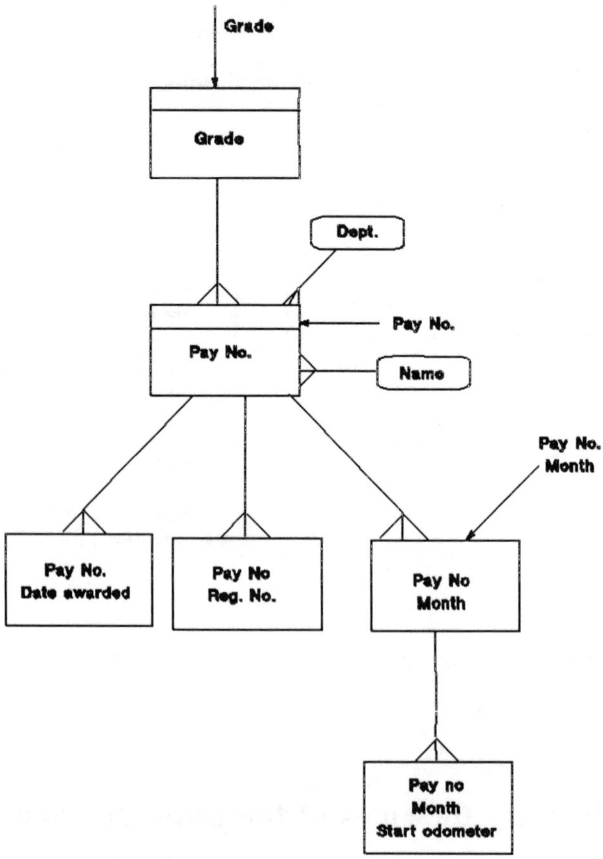

Figure 14.4 Identification of the roots of physical groups.

14.3.4 Identify the allowable physical groups

We can now identify the allowable or valid physical groups for each non-root entity. A non-root entity is only placed in a physical group if one of its mandatory masters is in that group. Where a non-root entity is a direct access point and could be placed in more than one such physical group, it should be placed with the master whose key is part of its own key.

The example in Figure 14.5 shows that there are only two allowable physical groups. There are only two root entities. 'Employee' has all the non-root entities as detail, so they belong to the physical group headed by 'Employee'.

In a more complex example there will be some details with more than one master which could belong to more than one physical group. The diagram should show the possible member entities to be grouped with each root entity.

14.3.5 Apply least dependent occurrence rule

The least dependent occurrence rule deals with those entities which can belong to more than one physical group. The entity should be placed with the group in which it occurs least. This can be determined from the occurrence values shown on the relationship lines.

The physical data model should now be redrawn showing the physical groups. Each entity should belong to one group only.

14.3.6 Determine block size

The choice of block size is limited by the block sizes supported by the DBMS, the sizes of the most commonly used groups and the space taken up when the blocks are read into memory.

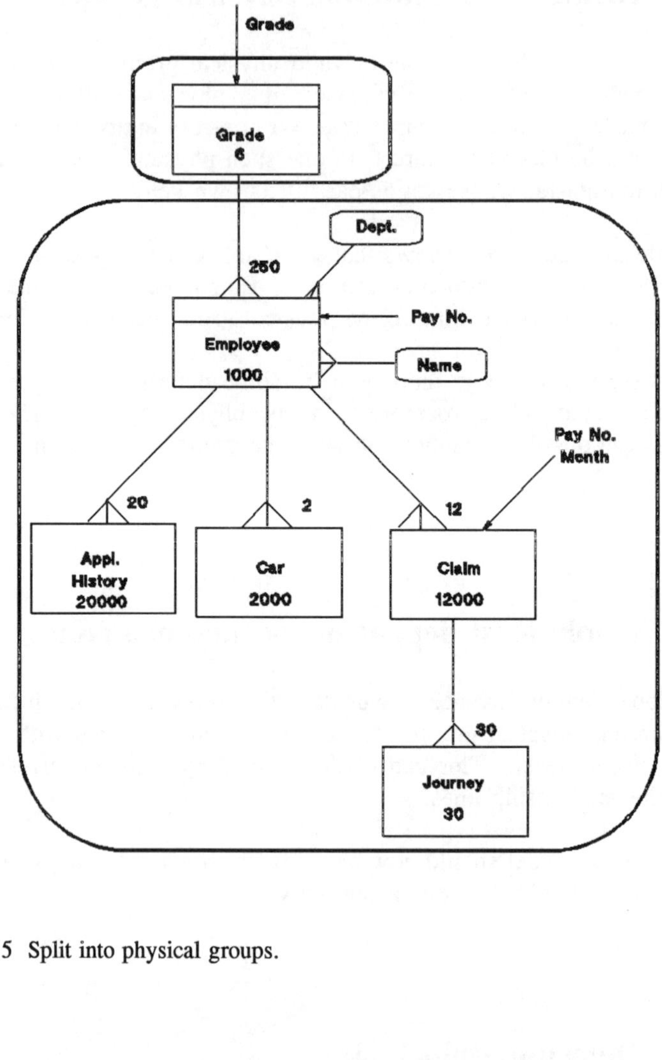

Figure 14.5 Split into physical groups.

14.3.7 Split the groups to fit the block size

The physical groups should be checked against the block size. Calculate the size of the data in each record by adding up the lengths of the data items given in the Entity Descriptions. Some assumptions must be made about the requirements for maintaining relationships and management of disk space.

The following assumptions have been made:

- each relationship takes 6 bytes in the master entity and six bytes in the detail entity.
- each secondary index entry takes 6 bytes (stored in index blocks, not data blocks)
- record overheads (header etc) are 6 bytes per record.
- assume blocks are only 60% to 80% full.

Where a physical group will not split into a block, the physical group must be split into two or more smaller groups. Work from the bottom of a physical group upwards to identify a sub-group which can be split off from the original group. The least dependent occurrence rule can be re-applied if groups are split.

In our example the two physical groups should not require splitting. See Figure 14.6 for an estimate of the data storage requirements for the Employee physical group. The Grade physical group contains only one entity with a record length of 23 characters.

14.3.8 Apply the product specific rules

The physical data design requirements have now been determined. The designer must determine how best to implement these requirements on the selected DBMS.

For instance, if the system is to be implemented on a relational DBMS product.

i) Each entity becomes a table

ii) Create a unique index for each table. Each index should consist of the key of the entity. For compound keys, the table is indexed by each part of its compound key

iii) Define an index for each foreign key

Record	Primary owner	Records per hierarchy	Data size	Record overhead	Relationship overhead	Space/ record	Space/ physical group	Record space/ block
Employee	——	1	259	6	24	289	289	289
Appl. History	Employee	20	19	6	6	31	620	620
Car	Employee	2	111	6	6	123	246	246
Claim	Employee	12	28	6	6	40	480	480
Journey	Claim	30	12	6	6	24	720	720
							Data total	2355

Figure 14.6 Data storage requirements for Employee physical group.

iv) Define an index for each secondary indexing requirement

v) For each non-root table, the index defined on the primary key of its owner is declared a clustering index.

The designer should select the facilities to be used and then apply the product specific rules to provide the first-cut Physical Design.

14.4 Tuning the design

The processes described so far in this Chapter are only a starting point in building the final physical data implementation. The design will need to be tuned by a designer with intimate knowledge of the final physical implementation. This tuning process will be aimed at optimising system objectives relating to file storage space, timing and recovery.

The process of design tuning is technical and specific to the selected implementation environment. A detailed treatment of this topic is beyond the scope of this book.

14.5 Place of Physical Data Design in SSADM

14.5.1 Requirements Specification

The Data Catalogue, Effect Correspondence Diagrams, Function Definitions, Required System Logical Data Model and Requirements Catalogue, produced or amended, during this module, are inputs to the Physical Data Design Technique.

14.5.2 Logical System Specification

The Enquiry Process Models, Update Process Models and Technical Environment Description produced during this module are inputs to the Physical Data Design Technique.

14.5.3 Physical Design

14.5.3.1 Step 610 Prepare for Physical Design

During this Step the facilities and constraints of the physical implementation environment must be identified. The product-specific data design rules should be specified. The design standards are documented using a Product Breakdown Structure and Product Descriptions.

14.5.3.2 Step 620 Create Physical Data Design

The Required System Logical Data Model is converted into a first-cut Physical Design using the Physical Data Design Technique as described in section 14.3. A Space Estimation is also produced.

14.5.3.3 Step 640 Optimise Physical Data Design

The Physical Data Design is optimised to meet the performance information contained in the Function Definitions and the Requirements Catalogue.

14.5.3.4 Step 660 Consolidate Process Data Interface

The optimised Physical Design is compared with the Function Component Implementation Map data access components to identify any mismatches in the view of data.

14.5.3.5 Step 670 Assemble Physical Design

The optimised Physical Data Design and the Space Estimation become part of the Physical Design Document.

14.6 Summary

The Required System Logical Data Model is transformed through a series of steps into a first-cut Physical Design for the selected implementation environment. The designer then tunes the design to meet the performance objectives described in the Requirements Catalogue and Function Definitions. The end result is the optimised Physical Data Design.

14.7 Keywords

Logical Design
Physical Design
Physical Data Design
Required System Logical Data Model
Physical Data Model
Allowable physical group
Product specific rules
Optimised Physical Design
Design tuning

First-cut design
Required entry point
Least dependent occurrence
Block size
Root entity
Access entry point
Performance objectives
Physical group

14.8 Exercises

14.8.1 Outline the activities involved in producing the first-cut Physical Data Design.

14.8.2 Prepare a first-cut Physical Data Design for the Telephone Directory System first described in Chapter 5, section 2. Select a suitable implementation environment from the facilities available to you.

14.8.3 Prepare a first-cut Physical Data Design for the Telephone Directory System described in Appendix 2. Select a suitable implementation environment from the facilities available to you.

CHAPTER 15
Physical Process Specification

15.1 Introduction

The final technique is the specification of the physical processes. This takes the logical specification of processes from the Logical System Specification and determines how best to implement these processes in the selected implementation environment. The Physical Process Specification technique provides a guide to the activities necessary in transforming the Logical Design into a specification which can be implemented using an application generator or a programmer to generate programs.

Physical Process Specification has four activities:

i) planning Physical Process Specification

ii) creation of the Function Component Implementation Map

iii) completing the specification of functions requiring procedural code

iv) developing the Process Data Interface

This Chapter gives a brief description of the activities involved in Physical Process Specification. An understanding of the selected physical environment is necessary to cover this technique in any depth and that is beyond the scope of this book.

15.2 Planning

The designer requires to study the selected implementation environment with regard to the processing elements of the system. The Processing System Classification is produced as part of this activity. The classification provides a guide to the features of the physical environment which will help in the development of standards for the conversion of the Logical Design into a Physical Design. For instance, the physical environment may impose some limitations on naming conventions. These require to be documented so that they can be adhered to during Physical Design.

15.3 Function Component Implementation Map

The Function Component Implementation Map is now created. This looks at all the fragments of processing required for the system. A fragment is a defined processing element which may be at any level from an operation (eg Read detail) upwards. The re-use of fragments is recorded on the Function Component Implementation Map which shows how the fragments fit together to form functions. The mapping of logical function components onto the physical design is also described.

The implementation plan for each function is completed and common processing within the system identified. Further detail is required for each function in the following areas:

i) success units

ii) syntax error handling

iii) controls and control errors

iv) physical input/output format

v) physical dialogue

In addition there are two areas to examine across the functions and to consider throughout this activity.

vi) duplication and common processing

Each screen, Input/Output process and common processing element must be fully documented. Detailed processing specifications are produced to include details such as: objectives, relationship with other processes, inputs and outputs, constituent processes, hardware requirements, references to file and record layouts, controls. Manual procedures should also be described.

15.3.1 Success units

A success unit is a group of sub-processes which must succeed or fail as a group. Keeping in mind the constraints of the implementation environment, the designer must decide on the most appropriate level of success unit for each function.

15.3.2 Syntax error handling

Each data item in the input data should have any syntax rules defined. A syntax error is an error detected in data input. The error might be a data item outside a specified range. For instance, in the Car Allowance System, 'Grade' would currently be specified as being in the range A to F. A suitable error message should be defined. 'Only grades A to F are defined' would be a suitable message for the above example. If the error messages are stored and retrieved from the database, they can be maintained without altering the programs, and re-used by several processes.

There may also be semantic errors in the stored data which are detected by the logical database processes. These were discussed as integrity errors in Chapter 14, Logical Database Process Design.

15.3.3 Controls and control errors

Controls and control errors require to be defined in two areas. The first is the navigation through the functions of the system and its associated error handling. The second is the control of data items using methods such as check totals.

15.3.4 Physical input/output format

Input/Output formats cover two major areas. The first is covers dialogues. The second is concerned with reports.

Physical Design adds many device or message type constraints on Input/Output Design. All the physical Input/Output formats must be specified to include the Logical Input/Output Structures, error messages and reports. The design is further constrained by the requirements of the Application Style Guide.

15.3.5 Physical dialogue

Dialogues require further format specification to become physical dialogues. The Logical Dialogue Design is taken as the basis and is extended to include details pertinent to the physical environment. This would include further specification of screens, physical data groups, input views of a physical data group, additional error handling components, and navigation paths through dialogues.

The logical data groups defined in Dialogue Design must be mapped onto the physical screens. A screen may contain one or more data groups. The redefinition of logical data groups as physical data groups may require some changes to screen design. A physical data group is a group of data items which occupies a whole screen or a defined area within a screen. Some logical data groups are too large for one screen and require to be split. On some occasions the constraints of the physical environment will mean a logical data group cannot be directly implemented as a physical data group.

Data items should be clustered as a physical data group:

- to display data related to one entity
- for the entry of a single enquiry or event
- to ease navigation through a dialogue.

In the Car Allowance System, the event 'Register car claim' would require three physical groups of data. The first group would be the relevant details from the 'Employee' entity, the second would be the 'Claim' entity details. These two physical groups could be placed on one screen. Those claims undergoing a more detailed check would require a third physical group, 'Journey details', to appear as a second screen.

A number of different strategies can be used for Physical Dialogue Design. For instance if a physical data group contains more than one event or enquiry trigger and the data group can trigger several success units, then each event could be individually processed. If the physical data group can only trigger one success unit, then the group of events can be input and processed as a single unit.

The selected physical environment will constrain navigation through the data items in a dialogue. The designer may be able to make use of facilities to jump forwards and backwards through data items or groups of data items. There may be facilities to ease movement through the menu structure. These facilities need to be mapped onto the control tables defined in Dialogue Design (see Chapter 3, section 6.3).

15.3.6 Duplication and common processing

Unnecessary duplication of processing fragments should be identified and removed. Care should be taken that the maintainability of the system is not compromised.

A common process is an element of processing which is common to several processes. In the Car Allowance System the 'Calculation of allowance grade' is a common process since it can occur in more than one process or function, since a new user, change of car or change in job details could all cause a recalculation of the grade. Many common processes have already been identified by the time Physical Design is carried out.

15.4 Functions requiring procedural code

Functions which require procedural code must be further specified. Some physical environments, such as a 4GL or a 3GL report generator, generate a physical program entirely from a description of its input and output. The physical environment deduces the logic of the programs. Where this occurs a non-procedural specification is used.

If the physical environment cannot generate the necessary programs from a functions logical Input/Output Structures, then a procedural specification is required. A formal language for describing procedural processes is required. A Jackson Structure with operations and conditions attached is an example of a suitable formal language. The most important area to specify is the combination of logical processes into physical modules.

15.5 Process Data Interface

The Process Data Interface shows how the Logical Data Model maps on to the Physical Data Design. Access requirements for function components identified on the Function Component Implementation Map are compared with the optimised Physical Data Design and mismatches identified.

For each mismatch, the physical keys of master and detail should be identified. The sequence of physical accesses to provide the logical view required by the Function Component Implementation Map is then specified.

The handling of mismatches between the logical and physical views of the accesses is fully documented in the Function Component Implementation Map.

The Logical Database Process Design technique assumes the existence of a DBMS. The process specifications can be implemented in a non-database physical environment if a Process Data Interface is designed to handle the reading and writing of entities.

15.6 Place of Physical Process Specification in SSADM

15.6.1 Logical System Specification

The Logical System Specification provides the major inputs to Physical Process Specification. The Update Process Models, Enquiry Process Models, completed Function Definitions and Dialogue Design provide the main sources of information about processes and navigation through the system.

15.6.2 Physical Design

15.6.2.1 Step 610 Prepare for Physical Design

During this Step the facilities and constraints of the physical implementation environment must be identified. Standards are developed for the use of the physical processing system.

15.6.2.2 Step 630 Create Function Component Implementation Map

During this Step the components of functions that are not included in the Logical Design are specified. This includes syntax error handling, physical input/output formats and physical dialogues. The Function Component Implementation Map is created.

15.6.2.3 Step 650 Complete Function Specification

This Step produces program specifications for the components of a function that require to be specified procedurally.

15.6.2.4 Step 660 Consolidate Process Data Interface

The data access identified on the Function Component Implementation Map is compared with the Physical Data Design to identify differences in the view of the data.

15.7 Summary

The Physical Process Specification Technique takes the Logical Design of processing requirements and transforms this into a Physical Design for the selected implementation environment. The end product is a set of non-procedural specifications which can be input to an application generator to produce program code, and a set of procedural specifications which can be given to a programmer to code.

15.8 Keywords

Function Component Implementation Map
Processing System Classification
Function Definitions
Update Process Models
Enquiry Process Models
Dialogue Design
Physical implementation environment
Process Data Interface
Function specification
Procedural
Non-procedural
Fragment
Common processing
Success unit

15.9 Exercises

1. Outline the purpose of the Function Component Implementation Map.

2. Can you identify any further common processing in the Car Allowance System Case Study?

3. Explain the difference between a procedural and non-procedural specification.

Appendix 1

The Structural Model of SSADM

MODULE FS - FEASIBILITY STUDY ACTIVITY DESCRIPTION

Objectives

To establish whether a proposed information system can meet the specified business requirements of the organisation.

To establish the business case for the proposed information system, and enable the project board to decide whether to commit resources to a more detailed study.

To determine whether to proceed in a different direction from that envisaged in the IS Strategy.

To enable the project board to select from a range of business and technical options, and to identify the projects necessary to implement the chosen option.

Summary

A Feasibility Study is a short assessment of a proposed information system to determine whether the system can effectively meet the specified business requirements of the organisation, and whether a business case exists for developing such a system.

A Feasibility Study is recommended as a preliminary to a Full Study (Requirements Analysis, Requirements Specification, and Logical System Specification) for all projects except those of low risk. It will frequently but not necessarily follow an IS Strategy Study. The scope of the feasibility study activities will often extend beyond those supported by SSADM techniques and described in the activity descriptions. The SSADM techniques primarily assist the identification of information system requirements and the assessment of technical feasibility. The Feasibility Module activities do not describe the other aspects of feasibility in detail, and these standard activities will need to be supplemented in Step 010 (Prepare for the Feasibility Study) according to the type of study being undertaken.

The current and required environments are studied and documented only in sufficient detail to enable a Problem Definition Statement to be developed and agreed with the project board, and for Business System Options and Technical System Options to be identified.

Participants

Feasibility study team, including those with project management and analysis skills, user participants and specialist advisers.

Preconditions

- **Management Authorization**
  Agreement to scope of investigation
  Agreement to problem definition
  Feasibility option selection
- **Inputs**
  Project Initiation Document
- **References**
  Business Objectives
  Business plans
  IS Strategy statement
  IS Strategy planning working paper
  Management and technical policies
  Organisation charts
  Project portfolio

Products

Feasibility Report

Activities

Stage	Step	Description
0		Feasibility
	010	Prepare for the Feasibility Study
	020	Define the Problem
	030	Select Feasibility Options
	040	Assemble Feasibility Report

MODULE RA - REQUIREMENTS ANALYSIS ACTIVITY DESCRIPTION

Objectives

To determine the scope of the application

To establish how to integrate the IT component with other needs.

To form a view of overall system costs and benefits.

To confirm the viability of continuing further.

To gain user ownership of the requirement.

Summary

SSADM Requirements Analysis is driven by requirements definition and Business System Options. These place the Study in the context of the future System. Requirements are documented in the Requirements Catalogue and are expressed in terms of system objectives. These are related to levels of service, security considerations and overall functionality. Each is expressed in as quantifiable a way as possible. This greatly helps the user organisation verify the acceptability of all products developed by the team.

The Requirements Catalogue is supported by models of the current environment - Data Flow Models of current functionality and a Logical Data Model of the information used in current services.

Business Systems Options are presented for management to choose the scope of the required system functionality, and to commit to its planned costs.

Participants

Requirements analysts with both SSADM and business knowledge; users; IT service providers; staff representatives.

Preconditions

- **Management Authorization**
  Project Initiation Document
  Requirements Analysis Module Plans
  Requirements Analysis controls
- **Inputs**
  Project Initiation Document
  Feasibility Report
  Reports from previous studies
- **References**
  Business Objectives
  Data descriptions from current environment
  Forms and documents from current environment
  Management and technical policies
  Procedure description from current environment

Products

Analysis of Requirements
Business Systems Options
Selected Business System Option
Project and analysis scope

Activities

Stage	Step	Description
1		Investigation of Current Environment
	110	Establish Analysis Framework
	120	Investigate and Define Requirements
	130	Investigate Current Processing
	140	Investigate Current Data
	150	Derive Logical View of Current Services
	160	Assemble Investigation Results
2		Business System Options
	210	Define Business System Options
	220	Select Business System Option

MODULE RS - REQUIREMENTS SPECIFICATION ACTIVITY DESCRIPTION

Objective

To enable user management to issue a Requirements Specification of correct scope, adequate provision, and with measurable acceptance criteria to enable a Logical System Specification to be developed under a contractual agreement by a design team. It is vital that the Requirements Specification has full user ownership by the time it is issued.

Summary

The Analysis of Requirements is reviewed to take account of the Selected Business System Option using requirements definition, data flow modelling and logical data modelling techniques to adjust the Requirements Catalogue, data and process models and to expand their detail.

The Data Flow Diagrams are subsequently transformed into Functions and I/O Structures formally specified. The Logical Data Model is enriched and validated by relational data analysis and entity life history analysis. Events are specified in detail, and defined in terms of Effect Correspondences. These and the Enquiry Access Paths give a detailed set of access requirements to fully underpin the Logical Data Model.

The aim is to express requirements in detail, and with objective measures which are embedded in the components of the Requirement Specification (Function Definitions, Logical Data Models) linked to the Requirements Catalogue.

Participants

Requirements Specification team including data modellers and analysts, functional modellers, entity life history practitioners and other specialists in requirements areas such as capacity planning, security and prototyping.

Preconditions

- **Management Authorization**
  Stage 3 controls
  Stage 3 plans
- **Inputs**
  Analysis of Requirements
  Installation Style Guide
  Prototyping Scope

Products

Command Structures
Menu Structures
Prototyping Report
Requirements Specification

Activities

Stage	**Step**	**Description**
3		Specification of Requirements
	310	Define Required System Processing
	320	Develop Required Data Model
	330	Derive System Functions
	340	Enhance Required Data Model
	350	Develop Specification Prototypes
	360	Develop Processing Specification
	370	Confirm System Objectives
	380	Assemble Requirements Specification

MODULE LS - LOGICAL SYSTEM SPECIFICATION ACTIVITY DESCRIPTION

Objectives

To enable management to select the technical environment which offers the best value for money in meeting the requirement.

To provide a physical design team with an implementation independent non-procedural detailed specification of required functionality, adequately documented with objective measures.

Summary

There are two parallel streams of activity in this module. In Stage 4, the Business Systems Option and the Requirements Specification are translated into a range of options for implementation. Languages, developed environments, implementation platforms and packages are compared and costed. Management selects the option which offers best value for money.

The parallel stream is to further detail the Requirements Specification into implementable components which define functionality in terms of operations within formal enquiry and update specifications.

Participants

Two teams:
- analysts and industry experts to produce Technical Systems Options. This may particularly require capacity planning and security specialists.
- process designers.

Preconditions

- **Management Authorization**
  Logical System Specification Module Plans
  Logical System Specification Module controls
  Technical system option selection

- **Input**
  Evaluated capacity planning information
  Installation Style Guide
  Project Initiation Document
  Requirements Specification
  Selected Business System Option

- **References**
  Audit standards
  Estimates for design and implementation activities
  Information on existing and planned IT infrastructures
  IS strategy policies (for hardware and software)
  IS standards
  Other business areas' plans
  Security statements (for hardware and software configuration) and standards

Products

Logical System Specification

Activities

Stage	**Step**	**Description**
4		Technical System Options
	410	Define Technical System Options
	420	Select Technical System Options
5		Logical Design
	510	Define User Dialogues
	520	Define Update Processes
	530	Define Enquiry Processes
	540	Assemble Logical Design

MODULE PD - PHYSICAL DESIGN ACTIVITY DESCRIPTION

Objective

To specify the physical data, processes, inputs and outputs, using the language and features of the chosen physical environment and incorporating installation standards.

The resulting design should provide everything needed to decide how application development should be taken forward. User management will need to agree this with service providers in both system construction and operations.

Summary

Physical design addresses the following activities:

- prepare for physical design
- learn the rules of the implementation environment
- review the precise requirements for logical to physical mapping
- plan the approach
- complete the specification of functions
- incrementally and iteratively develop the data and process designs, using a cycle of:
- design
- test against objectives
- optimise
- review

This Stage has two main strands; data and processing. Initially the physical environment is classified by the facilities and features it provides for both data and processing.

Within the data strand an initial physical data design is produced, using rules of thumb applicable to any DBMS or file handler. This is converted to a product specific data design. Timing and sizing is carried out on this design and if necessary changes made to the design to meet performance and space objectives.

A Physical Design Strategy is developed. This includes a definition, for the physical environment, of how process specification is to be approached and a definition of the style of program specifications.

The physical design procedures are intended to be used in conjunction with the product specific guides provided by suppliers.

Participants

Physical design team with expertise in mapping logical design to physical environment, function component implementation mapping, database tuning.

Preconditions

- **Management Authorization**
  Agreement to physical design strategy
  Stage 6 controls
  Stage 6 plans
- **Inputs**
  Installation development standards
  Logical System Specification
- **References**
  Physical Environment Specification

Products

Physical Design
Application Development Standards

Activities

Stage	Step	Description
6		Physical Design
	610	Prepare for Physical Design
	620	Create Physical Data Design
	630	Create Function Component Implementation Map
	640	Optimise Physical Data Design
	650	Complete Function Specification
	660	Consolidate Process Data Interface
	670	Assemble Physical Design

Appendix 2

Case Study
Student Administration System

1. Introduction

Your institution has gained funding for a one year postgraduate course. The future funding for this course is uncertain and, for various reasons, your institution's normal admissions and student records system can not provide the facilities you urgently require. The system must handle certain information about admissions and maintain student records once a place has been granted. Course assessment and examination records must also be maintained.

2. Constraints

The system must run on the IBM compatible PC used in the office. This system has 1 Megabyte of RAM and a 40 Megabyte hard disk. A high density 3.5 inch disk drive is available. A laser jet printer is already provided. The software available is an integrated package providing word-processing, spreadsheet, database and communications facilities. The system should be menu driven and require the minimum of training in the use of the package. No extra hardware or software can be provided to support this system.

The only standard form available is the letter-headed stationery already in use in the department. The budget does not permit the pre-printing of any further forms.

3. Users

The system users will be the Course Organiser, departmental office staff and course lecturers.

4. Course Structure

An examination of the course documentation provides the following information. The course is in three parts:

Part 1	This part runs for 12 weeks during the Autumn term and consists of four modules which must be taken by all students. Each module is assessed by two assignments.
Part 2	This part runs for 10 weeks during the Spring term. Students take two core modules and two modules from a selection of options. The part 2 modules are assessed by a mixture of assignment and examination. The weighting between assignment and examination can differ between modules.
Part 3	This part runs for six months for MSc students. They continue the study of one of their part 2 options in more detail and sit an exam in June to assess the part 3 work. In addition they must prepare a dissertation based on a project with a local firm. Postgraduate Certificate students carry out a project based on one of their term two options. The project must be submitted by the end of June. These students attend no classes during part 3.

5. Assessment

Students must pass part 1 to progress to part 2. A pass is an average of 45% across all the part 1 subjects. Referred assignments are set where students have failed to achieve this pass mark. The total percentage mark for part 1 (ie average of all subjects) carries a weighting of 0.1 for the final assessment at the end of part 3.

Students must achieve an average of 60% across all modules to progress to the MSc course, referred work can be set if a student has 50% on average, or greater. Students who do not meet this standard can be considered for the certificate course if their average mark is 45% or greater. Referred work can be set for students who do not meet this standard. Part 2 carries a final mark weighting of 0.3 for MSc students and 0.5 for certificate students.

The MSc students must pass their option and their dissertation. The option contributes 30% of part 3 marks, the dissertation 70%. A student with an average of 60% or more on their average final mark is awarded a degree with merit, an average of 70% or more gives a degree with distinction.

6. Admissions procedures

Students phone in for an application form. Some students receive a pack containing the form from the agency sponsoring the course. Records require to be kept for all applications received containing:

applicant's name, home address, term address (where relevant), phone number (if any), sex, age, a code indicating how they heard about the course, a code indicating whether applicants are currently undergraduates, employed, unemployed, women returners etc. This information is required to monitor the balance of applications and the best sources for publicising the course.

All applicants who meet the minimum requirements for the course are invited for interview and the result of the interview is recorded on the applicants record:

accept, reject or waiting list with a priority ranking.

A letter is sent to candidates giving the result of the interview. The candidate must write in to confirm acceptance of a place and acceptance/rejection is recorded on the applicant's record. If a reason for rejecting a place is given this is also recorded.

All students who have accepted places on the course are sent a pack of information before the course starts.

7. Student records

When students register on the course their applicant's record is updated with current addresses and the following additional information is required:
source of funding, tutorial group for core options, personal tutor's name.

During part 2 student options must be added to the record. During part 3 the title of the student's project or dissertation is recorded along with the name of the supervisor. MSc students also have the industry sponsor details recorded (contact name, position, company name, address, contact phone number). The part 3 option must also be recorded for MSc students.

Assessment marks are recorded for all students.

8. Hardcopy output required

- Class list in alphabetical order
- Tutorial lists in alphabetical order
- Option lists giving students in alphabetical order
- List of Certificate students in alphabetical order
- List of MSc students in alphabetical order
- Assessment marks for each subject in alphabetical order of student.
- Assessment sheets for each part giving the total marks for each student in each subject and the average mark for each student. The average mark for all students for a particular subject, and for the overall marks, should be printed at the bottom of the page.
- At the end of part 2 the exam board needs a printout which clearly identifies MSc candidates, Certificate candidates and failures. Referrals are at the discretion of the exam board.
- At the end of part 3 the exam board needs separate printouts for Certificate and MSc candidates.
- Pass lists for each part to be displayed on the departmental noticeboard.
- Standard letters to applicants for interviews, offers etc.
- Analysis of applications for the course committee and the sponsoring agency.
- Any other documentation which would ensure the smooth running of the course.

9. On-line enquiries

The course leader may wish to see an applicant or student record at any time.

Index